THE
ART OF THE
ISLAMIC GARDEN

THE
ART OF THE
ISLAMIC GARDEN

EMMA CLARK

The Crowood Press

First published in 2004 by
The Crowood Press Ltd
Ramsbury, Marlborough
Wiltshire SN8 2HR

www.crowood.com

British Library Cataloguing in Publication Data
A catalogue record for this publication is available
from the British Library.

ISBN 1 86126 609 X

Photograph previous page: Courtyard Garden,
Damascus (Maktab 'Anbar)

Designed and edited by
Focus Publishing
11a St Botolph's Road
Sevenoaks
Kent
TN13 3AJ

Printed and bound in Singapore
by Craft Print International

Dedication
To my Mother,
A true gardener

Contents

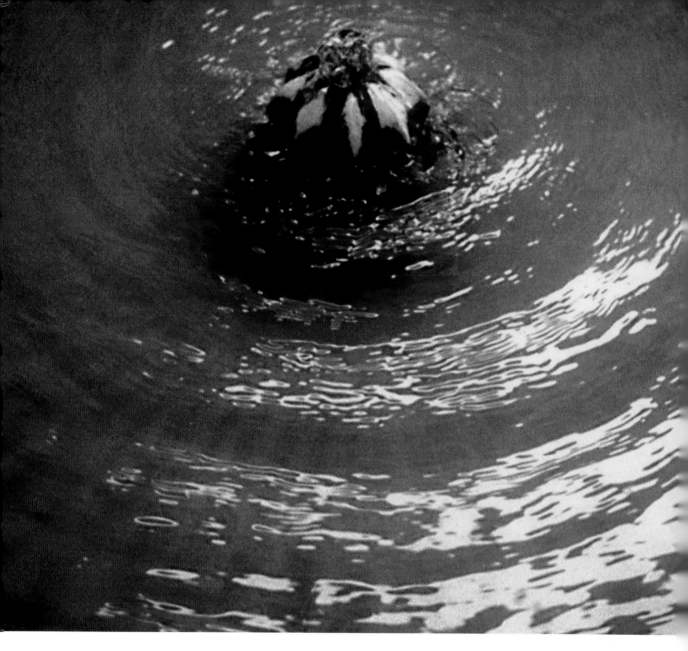

Fig. 1. The fountain is in the Alhambra Palace, Granada.

The inscription above reads 'Bismi'llah al-Rahman al-Rahim' *(In the name of God the Most merciful the Most Compassionate).*

Preface

Even a glimmer of understanding of traditional Islamic art and architecture clearly reveals that its beauty is not simply surface decoration but is a reflection of a deep knowledge and understanding of the natural order and of the Divine Unity that penetrates all of our lives. This profound revelation was the principal reason that led me to enter the religion of Islam. There is no separation between the sacred and profane in a traditional Islamic society (or any traditional society, i.e. one that is centred on a transcendent principle) and this means that everything, not just the ritual prayer (*salat*) performed five times a day, is touched by the sacred. Everything that we do in daily life, from washing to eating to conducting business or growing plants, is performed in the full knowledge and faith that it has a 'meaning in eternity'.[1] So the underlying theme of this book is that the traditional Islamic garden, like all traditional Islamic art, has a profound message for all those 'people who reflect'[2] – that of being a reminder of who we are before our Maker.

Studying Islamic art and architecture, and completing a master's thesis on the Islamic garden and garden carpet at the Royal College of Art,[3] opened my eyes to the meaning of art. Understanding something of the religion of Islam in general and Islamic art in particular, it became clear that all art, to a greater or lesser degree, should be the vehicle of a message of hope:[4] it should remind us of what it means to be human, of our place in the universe and our role, as is said in Islam, as God's vice-regent (*khalifat 'Allah*) on earth. It could be argued that any garden, since its main ingredient is God's creation, carries this message, reminding us as it does of the beauty and unity of nature, especially in built-up environments – and by and large this is true. However, a garden constructed according to traditional principles, such as the Islamic *chahar-bagh* or four-fold garden, can be a much more potent testimonial than a garden planned with no such principles in mind. That is the main theme of this book.

In the increasingly difficult times in which we live, it is good to be reminded that gardens and nature transcend nationality, race, religion, colour and ideology: the Islamic garden is not only for Muslims – its beauty is apparent to everyone, especially to those 'people who have sense'.[5] The media shows a side of Islam that has little to do with its inward aspect, an aspect that is shared by the other two great monotheistic religions – that of moving closing to God. The Quran is a sacred presence to Muslims and its references to nature, like its description of the paradise gardens, are worth considering carefully when looking at the meaning of the Islamic garden or if considering making one yourself. It is hoped that this book, in revealing something of its design and cosmology, goes a little way towards throwing some light, not only on one of the great achievements of the Islamic civilization, but also on the beauty of the religion itself.

Today it is estimated that out of the approximately six billion people in the world, over one billion of them are Muslims and it is also estimated to be the fastest growing religion in the world.[6] One journalist wrote in 1979, 'No part of the world is more hopelessly and systematically and stubbornly misunderstood by us than that complex of religions, culture and geography known as Islam'.[7] However, since then quantities of books have been published on understanding Islam,[8] and certainly knowledge of this religion and culture has increased considerably. Teaching about Islam and the Islamic civilization in the Western world is also fairly widespread now, if not exactly mainstream. Twenty-five years ago in the United Kingdom we were taught about Christianity at school and nothing else. Today, most primary schools teach something of the other world religions, and I find children and teenagers under 20 years old know far more about Islam – and other religions – than their parents and grand-parents. In our cosmopolitan and 'multi-cultural' societies, the only way of combating ignorance, prejudice and fear is intelligent education about religions and cultures of the world other than our own.

The Visual Islamic and Traditional Arts Programme (known as VITA) at The Prince's

Foundation where I am a tutor and lecturer, was founded in 1983 for the purposes of teaching, not only the principles and practice of the Islamic arts and crafts, but also the arts of the other great traditions of the world. Gradually, in the past few years an increasing number of people involved in education both at home and abroad are coming to VITA for advice on Islamic art teaching programmes for schools and higher education.

Through art, beauty and nature, tolerance and understanding will hopefully increase. As everyone connected to the horticultural world knows there has been a huge surge of interest in the last ten years or so in anything and everything to do with gardens. Hopefully, a love of gardens may encourage some people to learn more about the religion and culture that has produced some of the most beautiful gardens in the world.

Acknowledgements

I would first of all like to thank Khalid Seydo very much indeed, not only for his drawings (Figs. 62, 74a-74d, 231) but also for the hours he generously spent in reading the text and making helpful (usually!) comments. Secondly, many thanks to Emma Alcock for all the trouble she took with her drawings (Figs. 5, 6, 30, 58, 59, 114, 136). I would also like to thank Dr. Khaled Azzam very much for his invaluable editorial comments.

I am extremely grateful to Mike Miller, principal designer of The Prince of Wales' Carpet Garden and former managing director of Clifton Nurseries. He has been unfailingly helpful and generous with information and advice as well as providing photographs and plans of the Carpet Garden at both Chelsea and Highgrove.

I would like to express my gratitude to HRH the Prince of Wales who kindly allowed me to use his Carpet Garden as a case study in the design and making of a traditional Islamic garden in rural England. I would like to thank his staff as well, namely: David Howard, head gardener at Highgrove, Patrick Harrison, Nigel Baker and James Kidner.

I am indebted to the following friends and relatives who have been incredibly supportive in one way or another, giving editorial, practical and scholarly advice – from invaluable comments on the text and on geometric and garden design to Quran and *hadith* exegisis, as well as the identification of plants and allowing me to wander around their gardens – (in alphabetical order): Ms Fatma Azzam, Mr Nigel and Mrs Heather Alford, and Mr Martin Braund (three gardeners at Clovelly Court, North Devon), Mr Adnan Bogary and Mrs Summer Baghdady, Dr Harry and Mrs Laura Boothby, Professor Keith Critchlow, Mrs Jack Clark, Mr Jasper Clark and Ms Linda Rost, HRH Princess Haifa al-Faisal, Professor Richard Fletcher, HRH Prince Ghazi bin Muhammad and Princess Areej Ghazi, Mr Anthony and Lady Virginia Gibbs, Dr Julian and Mrs Alison Johansen, HRH Princess Johara bint Khalid, Ms Caroline Kinkead-Weekes, Mrs Debbie Lane for her great help at the Lindley Library, Dr Martin Lings, Mr Mustafa and Mrs Haajar Majzub, Mr. Khalil Martin, Dr Toby and Mrs Farhana Mayer, Mr Minwer al-Meied, Dr Jean-Louis Michon, Mr Khalid and Mrs Pascal Naqib, Professor Seyyed Hossein Nasr, Dr Hilali and Mrs Samya Noordeen, Professor Abdullah and Mrs Tybah Sharif-Schleiffer, Dr Reza and Mrs Nureen Shah-Kazemi, The Rickett family, The Hon John Rous, Dr Philip Watson, and the Zinovieff family.

Picture Acknowledgements

I am also indebted to the following colleagues and friends who have so kindly provided images: Paul Marchant (Figs. 17, 19, 41, 34), Taimoor Khan Mumtaz (Fig. 116), Kamil Khan Mumtaz (Fig. 138), Sajjad Kauser (Figs. 18, 131, 137), Professor Jonas Lehrman (Figs. 139, 140, 141), Michael Miller (Figs. 206, 207, 211, 213, 221, 226), Safina Habib (Fig. 25), Ririko Suzuki (Figs. 23, 84), Farid Aliturki (Fig. 66), and Patricia Araneta.

The British Library Oriental and India Office Collections (Fig. 26), The Al-Sabah Collection Kuwait National Museum (LNSIOR) Courtesy of Gulf International (Fig. 210), and Christie's International (Fig. 102).

Finally, I would like to express my profound respect and gratitude to all those gardeners, mostly anonymous, who tend their gardens with painstaking love and care: they receive little outward show of thanks but provide more beauty and solace to uplift the spirit of many a passing soul than they are aware; and of course all thanks to the greatest gardener of them all, Mother Nature.

Al-hamdu li'Llah rabi'Allah 'min.

Introduction

This book offers an introduction to the design, symbolic meaning and planting of the traditional Islamic garden, as well as giving some practical ideas for those interested in making one for themselves – in the United Kingdom or elsewhere with a similar climate. It is not a history of Islamic gardens or a geographically comprehensive survey of them. Some may be inspired to make one of these gardens as a reminder of time spent abroad in countries as diverse as Morocco, Syria, Iran, India or Spain; or Muslims may wish to make one as a reminder of the gardens in the country of their birth or their relatives' birth. Obviously it is not necessary to be a Muslim to make an Islamic garden, just as it is not necessary to be a Buddhist to make a Japanese Zen garden or a Christian to make a medieval knot garden. However, there is no doubt that it is far more enriching for the garden-maker or designer, when embarking on such a garden, to have some understanding of the culture that gave birth to it in the first place.

This book does not contain strict blueprints for designs but rather flexible ideas deriving from a fundamental theme – that of the *chahar-bagh* (from the Persian *chahar* meaning four and *bagh* meaning garden), as well as recommendations for planting. The classic *chahar-bagh* is the four-fold garden constructed around a central pool or fountain with four streams flowing from it, symbolically towards the four directions of space. Occasionally, the water is engineered to flow both from the central fountain 'outwards', as well as travelling 'inwards' from fountains placed at the 'four corners' towards the centre – as can be seen in the Court of Lions at the Alhambra (Fig. 6 and see Figs 31 and 32). Often paths are substituted for water. This could be said to be the quintessential plan of an Islamic garden – and there are many interpretations of it across the Islamic world, for example, it can be rectangular and not square (the Patio de la Acequia at the Generalife, Figs 40, 52 and 56) and it can be repeated on a kind of grid system, following irrigation channels (the Agdal

Fig. 2. Jardin Majorelle – Ironwork window-grille set within carved plaster surround.

Fig. 3. Courtyard, Azem Palace, Damascus.

Fig. 4. Generalife gardens, Alhambra Palace, Granada.

gardens near Marrakesh); its symbolism is not particular to Islam but of a universal nature, founded upon a profound understanding of the cosmos – this is examined in Chapter 1. The plan can be adapted for your own garden according to individual circumstances and requirements, while the underlying meaning of being a reflection of the heavenly gardens remains the same and is relevant to all, Muslim and non-Muslim alike.

We all have different starting-points for our gardens depending on the size, situation (urban, suburban or rural), aspect, climate, soil and so on, so suggestions

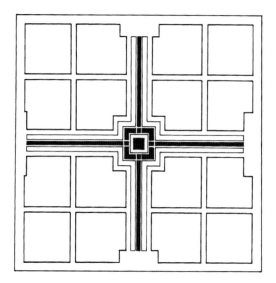

Fig. 5 (above). Fundamental chahar-bagh *(four-fold garden) plan, after the Taj Mahal garden.*

Fig. 6 (right). Court of Lions, Alhambra: water flows both from the central fountain into the rill below and from four fountains, one on each side of the court, towards the centre – reflecting the four rivers described in the gardens of paradise in the Quran: one of water, one of milk, one of honey and one of wine (see Chapter 2).

are made in Chapters 5 and 6 for a variety of trees, shrubs, plants and flowers, which may suit a more northern climate at the same time as being appropriate for an Islamic-inspired garden. Crucially, the fundamental four-fold lay-out should be retained, together with water in some form or other (see Chapter 4). It should be made clear from the outset that this kind of garden is a formal garden and on the whole is easier to adapt to an urban situation rather than a rural one. However, it is certainly possible to create a formal *chahar-bagh* in the countryside, providing it has some kind of separation from its surroundings – in the form of walls or high hedges, creating a 'room' for it. The case study in Chapter 7, HRH The Prince of Wales' carpet garden at Highgrove, demonstrates how well this can succeed.

There is no substitute for actually visiting Islamic gardens around the world for a greater understanding and appreciation of them. The ones we are mainly looking at for inspiration are those created from approximately the tenth to the end of the seventeenth centuries, in the countries most

obviously categorized as the traditional Islamic world: north African countries, the Near and Middle East, Turkey, Persia (present-day Iran) and the Indian sub-continent.[8A] The majority of the most outstanding Islamic gardens were created before the beginning of the eighteenth century when the influence of the Western European gardening traditions began to be felt.[9] Until this time, from around the middle of the sixteenth century onwards – and at least a century earlier in Spain – this situation was in reverse: it was European gardens that were influenced by Eastern gardens, experiencing a kind of revolution, not so much in design as in plants and planting. This was initiated by the great number and variety of new trees, shrubs and flowers introduced from Turkey and further East by diplomats and travellers keen to find out more about the powerful and fast-expanding Ottoman empire.[10]

However, to return to one of our main purposes here, that is, to look at some Islamic gardens which have survived until today for inspiration. A glance at just a few of these great gardens[11] – from the expansive

Fig. 7. The garden of the Dar Batha Museum, Fes, showing paths forming the chahar-bagh.

Achabal gardens (Kashmir) and the Bagh-i-Fin (Persia), to the more intimate gardens of the Alhambra and Generalife (Spain) and the courtyards of old Damascus and Fes – demonstrates the emphasis on water and shade, as well as on the strong integration between architecture and landscape, which distinguishes them from the gardens of the northern European tradition. In a North European country such as the United Kingdom the emphasis is, understandably, less on water and shade than on sun and the longed-for south-facing border. Indeed, most people still, in spite of all the health warnings, rush to bask in the sunshine as soon as it makes one of its rare appearances. It was only after visiting Iran and spending time in cafés at the foot of the mountains north of Tehran that I really began to understand the importance of water and shade, and to absorb the atmosphere of what an Islamic garden means. Here, cheap metal divans are placed across fast-running streams; rugs and cushions are laid out on the beds so that the visitor can sit cross-legged or lie on them and wait to be served with water-melon, tea and perhaps *shisha* or *argile* (water-pipe). Then one sinks back into the cushions looking up at the leaves of the *chenar* tree (*Platanus orientalis*) filtering the sunlight, listening to the sound of water running over the pebbles below and the phrase from the Quran, 'Gardens underneath which Rivers flow,'[12] is really brought alive. The experience is truly a foretaste of the Paradise gardens which all Muslims, and others too no doubt, hope to be their final resting-place.

When observing the formality of the *chahar-bagh* across the Islamic world, it is worth noting a fundamental difference between the gardens (the larger ones we are referring to here) of England and

Europe, and the Islamic gardens: Muslims, indeed anyone brought up in a hot country, do not on the whole, like to walk purely for pleasure.[13] First of all, it is generally too hot and secondly, what is the point of walking if you do not have a necessary destination in mind? As the reader who has stayed in a hot country for any length of time will know, this is completely understandable. Thus, after the two vital elements of water and shade, another important consideration (along with geometry, discussed in Chapters 2 and 3) is a place to sit: a pavilion at one end or in the centre, preferably somewhere near the water in order to catch a cooling breeze. Sir John Chardin's (ambassador to Persia in the seventeenth century) observation that 'The Persians don't walk so much in Gardens as we do … they set themselves down in some part of the

Fig. 8. Café at the foot of the mountains just north of Tehran. Guests sit or recline on metal beds covered in rugs, which are placed straddled over a fast-flowing stream.

garden ... and never move from their seat till they are going out of it,'[14] is very relevant in understanding the ambience of the Islamic garden. It is far more focused on rest, relaxation and entertainment, as well as quiet contemplation, than a garden in England in which it is only possible to sit for two or three months of the year, the rest of the time being a damp, if beautiful, place to walk. In fact, Francis Bacon (1561–1626) commented the opposite about England, 'It is very pleasant to be outside but not pleasant enough to sit still'.

Intention

When studying the art, architecture and landscape of another culture, in particular the Islamic culture, the intentions and mentality of all those skilled craftsmen, artists and designers who created them should be taken into account. In Islam the intention of a person is profoundly important. There is a *hadith* (a Saying of the Prophet Muhammad),[15] which says that if anyone has intended a good deed and has not carried it out then God writes it down as a full good deed, but if he has intended it and has carried it out then God writes it down 'as from ten good deeds to seven hundred times, or many times over'.[16] This recalls a lesson that an English gardener, apprenticed in the art of Japanese gardens, brings across vividly in his book on Japanese

gardens, when he learns the importance of how to approach a task: 'The lesson that the spirit with which one performs any task, no matter how "menial", is more important than getting it done cannot be ignored ... the essence of that spirit is to be "centred" '.[17] The apprentice needs to 'centre' himself before executing his craft and this means, very briefly, that the soul needs a certain discipline and maturity before proceeding to a more sophisticated level of the craft. This could well be applied to a student or apprentice of any traditional art or craft, especially in Islam where a good intention is so highly rewarded. As will be mentioned more than once in this book, the crafts and the spiritual orders in Islam, as with the medieval craft guilds of Christendom, were closely allied.

Therefore, the intention or the spirit behind creating a garden is fundamentally important in both understanding gardens made by others and in a garden made by oneself. There is no doubt that a person's surroundings both reflect the soul of that person as well as, conversely, having an effect upon that person's soul. As the Buddha said, 'If a man's mind becomes pure, his surroundings will also become pure'.[18] At the same time, if the surroundings are 'pure' – the greatest example being virgin nature and, secondarily (in the absence of sacred architecture), a beautifully-ordered garden – it will help the soul of the person within those surroundings towards a certain inward tranquillity, if not necessarily 'purity'. The kind of purity the Buddha is referring to requires life-long disciplined spiritual work, a path for which only some are destined. Few would argue that it is easier to feel peaceful and contemplative in a beautiful garden or virgin nature than in a city with tall buildings, deafening traffic and crowded streets.

Fig. 9. The 'Garden of the Sultana' showing pavilion and water, Generalife gardens, Alhambra.

Types of Gardens

Apart from the *chahar-bagh* mentioned above there are several other garden types in the Islamic world, the main distinction being between the larger outward-looking gardens and the smaller inward-looking courtyard ones. The larger ones are generally known as *bustan* (the Persian word for 'orchard') and may have formerly belonged to palaces, such as the Jardin Menara or Jardin Agdal, now public gardens on the outskirts of Marrakech. They both consist of vast still pools surrounded by olive groves, fruit trees and palm groves. The largest, the Jardin Agdal, could be said to be a *chahar-bagh* multiplied many times over, in that its enormous central expanse of water is surrounded by smaller irrigation pools with geometric water-channels running between them. The whole area is surrounded by walls within which are seemingly endless square plots of fruit trees – oranges, lemons, apricots, figs and pomegranates – all divided geometrically by the irrigation channels and with raised walkways and avenues of olive trees in between. These large gardens are not flower gardens as we understand them, but cool, green places for sitting in and picnicking under trees near water while children play. Another famous large open garden, this one focused almost entirely on terraces of water and pavilions, is the Shalimar Gardens in Lahore, built in the seventeenth century by the Mughal Emperor Shah Jahan (see Chapter 4 and Fig. 116).

The smaller gardens are usually formed by the courtyards of the inward-looking traditional Arab-Islamic house. These are all adaptations of the *chahar-bagh* form and can vary in size from small, as in approximately six metres square, to as large as twenty metres by about fifteen. In old Damascus, the large houses of the rich officials, such as the Palace of As'ad Pasha al-Azem, contain a series of courtyards ranging from the largest, approximately twenty-five by twenty metres, to the smallest, which is about seven metres square, all with fountains or pools. Al-Azem governed Damascus for fourteen years and made such a huge fortune that when it was confiscated by the Ottoman Sultan in 1758, the currency of the Empire had to be re-valued! Maps of traditional Islamic cities such as Damascus, Fes or Aleppo are fascinating to look at: there are no main roads or open spaces, just an extraordinary dense

Fig. 10. Menara Gardens, Marrakech.

Fig. 11. Agdal Gardens, Marrakech.

Fig. 12. Menara Gardens – picnicking under the olive trees.

Fig. 13. Traditional courtyard house, Marrakech.

Fig. 16. Large central courtyard, Azem Palace, Damascus.

Fig. 14. Riyadh al-Arsat, Marrakech, a small area in this large courtyard garden.

Fig. 15. One of the smaller courtyards, Azem Palace, Damascus.

network of narrow winding lanes and alleys and the courtyard squares of houses, every so often divided into neighbourhood quarters each with its own mosque and bread oven. The map of Damascus made by the French in the 1930s shows that each house has its own courtyard, fountain and trees.[18A] Many travellers have observed the contrast between the dark narrow streets and the high and seemingly impenetrable outer walls of the houses with the brilliance of the courtyards within. 'Are you disappointed, as you tread these streets by these repulsive walls? Do you tremble lest the dream of Damascus be dissolved by Damascus itself?' wrote an American melodramatically in 1852, continuing, 'Oh little faith! Each Damascus house is a paradise!'.[19]

Another type of garden is the *gulistan* or rose-garden, which may take up one area of the *bustan,* or may simply consist of a wall or arbour with climbing roses or a few shrub roses in a courtyard. The word *gul* is used as a general term for flower in Persian, as well as specifically for the rose. An abstracted version of a *gul* is the dominant motif in many tribal carpets, from Baluchistan to Anatolia through to the wide range of Turkomen rugs and carpets.

Then there is the mausoleum garden, a form which came into its own in Mughal India. This is a variation on the *chahar-bagh* theme; instead of a pavilion for sitting in, the tomb of the deceased is placed in the centre of a large *chahar-bagh,* symbolizing the meeting of the immortal soul with God at death. The mausoleum gardens look outward from the centre toward the four directions of space. Three of the most famous examples are: the mausoleum of Itimad ud-Dawlah, who was the Lord High Treasurer under the Mughal Emperor Jahangir (1605–27); the tomb of Jahangir himself; and the Taj Mahal. The Taj Mahal, built by Shah Jahan for his wife, Mumtaz-I-Mahal, is the supreme example of a mausoleum garden, the tomb itself set at the head of the *chahar-bagh* looking down its main axis towards the raised pool in the centre.

Rawdah literally means 'garden' in Arabic but the term is applied specifically to the small area in the Prophet's mosque at Medina between his tomb and the pulpit (*minbar*). It is called this because of the Saying of the Prophet, 'Between my house and my pulpit is a garden [*rawdah*] of the gardens of paradise'. Today, when worshippers visit the mosque at Medina, this area is always the most crowded, since everyone longs to be with the Prophet in his garden in Paradise.

All of the above gardens may employ the *chahar-bagh* geometric design in some form or other and in the larger ones, such as the Jardin Agdal, it may be repeated several times to form a regular grid pattern. This is clearly shown in the great classic garden-carpets such as the Aberconway (Fig. 210) in which the bird's-eye view allows the onlooker an

Fig. 17. The tomb of Itimad ud-Dawlah, Agra, at the centre of a chahar-bagh.

Fig. 18. Jahangir's tomb showing four-fold design of garden with large square central pool, Lahore, Pakistan.

all-encompassing vision. The ordered geometric lines are either irrigation channels or paths and the square or rectangular plots usually contain one specific fruit tree or vegetable each. The separation between the flower garden and the *potager* or vegetable garden was not as strictly imposed as seems to be the case in many of the ninteenth-century estates in England and Europe. In the Victorian era, the separate walled vegetable garden became an important feature of the 'stately home' and it is only relatively recently that mixing flowers with vegetables has come back into fashion. Of course, the cottage garden of rural labourers at this time contained vegetables, fruit and flowers – indeed, flowers were only for the fortunate ones who could spare a little ground from their vegetable-

Fig. 19. The Taj Mahal at the head of a large chahar-bagh.

patch (see Chapter 6). A good example of the recent mixing of flowering plants and produce is the walled garden at Highgrove, which echoes the Islamic – and, as we shall see in more detail in the next chapter, universal – theme of the four-fold design with a pool in the centre. Arbours of roses and tunnels of sweet peas form part of the symmetrical lay-out with fruit and vegetable plots in between.

The Quran, Symbolism and Plato

In the modern world there is a sharp division between everyday life with all its material requirements and preoccupations, and a spiritual life – if we are fortunate enough to have one. For very many people living in the Western world, the former has all but destroyed the latter. In Islam, as in the other two Abrahamic religions,[20] man[21] is seen to have fallen from his primordial state in the Garden of Eden when he was at peace with his Lord and in a state of unity with Him and the cosmos. In order to regain this primordial state of unity with God, man needs all the help possible to remind him of his theomorphic nature and his role as vice-regent (*khalifat 'Allah*) of God on earth. Human beings are forgetful, becoming so immersed in the details of earthly existence that we no longer recognize the signs that can jolt us back to remember what it means to be human. One of the greatest of these signs is Nature herself. The Quran points out many times over, the importance of 'signs' or 'portents', 'symbols' or 'similitudes' (variously translated from the Arabic word *aya*) in the natural world, none of which are too small or too trifling to be a reminder of God – from a date-pip to a gnat ('God is not ashamed to strike a similitude even of a gnat or aught above it', Quran, II:24). *Aya* is also the word for a verse of the Quran, implying that every verse is a sign of God. Indeed, this is the case, since in Islam the greatest miracle is the Holy Quran itself, the Word of God made manifest. It is generally agreed that the Quran, being the 'Word made Book' corresponds to Jesus Christ in Christianity, who is the 'Word made Man'.

In Plato's 'Theory of Art',[21A] he suggests, through the dialogue about the bed, that he considers everything created by the carpenter or the painter or other artists as being at a 'third remove from reality'.

Fig. 20. Virgin Nature, the greatest sacred art. In the Quran there is a constant refrain that we should meditate upon Nature, since her beauty and diversity is one of the great symbols that open a door towards the Creator.

Their objects are simply distant representations of the 'throne of truth'. The 'true form' or archetype was made in Heaven (by, in monotheistic terms, God Himself) and therefore everything in the created world including plants, animals, the earth and sky and the planets, are reflections or mirror-images of these heavenly archetypes. Islam embraced the Platonic tradition, and those who understand, those 'people who reflect' (a phrase repeated throughout the Quran) see through the phenomena of the natural world in all its infinite glory to the underlying truth: Nature, as a sign of God, both veils and reveals. So the beauty of the natural world is one of God's greatest symbols and through meditation on its glories we can, as with all true sacred art, retrace a path back to Truth. This is indeed what sacred art is centred upon – as Plato is famously credited with saying, 'Beauty is the Splendour of the True'.[22] In Islam there is no beauty outside of God[23] and all traditional art across the Islamic world, demonstrates, to a greater or lesser extent, the truth of this and of Plato's words. In a general sense, the traditional Islamic *chahar-bagh*, the archetype of which are the paradise gardens described in the Quran (see Chapter 1), is itself one of these symbols. It is a means whereby we are roused from a passive, unquestioning acceptance of the sensory world to an awareness of both the immanence and the transcendence of God.

Islamic Gardens in a Different Environment

The Islamic garden, as is well-known, was born in a hot climate. Although snow falls in many areas of the Islamic world, such as Turkey, parts of Jordan and Iran, and temperatures can reach well below zero, there is nevertheless a far greater amount of heat and sunshine than in northern climates. So the gardener or designer will understand from the outset that simply emulating the gardens of the East, such as Bagh-I-Shazdeh (the Prince's garden) in Mahan, Iran or those nearer to home such as the courtyards and gardens of the Alhambra and Generalife (Figs 21, 24 and 28–29) is neither possible nor necessarily desirable in a damper climate. What is possible and desirable in our increasingly 'multi-cultural' world, is a merging of Islamic design principles – speaking as they do of a universal vision of the cosmos – with northern climactic conditions. The results will hopefully have a strong appeal to people from whatever background, country or religion at the same time as encouraging an awareness of the beauty and underlying universality of what is often considered an alien culture.

The principal elements of all Islamic gardens, of whatever type and wherever they may be, are water and shade; so, much thought is required in making such a garden in a climate where heat from the sun is the sought-after and cherished element, while water and shade are plentiful and taken for granted. Therefore, on one level, the garden designer is searching for a new language of gardening, a marriage of Islamic design principles with planting more appropriate to northern climes. On a more profound level the person wishing to make an Islamic garden may be attracted by its role as a kind of sanctuary on earth, as well as being a foretaste of the Heavenly Gardens.

The great appetite for learning about different gardening traditions today is a sign that many people genuinely want to understand something of the cultural and spiritual vision that gave birth to some of these traditions. Essentially, the Islamic garden, like the Zen Buddhist garden, is an embodiment of a spiritual vision. Based as it is on the universal laws of Nature and the cosmos it may inspire people from a wide variety of backgrounds and geographical locations to interpret its ideas for themselves. The universal vision embodied by the Islamic garden may speak to everyone from whatever background, country or religion.

Hopefully, in the following chapters, the reader may learn something of the important symbolism of the Islamic garden as well as its design principles and how to combine these with suitable planting in order to create this 'new language'. These principles may be adapted to a site but should not be fundamentally changed, since this would upset the underlying meaning. The planting is more flexible and can be altered according to the climate, soil, aspect and other environmental considerations without the design principles being altered significantly.

Fig. 21. Pool garden at the Alhambra.

On conquering different countries, the religion of Islam to a certain extent embraced these countries' very varied cultures and in turn transformed them. This is true of the art, architecture and way of life all over the diverse regions of the Islamic world. It is interesting to observe that in the countries where Islam has recently spread, such as Northern Europe and North America, the mosques that have been built in the last thirty to forty years are by and large not examples of good design.[24] Perhaps more time is needed to understand how to combine traditional Islamic design with the indigenous architecture and materials of these countries, as well as with modern western design in general. With gardens it should be an easier task to marry the two forces together in a pleasing, harmonious and meaningful way. After all, Islam has spread to widely differing countries and climates, from Africa to Turkey to Indonesia and China, so it is a religion and culture that is flexible and is used to adapting local art to its own quintessentially Islamic spirit and vice-versa. Now it is the turn of more northern countries to absorb and interpret the Islamic vision within indigenous

gardening traditions to create something identifiably Islamic and yet at home in the country concerned. There are few examples to cite here, the most well-known probably being the carpet garden at Highgrove (see Chapter 7; there is also the Mughal-inspired garden at Manningham Park, Bradford). This works well, largely because, as mentioned above, it is secluded behind walls and does not attempt the impossible – to blend into the very English garden surroundings. This is in keeping with the Islamic idea of creating a sanctuary, one of the features of the desert gardens, and the Persian *pairidaezas* (hunting-parks) both areas isolated from their surroundings by boundary walls and planting.

So, what is an Islamic garden exactly, and in what ways does it differ from, or is similar to, other gardens? How can we apply its principles and ideas to our own gardens? It is hoped that this book will answer some basic questions as well as offering some explanation of the more esoteric meaning underlying the form and function of the Islamic garden. Hopefully, also, readers may be inspired to take up some of the ideas and apply them to their own gardens. When thinking about the Islamic garden and how it may be possible to design and make your own, it is inspiring to read the words of one of the greatest garden designers and writers of the last century, Russell Page:

Fig. 22. The walls of the Carpet Garden at Highgrove, from the Orchard Room side. They are constructed from local stone with rendered and painted concrete – to give a Cotswold–Mediterranean look with an almost Aztec sense of mass!

When I come to build my own garden it can scarcely take another form than the one which is a reflection of its maker. If I want it to be 'ideal', then I too must set myself my own ideal, my own aim. Now, as for a painter or a sculptor or any artist comes the test – what values does the garden-maker try to express? It seems to me that to some extent he has the choice. He may choose the easy way and design a garden as a demonstration of his technical skill and brilliance, go all out for strong effects or see the problem as one of good or bad business and so plan accordingly. Or he may try to make his garden a symbol and set up as best he can a deliberate scaffolding or framework which nature will come to clothe with life.[25]

This last sentence puts the making of an Islamic garden in a nutshell, since ultimately the *chahar-bagh* is a symbol, a symbol of the Heavenly Gardens. Hopefully, this book will give the reader ideas for setting up the framework for the symbol and for clothing it with life.

The Chahar-Bagh in the Modern World

One of the main objectives of this book is to show that, in an increasingly urban society, the traditional Islamic four-fold garden, the *chahar-bagh*, could be developed in the United Kingdom and northern Europe, and other parts of the world with a similar climate. There is increasing evidence that more people are finding that a garden, however small, can become a source of sanity in an increasingly complex and frenetic world. The emphasis of the Islamic garden on peace and contemplation is what many city dwellers find most attractive about it. In desert regions, the inhospitable environment is shut out by means of high walls and evergreen trees – usually conifers of some sort, as they can withstand the wind and lack of water – to create a sanctuary within. In the

Fig. 23. The Paris Mosque, a good example of a twentieth-century mosque and courtyard in Europe, built in traditional North African style.

modern city today the same principle holds true, that of shutting out the environment: but instead of the purity of the hard, empty, arid desert, it is the noisy, polluted, traffic-ridden, crowded streets. In fact the traditional Arab-Islamic town house (Fig. 13), still to be seen in the *medina* (old city) of some Muslim towns such as Fes, Rabat, Marrakech or Aleppo, was always built a around a central courtyard, separated from the city by high walls. The focus of these courtyard houses (the courtyard being a miniature garden) is inwards and upwards, symbolically towards the heart and towards God. This courtyard was, and still is, the inner sanctum, the heart of the house reserved for the family. As the great Egyptian reviver of traditional architecture and city-planning, Hassan Fathy, wrote, 'The best definition of architecture is one that is the outcome of the interaction between the intelligence of man and his environment, in satisfying his needs, both spiritual and physical'.[26] Today, an inner sanctum can be recreated in the back or front garden of many an urban dweller.

CHAPTER 1

History, Symbolism and the Quran

The first Muslims came from the Arabian desert: the Prophet Muhammad himself, like most young Arab boys at that time (sixth century AD) spent his early childhood brought up by a foster-mother from one of the nomadic desert tribes. It was believed that the demanding desert environment and nomadic way of life would instil the virtues of steadfastness, strength and courage into boys at an early age, which would stand them in good stead in adulthood. As far as is known, there is no history of gardens as we understand them in Arabia at this period: a date palm tree (*Phoenix dactilifera*) and water – the oasis – was a garden. It was not until Islam conquered other countries with civilizations of their own, in particular, Persia, that the Islamic garden can be said to have been born. Here, Islam absorbed the already well-established tradition of hunting-parks (*pairidaeza*) and royal pleasure gardens and invested them with a whole new spiritual vision.

A glance at the art and architecture of the Islamic world clearly shows the tremendous variation of artistic expression – from the Kairouine mosque in Fes, to the Ibn Tulun mosque in Cairo, to the Friday Mosque in Isphahan, to take just three examples; and they all have rich art and craftsmanship adorning them. Each geographical location with its indigenous people, cultural characteristics and gifts, has adapted the Islamic vision and principles to achieve pinnacles of art that are both reflections of the land in question but which are recognizably true manifestations of the Islamic spirit; and this is no less true with Islamic gardens. Across the Islamic world these gardens show a great variation of style, reflecting practical and environmental factors, as well as indigenous cultural ones: factors such as topography, availability of water and purpose or type of garden. These range from the vast open gardens, such as the spectacular Shalimar Bagh ('Abode of Love') in Kashmir where water can be collected and channelled from the mountains, to

Fig. 24. The 'Garden of the Sultana' in the Generalife gardens.

the smaller, inward-looking courtyard gardens (which are our main interest here) of traditional cities such as Fes or Damascus. Like Islamic art and architecture, however richly varied these garden styles may be, they nevertheless retain the same principles and are expressions of the Islamic spirit.

If the individual gardener or designer skilfully links together Islamic design with local factors such as climate, materials, architecture and gardening traditions, then there is no reason why Islamic gardens should not succeed in a wide range of geographical areas in the world – from the South of France to Scotland, or from Venezuela to Canada. However, as this book is at pains to point out, making a successful Islamic garden in a part of the world that seems alien to the concept, requires some knowledge of its history, symbolism, planting traditions and variety of styles across the Islamic world. Thus, understanding of the cultural context is helpful and important when looking for inspiration and practical ideas.

History

The idea that Paradise is a garden is a very ancient one. It pre-dates Islam, as well as Judaism and Christianity and the Garden of Eden by centuries, seeming to have its origins as far back as the Sumerian period (4000BC) in Mesopotamia. Here, a paradise garden for the gods is mentioned in the first writings known to man. The Babylonians (c.2700BC) later described their Divine Paradise in the Epic of Gilgamesh: 'In this immortal garden stands the Tree... beside a sacred fount the Tree is placed'.[27] So already we have the two indispensable elements of the Paradise Gardens of Islam: water and shade. In the Quran these gardens are called the *jannat al-firdaws*, *jannat* meaning 'gardens' and *firdaws* meaning 'paradise'. The word *janna* (singular) can also mean 'paradise'. All the other words mentioned describing gardens such as *chahar* ('four'), *bagh* ('garden'),

Fig. 25. Palm grove, Medina.

the popular idea of paradise is a desert island with a palm tree!) it is all too easy to take water for granted and be unaware of how much a lush garden with a green canopy of shade and flowing water means to inhabitants of countries with baking hot desert climates. It is no accident that green is the colour of Islam – it is the colour used over and over again to describe the gardens of paradise, where the faithful recline on 'green cushions' in 'green shade'.[29] Not only is it the colour of all vegetation, appearing young and fresh in the Spring, symbolizing growth and fertility, but it is the antithesis of the monotonous sandy-browns of the stony desert; it offers a longed-for soothing and gentle relief to the eyes. A famous English gardener writing at the beginning of the twentieth century gives a very evocative description of the unavoidable heat and longing for coolness and green foliage when trekking in Iran:

> Imagine you have ridden in summer for four days across a plain; that you have then come to a barrier of snow-mountains and ridden up that pass; that from the top of the pass you have seen a second plain, with a second barrier of mountains in the distance, a hundred miles away; that you know that beyond these mountains lies yet another plain, and another; and that for days, even weeks, you must ride with no shade, and the sun overhead, and nothing but the bleached bones of dead animals strewing the track. Then when you come to trees and running water, you will call it a garden. It will not be flowers and their garishness that your eyes crave for, but a green cavern full of shadows and pools where goldfish dart, and the sound of a little stream.[30]

bustan (orchard) and *gulistan* are *farsi* words (the Persian language), clearly indicating where the earthly form of the Islamic garden originated. It was the unique impact of the Islamic revelation on the ancient Sassanid and Achaemenian civilizations of Persia with their *pairidaezas* (walled hunting-parks) and sophisticated irrigation systems, such as those of Cyrus the Great's gardens at Pasargardae, that ultimately brought the Islamic garden into being. The English word 'paradise' itself comes from the ancient Persian word *pairidaeza*, *pairi* meaning 'around' and *daeza* meaning 'wall'.

There are many references to the fountains, flowing waters and perfect temperate climate in the descriptions of paradise in the Quran, where the blessed shall be shaded by 'thornless lote-trees and serried acacias' and 'palms and vines'.[28] In hot and dry environments, water is understandably viewed, whether rain or a spring, as a direct symbol of God's mercy and rain is described throughout the Quran as a mercy and as life-giving (see Chapter 4). To those brought up in countries where rain is frequent (and

The Persians, as noted above, were one of the earliest peoples to cultivate gardens, parks and hunting-grounds – their *pairidaezas* by definition were walled areas. Thus we immediately have the idea of an area isolated from its surroundings, shutting out a difficult environment to protect an area of fertility and ease within. It is in the nature of paradise to be hidden and secret, since it corresponds to the interior world, the innermost soul – *al-jannah* meaning 'concealment' as well as garden,[31] echoing the *hortus conclusus* of the medieval monastic garden. Thus the *chahar-bagh* is often represented in exquisite miniature paintings as

Fig. 26. Persian miniature showing high walls surrounding a house and garden, late-fourteenth century.

surrounded by high walls. The courtyard of a traditional Arab-Islamic house in a city is a *chahar-bagh* in miniature; there may not be room for many plants and flowers but there is always water, usually a small fountain in the centre with possibly one palm tree or some plants in pots. These houses are often quite high with four stories or more and a flat roof on which one can sleep on hot summer nights. The windows rarely open out onto the street; instead, they look inwards, usually with balconies, to the courtyard and the miniature paradise garden within. When entering one of these houses, in order to maintain privacy from the street, the entrance corridor bends so that passers-by cannot peer in too far.

The plan on which the Arab-Islamic house is based, also the plan of the *chahar-bagh*, is inherited from the ancient prototype originating in Mesopotamia. Here they made maximum use of what little water was available and built their houses of mud-brick around enclosures or courtyards with a fountain or small pool in the centre. This kept the adverse conditions outside, while simultaneously creating a cooler, cleaner, refreshing refuge within. Under Muslim direction, this architecture also reflected the clear separation between the public and private domains in a traditional Islamic society. This distinction between the public and private domains became one of the principles of traditional Islamic architecture and, by extension, the traditional Islamic four-fold garden. The house opens inwards to the heart rather than outwards towards the world. The heart, the courtyard, represents the inward (*batin*), contemplative aspect of human nature. The modern villa-type house, in contrast, represents the opposite, the outward (*zahir*), worldly attitude. The traditional house may be in the middle of the bustling *medina* (old city) – of Marrakech for example – but when the door to the street is shut the visitor enters a totally different world: it is immediately quiet since the high, thick stone walls keep out the noise and bestow a kind of muffled silence on the interior, not dissimilar to entering a church. The gentle murmur of a fountain in the centre draws the visitor in, contributing to the atmosphere of inward reflection. At night these small courtyards (often about six metres square or less) are quite magical: sitting on a rug or cushion on the stone floor, one's gaze is inevitably drawn upwards to the stars in the sky. It is a beautiful example of how traditional architecture can affect a whole way of life and have an impact upon the soul.

Fig. 27. Riyadh El-Arsat, Marrakech, fountain at centre of four paths.

'As desert dwellers, the notion of invisible hands that drove the blasts that swept the desert and formed the deceptive mirages that lured the traveller to his destruction was always with them,' writes one religious scholar.[32] So, for the pre-Islamic Arabs, accustomed as they were to living in a hostile environment, the smallest drop of water or the slightest indication of nature's greenness was considered precious and sacred, its rare appearance the work of 'invisible hands'. To them the oasis was a garden. So an extension of this oasis, more water and more trees, as mentioned in the Quran, was miraculous and heaven-sent. They already revered Nature as life-giving and as a sign of the mysterious power that guided the universe, and were familiar, as it were, with the unseen world of the spirit. Thus, when the Quran was revealed to the Prophet Muhammed in the early part of the seventh century AD, with its promise of gardens of paradise to the faithful and righteous, it was perfectly natural for the Arabs to accept this. The religion of Islam reconfirmed ancient and universal truths, imbuing them with a rigorous spiritual vision focused on one single invisible God. So when the Arab Muslims conquered Persia, Syria – Damascus in particular – and Spain, all countries with an abundance of water compared to Arabia, it is not surprising that they believed they had found their earthly paradise.

The Quran and Symbolism

There are many references in the Quran to the paradise gardens, the *jannat al-firdaws* promised to 'those who believe and do deeds of righteousness'.[33] Various epithets are attached to the word *jannat* (gardens) in order to describe the qualities that they possess: for example, *jannat al-khuld*[34] – *khuld* meaning immortality or eternity; *jannat al-naim*[35] – naim meaning bliss, delight or felicity; *jannat al-ma'wa*[36] – *ma'wa* meaning refuge, shelter, abode. Also *jannat 'Adn*[37] is mentioned – the Garden of Eden, suggesting the peace and harmony of mankind's primordial state. From these descriptive words attached to *jannat*, we see that the Islamic paradise gardens are not only blissful and eternal, but they are also a refuge or sanctuary, a sheltered and secure retreat (*khalwa* meaning 'retreat' is also a term used) far away from the disquiet of the world. However, the phrase most often used (over thirty times) is *Jannat tajri min tahtiha al-anhar*, 'Gardens Underneath which Rivers Flow'.[38] Even in translation the repetition of this phrase has a soothing rhythm to it and, closing one's eyes, it is possible to imagine being in a garden with water flowing through it (Figs. 29, 31 and 40).

'But the God-fearing shall be amongst gardens and fountains.'[39] Rivers flowing, water and fountains are the most powerful and memorable images one retains after reading the portrayals of the paradise gardens in the Quran. There is no doubt that the reason that water is the essential element in an Islamic garden is both because of the lack of it in the desert lands of Arabia and because of the importance placed upon it in the Quran (see Chapter 4). The Almighty knew that in order to tempt his flock back onto the 'straight path' (*al-sirata mustaqim*),[40] He must promise them rewards in the Afterlife that they would understand and desire and which they already revered for their life-giving properties – such as water and shade. Islam gave the first Muslims the knowledge and faith that these two elements, together with the rest of the natural world, were not to be worshipped for themselves alone: they must be revered for what they represent. Nature and beauty are outward symbols of an inward grace. Throughout the Quran the faithful are exhorted to meditate upon these signs or symbols, since everything in the created world is a sign or symbol of God: 'So God makes clear His signs for you; haply you will

Figs. 28 (top right) and 29 (bottom right). Gardens in the Generalife at the Alhambra.

understand.' (II:243) The Quran also refers to the mediocrity and ephemeral nature of this lower life compared to the happiness of the life everlasting and the gardens of paradise: 'The present life is naught but a sport and a diversion ... the world to come is better and more enduring.' (XLVII:38)

Human beings would cease to be truly *muslim*, literally in submission to God, if they were to revere the created world as an end in itself (see page 33). The world should be seen for what it is – an illusion (*maya* in Hinduism) that both veils and reveals the archetypal heavenly world. When a civilization is centred on the sacred, whether it be Islamic, North American Indian or medieval Christian, the practical is always inextricably linked to the spiritual. This is the language of symbolism – linking the everyday practical activities back to their heavenly archetype. But human beings are forgetful and need to be continually reminded that the things of this world are transparent and not an end in themselves. This is where, firstly, religion[41] comes in, and secondarily, sacred art. The Islamic garden can be seen as a kind of open-air sacred art, the content, form and symbolic language all combining to remind the visitor of the eternal, invisible realities that lie beneath outward appearances.

Jannat tajri min tahtiha al-anhar, 'Gardens Underneath which Rivers Flow': the idea of water flowing 'underneath' probably arose from the demands of a desert existence where the only source of water for most of the year was from the oases or underground irrigation systems such as the *qanats* in Persia. In the gardens themselves, the water is to be seen and experienced; in order to irrigate the flower-beds, it has to flow in straight channels and rills, often under the pathways, thereby giving the visitor the impression of actually being in a garden 'underneath which rivers flow'. On a more profound level, water flowing underneath suggests the nurturing of the 'garden

within', the 'Garden of the Heart', by the ever-flowing waters of the spirit, which serve to purify the soul of those on the spiritual path (*al-tariqah*). Indeed, water is symbolic of the soul in many sacred traditions, its fluidity and constantly purifying aspect is a reflection of the soul's ability to renew itself, yet always remain true to its source (see Chapter 4). The apparently endlessly flowing water in the Shalimar Gardens in Lahore or the gardens of the Generalife at the Alhambra are some of the most evocative representations of the Islamic gardens of paradise anywhere in the world: the sound of water not only muffles the voices of other people but has the miraculous effect of silencing one's own thoughts and allowing an overwhelming sense of peace to descend.

In Islam there are two main divisions in the Afterlife, heaven or paradise, and hell: the division between those who are saved and those who are not saved – and within these there is a hierarchy of many degrees.[42] It is written in the Quran: 'Whoso followeth My guidance, there shall no fear come upon them, neither shall they grieve'.[43] So the faithful and righteous may be sure to enter the paradise gardens, havens of such sublime beauty and happiness that only a foretaste of them can be experienced on earth. This foretaste is achieved in some of the great Islamic gardens across the world, several of which are observed in this study; and hopefully, with love and care, may also be achieved on a more modest scale in your own Islamic garden.

The following are some brief extracts to give an indication of the sense of rich abundance and blissful delight that a fuller reading of the Quranic descriptions of the gardens of paradise, (*jannat al-firdaws*) gives:

'Therein they shall recline upon couches... Immortal youths shall go about them, when thou seest them, thou supposest them scattered pearls, when thou seest them then, thou seest bliss and a great kingdom.'[44]

In Paradise there is 'no idle talk... no cry of lies'; 'no babble'; 'only the saying "Peace, Peace"'.[45]

'We shall strip away all rancour that is in their breasts; as brothers they shall be upon couches set face to face.'[46]

There is a perfect temperate climate, 'they shall see neither sun nor bitter cold'.[47]

There will be cool pavilions, couches, cushions and carpets and silk attire, 'green garments of silk and brocade'.[48,49]

Weariness is unknown in this paradise, 'there shall be repose and ease... no fatigue there shall smite them'.[50]

Fruit will be in abundance; 'produce is eternal... such fruits as they shall choose and such flesh of fowl as they desire'[51] will be provided.

Gold and silver jewellery will be worn and 'sweet potions' will be drunk from 'vessels of silver' and 'goblets of crystal'[52] and they are of such purity that there are no after-effects, 'no brows throbbing, no intoxication'.[53]

An essential element of the gardens of paradise is that they are eternal, that the righteous are there forever, 'therein to dwell for ever; that is indeed the mighty triumph'.[54]

Finally, and movingly, the Lord rewards the faithful for remembering Him on earth: 'And their Lord shall give them to drink a pure draught. "Behold this is recompense for you, and your striving is thanked."'[55]

The wonderful joys and delights of the gardens of paradise as depicted in the Quran give the faithful a clear idea of the heavenly reward for their 'striving'. They transport the reader or listener to the heavenly realms, to a place of infinite and surpassing peace and felicity, which only the most dedicated spiritual seekers can reach on earth. This may only be achieved through the constant and sincere remembrance of God (*dhikr 'Allah*), through the nurturing of the garden within, the garden of the heart. This is the domain of the Sufis,[56] those who concentrate on the inward or mystical aspect of Islam and who understand profoundly that the visible world is a symbol, a transient mirror-image of an invisible eternal reality.[57]

Design and Symbolism: the Number Four

Although the four-fold garden design is used in other traditions, most notably the Christian where the monastic herb garden and the 'cloister garth' spring to mind, as well as most Oxford and Cambridge colleges, there is still no doubt that in most people's minds the classic *chahar-bagh* design is

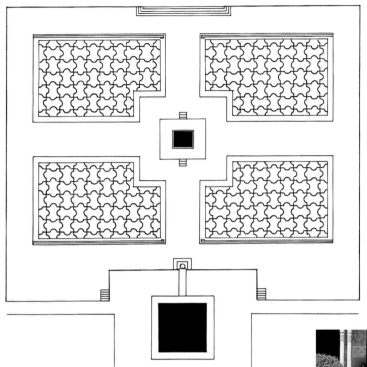

Fig. 30. Plan of the Anguri Bagh, part of the Red Fort at Agra.

describing his ascent to heaven (*miraj*) the Prophet Muhammad speaks of four rivers: one of water, one of milk, one of honey and one of wine. These four rivers are also mentioned in the gardens of paradise described in the Quran: 'Rivers of water unpolluted, and rivers of milk whereof the flavour changeth not, and rivers of wine delicious to the drinkers, and rivers of clear-run honey'[60] and in Genesis it is written, 'And a river went out of Eden to water the garden and from thence it was parted into four heads'.[61] Titus Burckhardt's description of the Court of Lions at the Alhambra is worth quoting in full here:

quintessentially Islamic. This quadripartite plan developed from a combination of the ancient pre-Islamic Persian prototype and the gardens of paradise described in the Quran and the Sayings of the Prophet.[58] Also, inherent within the number four is a universal symbolism based on an understanding of the natural world. It encompasses the four cardinal directions, the four elements and the four seasons. The cube, the three-dimensional form of the number four, represents solidity, the Earth.[59] The four-fold plan also recalls the fundamental *mandala* of the Vedic tradition, which is divided into nine squares and symbolizes the terrestrial realm. Tibetan Buddhist *tangkas* are also based on a square diagram within a circle, representing the earth encircled by heaven. The religion of Islam emphasized these ancient, widespread and universal truths, and invested them with a new spiritual understanding. In

Fig. 31. The Court of Lions, Alhambra.

Fig. 32. The Court of Lions, Alhambra.

but certainly they would all have been intuitively aware that the bounties of nature came from the Almighty: 'Surely in that are signs for a people who consider'.[63]

As with all the crafts/arts, including architecture and gardens, there would have been a master-craftsman who first conceived of the design and who would oversee the project as it developed. He would also have had some knowledge of the symbolic significance of his designs and would have worked in close collaboration with the ruler. It was the sultans and princes who initiated most of the large-scale gardens that still survive today. The great architect Sinan worked closely with Suleyman the Magnificent. At the Alhambra, Muhammad V was the patron who initiated the Court of Lions and who would have understood much of the profound meaning of the four-fold pattern. Interestingly, the word 'patron' comes from the Latin *patronus* meaning 'father' and implies care and protection as well as support and guidance. The word 'pattern' or model upon which a thing is designed also has its origins in *patron* and *patronus* – all reinforcing the idea (partly inherited from Plato) that everything on earth has its divine model or archetype in heaven.

The plan of the heavenly garden always includes the four rivers of Paradise flowing towards the four quarters of Heaven, or from them towards the centre. The water courses of the Court of Lions are fed from the two halls to the north and south and from the two stone canopies at the west and east end. The floor of the halls is set higher than the garden, and so the water, which flows from round basins, runs down over the threshold towards the fountain, where it collects around the lions and soaks away... The fountain itself with its twelve lions supporting a basin spewing water is an ancient symbol which reached the Alhambra from the pre-Christian Orient by way of all kinds of intermediary links. For the water-spewing lion is none other than the sun, from which life gushes forth, and the twelve lions are the twelve suns of the Zodiac, twelve months that are all present concurrently in eternity. They support a 'sea'... and this sea is the reservoir of Heavenly waters... The stone canopies, too, at opposite ends in the east and west of the garden, are also a part of the picture of the garden of paradise, for in the description of paradise, the Quran mentions high canopies or tents.'[62]

It is not known how many of the gardeners would have been aware of the profound meanings underlying the plan and construction of the gardens

Surat al-Rahman

In the Quran, not only are four rivers described but also, in the chapter entitled 'The All-Merciful' (*Surat al-Rahman*, Chapter LV) four gardens are described as two pairs. This is the longest reference to the gardens of paradise in the Quran and according to the commentator, these four gardens are divided into the first or lower pair which are the Garden of the Soul and the Garden of the Heart (reserved for the Righteous). The second and higher pair, 'and besides these shall be two gardens', is the Garden of the Spirit and the Garden of the Essence (reserved for the

Fig. 33. Centre of chahar-bagh, *Alcazar, Cordoba.*

with courtyard gardens integral to houses and public buildings. Moorish Spain has remarkable examples in the already mentioned courtyard gardens of the Alhambra Palaces and the gardens of the Generalife, as well as the gardens of the Alcazar in both Cordoba and Seville, which owe a great deal to their Muslim forbears. One glance at any of these gardens shows that they all have a fundamental element in common – water. Water, as is elaborated upon in Chapter 4, is the single most valuable and defining element in an Islamic garden. Just as there are rivers and fountains in the paradise gardens, so there are rivers, or rather channels or rills,

Foremost, *as-Sabiqun,* those who are closest to the Divine Presence). Each of these four gardens contains, respectively, its own fruit – the olive, the date, the fig and the pomegranate. There is a complex and profound symbolism contained in the four gardens of Surat al-Rahman which is not appropriate to go into any further here.[64] It is enough to emphasize that the *chahar-bagh,* the four-fold form of the archetypal Islamic garden, is not just a whim of design or a horticulturally convenient plan but is fundamentally a reflection of a higher Reality and a universal symbol of Divine Unity.

Development of the Chahar-Bagh

So the design of any of the famous Islamic gardens is based on the number four and the *chahar-bagh* became the principal symbol of the Quranic gardens of paradise. It was taken up and developed all over the Islamic world: for example, in Isphahan there is a road called the Avenue of the *Chahar-Bagh,* which in earlier times was lined with several beautiful four-fold gardens.[65] In India some of the great mausoleum gardens were built, such as that of Humayun, where the tomb is placed in the centre of the quadripartite plan, and the Taj Mahal, mentioned earlier, where the mausoleum is placed at one end, the *chahar-bagh* stretching out in front with a pool in the centre (Fig. 19). The beauty of these mausoleums and their gardens is quite breath-taking; however, it is probably unlikely that any reader will be intending to design one such as these – but who knows? More modest examples of *chahar-bagh*s are to be seen across the Islamic world in Morocco, Syria, Persia and Turkey,

Fig. 34. Humayun's tomb, India.

Fig. 35. A courtyard with chahar-bagh *lay-out, near the Suleymaniye, Istanbul.*

Fig. 36. The Alcazar, Cordoba, showing fountain at the centre of a chahar-bagh.

and at least one fountain, in the earthly gardens. Indeed, in many cases it is true to say that the geometric layout of a garden has been determined by the practical demands of irrigation, by the water-flow itself. In a traditional Islamic garden, as in all traditional Islamic art and architecture, there is never a distinction between what is carried out for practical purposes and its spiritual significance: they went hand-in-hand.

Peace

It is written in the Quran that the only word spoken in the gardens of paradise is 'Peace': 'There hear they no vain speaking nor recrimination. [Naught] but the saying "Peace, [and again] Peace"'.[66] One of the principal functions, therefore, of these earthly 'gardens of paradise' is to provide beautiful and harmonious

surroundings, a retreat from the world, where the soul can let go of distracting thoughts and be at peace. The word *Islam* is derived from the root s-l-m, which primarily means 'peace' but also means 'submission' or 'surrender', and taken together thus means 'the peace that comes when one's life is surrendered to God.'[67] The traditional greeting used across the world by all Muslims of whatever race, nationality, colour, background or age and regardless of whether any other words can be communicated, is *Asalaamu 'alaykum*, 'Peace be upon you', and the reply is, *Wa 'alaykum 'asalaam*, 'And upon you be Peace'. The two people greeting are each giving to the other a little echo of the paradise gardens. There is something extraordinarily beautiful about the courtesy, dignity and sobriety of this greeting, which is both warm and reserved at the same time: warm, in the sense that as two human beings before God – whatever station in life we are – we acknowledge each other as equals with respect;

reserved, because it requires no further communication: discretion and privacy is maintained and nothing further need be said.

So when we read that no words are spoken in the gardens of paradise except 'Peace', *salaam*, it seems completely natural. The search for paradise on earth is essentially the search for peace, not just peace from the world but more importantly peace from our own soul (*nafs*) – not the immortal soul, but the passional soul, the ego and all its desires. The much misused Arabic word *jihad* literally means 'struggle' or 'effort' and can take many forms such as a *jihad* against intolerance and discrimination; however, according to a saying of the Prophet Muhammad, the greater *jihad* (*al-jihad al-akbar*) is the war with our own souls. The longing, more often unconscious than conscious, for serenity of soul is like a vague memory of our primordial nature (*fitrah* in Arabic) when man was at peace with his Creator in the Garden of Eden and therefore at peace with his own soul. In order to regain this primordial paradise those seriously committed to the spiritual path (*al-tariqah*) must reach the state of constant remembrance of God (*dhikr 'Allah*) referred to earlier (page 28). The Islamic garden, the *chahar-bagh*, can be an aid in this remembrance; like all sacred art it provides a sanctuary as well as solace for the tired or troubled soul, putting worldly cares into perspective.

Parable

There is a powerful parable in the Quran (Sura XV111, *Al-Kahf*, The Cave) about a vain and proud man who is convinced that the beauty of his garden is all his own doing and that it will last forever, claiming, 'I do not think that this will ever perish; I do not think that the hour is coming; and if I am indeed returned to my Lord, I shall surely find a better resort than this.'[68] His companion is horrified at this arrogance and asks why he is not praising and thanking the Almighty for his beautiful and fertile garden, 'Why, when thou wentest into thy garden, didst thou not say, "As God will; there is no power except God"?' And this man, being faithful and righteous, can look forward to the heavenly gardens, 'yet it may be that my Lord will give

Fig. 37. Ablutions before prayer: the Shah Mosque, Isphahan.

me better than thy garden and loose on it [thy garden] a thunderbolt out of Heaven, so that in the morning it will be a slope of dust'.[69] Sure enough, because the arrogant one failed to acknowledge that he owed his good fortune to the generosity of his Lord, he was punished with a thunderbolt from heaven and his garden was destroyed.

It is perhaps this story that is elaborated upon by Washington Irving in one of his *Tales of the Alhambra* in which a wicked astrologer promises the Moorish King that he can make for him the elusive 'Garden of Irem [*Irem* or *Eram* meaning Heaven] one of the prodigies of Arabia the happy... Adorned with fountains and fish-ponds and groves and flowers and orchards laden with delicious fruit' but which, for most travellers, disappears like a mirage. According to the astrologer, the sumptuous garden was the creation of King Sheddad, the great-grandson of the Prophet Noah (*Nuh* in Arabic) who founded a stately city and when 'he saw its grandeur, his heart was puffed up with pride and arrogance, and he determined to build a royal palace with gardens that should rival all that was related in the Quran of the celestial paradise. But the curse of heaven fell upon him for his presumption. He and his subjects were swept from the earth, and his splendid city and palace and gardens were laid under a perpetual spell that hides them from human sight, excepting that they are seen at intervals, by way of keeping his sin in perpetual remembrance'.[70] In Shiraz

in Iran there is a garden with orange and lemon groves, cypress trees and a rose-garden called the Bagh-I Eram.[71] It was built in the nineteenth century and was no doubt inspired by the descriptions of the Heavenly gardens as well as this tale of the sumptuous garden, which is but a mirage – a reminder that however seductive the earthly gardens may be, they are but an illusion.

Tradition and Traditional Art

The merging of the sacred and secular is a crucial part of traditional Islamic culture, as it is of all traditional cultures.[72] Tradition means, briefly, the 'handing-over' of precious learning from one generation to another and can be traced back to its ultimate source in Divine Revelation. Besides the contemplative aspect of the Islamic garden, it is also true to say that it was for pleasure and love-making, political discussions and parties, as well as for growing vegetables and fruit. The garden was for resting and taking refuge in, and for delighting in the cooling and soothing properties of water; for the aesthetic and sensory delights of flowers, the scent of blossom, the song of the birds, as well as the protective shade of trees. All these things were enjoyed, not for their sake alone, but in the full knowledge that they were a reflection of the bliss of the heavenly gardens to come.

> If his [a Muslim's] house has no windows onto the street and is normally built around an inner

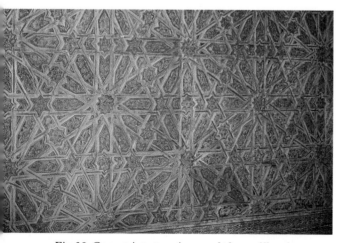

Fig. 38. Geometric pattern in carved plaster Alhambra.

court from which the rooms receive light and air, this is not simply in response to the frequently torrid climate of Muslim lands; it is clearly symbolic. In conformity with this symbolism, the inner court of a house is an image of paradise; when it contains a fountain and water-courses which gush forth to water trees and flowers, it does in effect recall the descriptions in the Quran of the abode of the blessed.[73]

Thus when one author writes that 'the conclusion that the Quran supplied the blueprint for Islamic gardens is methodologically fallacious' [73A] she is correct in that it does not offer a 'blueprint', that is, a practical guide to measuring out your plot as the Bible instructs Noah how to build the Ark. However, the Quran offers something incommensurably deeper and more powerful than a 'blueprint' – it offers the inward dimension, the *haqiqah*, Truth. This is no less than Divine Revelation with its emphasis on Unity, *al-Tawhid*. When combined with a knowledge and love of the natural world, as well as universal forms inherited from ancient civilizations, it resulted in the creation of a new art, an art that was beautiful because it was true. The criterion of traditional art is that it is has meaning – it performs a function – as well as being aesthetically pleasing.[74] 'Art for art's sake' has no place in the traditional world. The fact that *janna* means both garden and paradise is indicative in itself of this lack of distinction between the sacred and the profane.

The Concept of Unity

The concept of Unity, *al-Tawhid*, is the fundamental message of the Quran. In brief this is the awareness that 'there is no divinity save God',[75] which could also be rendered 'there is no reality save the Reality', that is, the only reality is God. Thus existence is entirely centred on the consciousness of Divine Unity and this means that everything in the created world – all of phenomena – is transparent; that is, behind the ephemeral beauty of the outward form lies the ineffable spirit within. It is this invisible, eternal and transcendent quality that gives the world of nature and all of manifestation its meaning: all else passes away. As Titus Burckhardt has written:

The most profound link between Islamic art and the Quran… lies not in the form of the Quran but in its *haqiqah*, its formless essence, and more particularly in the notion of *tawhid*, unity or union, with its contemplative implications; Islamic art – by which we mean the entirety of plastic arts in Islam – is essentially the projection into the visual order of certain aspects or dimensions of Divine Unity.[76]

The projection of the concept of unity into the visual order, through gardens, is the main subject of the next chapter.

Conclusion

Increasingly, people are attempting to create their own miniature paradise gardens, green and secluded places in which to soothe the soul. The *chahar-bagh*, with its emphasis on the contemplative dimension, may well offer some readers inspiration for their own courtyard gardens. Many writers across the centuries and across continents have conveyed beautifully the power of a garden to console and restore; for instance, John Donne begins his poem *Twickenham Garden* with: 'Blasted with sighs, and surrounded with tears, hither I come to seek the spring'. Spring suggests hope, renewal and rebirth, and in this garden the poet also 'receives such balmes as else cure everything'. Shakespeare often uses the analogy between the soul and the garden, as well as the heart and the garden, both universal themes explored by many a Persian poet, as we shall see later in the book. Hamlet compares his own state of mind to an untended garden: 'Tis an unweeded garden that grows to seed; things rank and gross in nature possess it merely.'[77] Just as one cannot neglect the garden for a moment since disease or predator will strike, so one cannot neglect one's own soul, so vulnerable is it to tempting and negative influences.

However, the main concern of this book is to make suggestions as to how the contemplative and peaceful atmosphere of a *chahar-bagh* may be captured in a garden created in northern Europe and countries with similar climates. In the next chapter we will look at the fundamental ground-plan and overall design of a *chahar-bagh*, and the chapters following will concentrate on the essential elements of the traditional Islamic garden: geometry and architectural ornament, water, trees and shrubs, and then plants and flowers. The final chapter is a case study of the 'Carpet Garden', an Islamic garden based on an original idea by HRH The Prince of Wales.

The traditional perspective, and this coincides with the Islamic view, that the garden is a place of beauty reflecting the beauty and love of the Creator, is sensitively summed up by one of the greatest of English gardeners, Gertrude Jekyll:

I try for beauty and harmony everywhere, and especially for harmony of colour. A garden so created gives the delightful feeling of repose, and refreshment, and purest enjoyment of beauty, that seems to my understanding to be the best fulfilment of its purpose; while to the diligent worker its happiness is like the offering of a constant hymn of praise. For I hold that the best purpose of a garden is to give delight and refreshment of mind, to soothe, to refine, and to lift up the heart in a spirit of praise and thankfulness.[78]

Fig. 39. Courtyard Garden, Damascus, showing large fountain at the centre of four intersecting paths (Maktab 'Anbar).

CHAPTER 2

Design and Layout

In this chapter the fundamental principals of design for an Islamic garden, primarily the *chahar-bagh*, are considered, together with how they may be applied to your particular space. Before embarking on designing an Islamic garden, you should consider carefully whether the space is suitable for such a project, as well as taking into account the aspect, soil, surroundings and so on. The underlying principles may be adapted or interpreted to fit successfully into the required site, providing that the overall sense of unity, discussed in the previous chapter and fundamental to all Islamic design, is kept uppermost in your vision.

A Sense of Unity

What is of the utmost importance when designing your garden is not simply to take a nice Islamic-style element or two, such as a fountain or some geometric-patterned tiles, assemble them and hope that (hey presto!) an Islamic garden will miraculously appear. This 'magpie' garden-maker is more likely to end up with a rather cluttered jumble of a garden, pleasing in parts but overall not very satisfying – and not truly Islamic. Islam, as mentioned before, is spread across widely diversified regions of the world, so an Islamic garden will look different in Malaysia from how it looks in Iran, say, or North Africa. However, as with Islamic art and architecture in general, wherever they may be in the Islamic world, and however varied is their appearance, they are unquestionably Islamic. This is because, as established in Chapter 1, they refer back to the all-embracing concept of unity, the principle underpinning all Islamic art, architecture and garden design. Through studying the language used by Muslim designers and gardeners of the past (primarily gardens from the tenth to the end of the

seventeenth centuries) a tremendous amount can be learned: looking at the way they employ geometry and water in their gardens and the proportion between these elements and the planting, as well as the harmonious relationship with the surrounding architecture – this is all vital. It can be seen that after the two primary elements of an Islamic garden, water and shade, comes the important third element, geometric layout. The fourth component is architecture – the linking of the house with the garden. In Morocco, for example, there is a particular type of house called a *riyadh*, which is a house with a garden attached, usually walled on

Fig 41. The tomb of Itimad ud-Dawlah, Agra.

Fig 40. Patio de la Acequia, Generalife.

three sides, the fourth side being the house.[79] In the larger Mughal and Persian gardens, architecture in the form of pavilions or 'kiosks' (a word probably derived from the Turkish) for sitting in were common features, often placed near the water for a cooling breeze; and the mausoleum gardens can be seen as a beautiful integration of the mausoleum building itself with its formal surrounding garden (e.g. the tomb of Itimad ud-Dawlah, Fig. 41). As Constance Villiers Stuart observed in the early twentieth century: 'In Persia and India a house or palace is always understood to be included under the name of garden, and the whole composition was closely and beautifully interwoven.'[80] This principle of the close interweaving of the house with the garden is crucial when beginning to lay out the ground-plan of your Islamic garden.

Beyond the different component parts of water, planting, geometry and architecture lies the secret force that draws them all together into a satisfying and harmonious composition: the concept of unity, *al-tawhid*, the profound message of the Quran, which penetrates every aspect of a practising Muslim's life. After spending some time contemplating a garden that exemplifies these principles, such as the Patio de la Acequia at the Generalife[81] (Figs. 40 and 52) or the smaller *chahar-bagh* in the Alacazar in Cordoba (Fig. 36) the visitor will begin to understand what is really meant by this; this unity gives the Islamic garden its special contemplative quality. It is evident in all traditional Islamic gardens, whether it is the vast Shalimar Gardens in Lahore or the more intimate courtyard gardens of Damascus or Fes (see illustration, page 16). 'In Islamic art, unity is never the result of a synthesis of component elements; it exists *a priori*, and all the particular forms are deduced from it; the total form of a building or interior exists before its parts, whether they have a static function or not.'[82]

So, how can we achieve a sense of unity in our own Islamic garden? There is no precise and definitive prescription: it requires first of all a certain commitment and responsibility on the part of the gardener (and client too if you are a garden designer) to understand something, however little, of the religious tradition that informs the design; and, second, to keep this in mind as you work out the practical logistics of fitting a design into a certain site.

Then, as with all creative work, much thought and contemplation is involved, as well as research, knowledge and a true love of the subject concerned – and prayer as well for many of us. Then, with a certain humility, inspiration will come *insha 'Allah* (God willing) – hopefully sooner rather than later! To be 'inspired' means literally to breathe in the divine spirit, to receive the breath of God. Inspiration needs a formal language to work with, to manifest the idea – and in creating an Islamic garden, besides being familiar with traditional Islamic architecture, design and gardens of the past, the most important language is that of geometry: this is explored later in the chapter and in Chapter 3.

Contemplative Apprenticeship

In former times in both the East and the West, and until recently in many parts of the East, the apprenticeship of a traditional craftsman lasted for many years (see Chapter 3). The apprentice would follow his master's teaching until he had reached the required level, both in technical expertise and in the disciplining of his soul, to progress further. Then, once he possessed to a high degree all the skills necessary for putting his ideas into practice, together with a certain transformation of his character, he would be allowed to design something of his own. It was the same in gardening, but today, as with every occupation, progress has been speeded up. In Japan, for instance, gardeners in the past would spend three years sweeping up leaves before being allowed to prune – now they are expected to prune from their first day.[83] The slow contemplative kind of training, it seems, is no longer practicable in the modern world. Nevertheless, the main point is that the more understanding and experience you have had of traditional Islamic art and design as a whole, or as a practitioner of geometry and/or as a gardener, the easier it will be to design your Islamic garden. As is true of the practice of all traditional arts and crafts, the success of the outcome depends on a combination of many elements: sincere intention, knowledge, experience, practical skill, a sense of the sacred and a sense of beauty, a certain 'emptiness' of heart or humility, and above all a real love of the work – all these are needed in some degree or other

Fig. 42. Court of Myrtles, Alhambra.

in order to be open to inspiration from Heaven and give this inspiration a physical form in keeping with the tradition.

This is not intended to put you off designing your garden but it is intended to stress the importance of doing some research and spending as much time as possible looking at photographs of Islamic gardens or, better still, visiting as many as possible. Only then can one really begin to understand the underlying unity that marks out an Islamic garden from other gardens. After spending many hours over many visits absorbing the atmosphere of the Patio de la Acequia in the Generalife, the Court of Myrtles and other courts of the Alhambra (such as the garden court of Lindaraja [Fig. 126]) the Azem Palace courtyards in Damascus – to name just a few, one thing became crystal clear: it was the profound love and understanding that the Muslim designers and craftsmen had of the harmonious relationship and proportion between the architecture, the geometric plan, the water and the planting – the integral unity of the whole. There is no doubt that this understanding came about because their whole way

of living, mostly unconsciously, was penetrated by the central message of the Quran: and it was this that made possible their astonishing achievements in the art of garden design.

A Sense of Order

Practically and symbolically, as it has been emphasized, a precise geometry centred around the primary four-fold layout is crucial when designing your *chahar-bagh*. Ways of employing geometry in the garden, apart from the basic layout, are suggested in the following chapter. There should be no winding sinewy paths in a traditional Islamic garden – the rhythmic element is provided by nature in the form of the foliage, plants and flowers. John Caie (1811–79), head gardener to the eighth Duke of Argyll at Inverary Castle, could have been a Muslim gardener in his keenness on order, stating, 'Order is the source of peace'. Order is paramount in an Islamic garden and is a reflection of the garden-maker's understanding of the laws of the cosmos. Unity manifests itself through order and the harmonious relationship between the geometric ground-plan, the planting, the water and the surrounding architecture. Sir Thomas Browne wrote that, 'All things began in order, so shall they end and so shall they begin again according to the ordainer of order and mystical mathematics of the city of Heaven.'[84] The religion of Islam brought with it a heightened sense of universal order and acute awareness that God and the universe, humankind and nature, are all linked in mathematical order and pattern. This pattern is manifested in nature, from the petals of flowers and the formation of leaves, to the infinite variety of snowflakes and the structure of crystals. Islamic art captures the order beneath the surface, the essence beneath the illusion. The Muslim gardener imposes order upon nature with a cosmological wisdom manifested through design and geometry.

When designing an Islamic garden words such as symmetry, balance, harmony and proportion spring to mind as well as order and geometry. Proportion means, essentially, the 'relationship between things or parts of a thing'.[85] Plato stressed the importance of understanding the underlying order of things, emphasizing that it is only through this that it is possible to know the divine order of the cosmos. The Arabs inherited the concept of the importance of order and, as is well known, it is the Arab Muslims who took on the mantle of Greek knowledge and translated and disseminated it all over Europe. This is true not only of the work of philosophers such as Plato, but also of scientific and horticultural works (see Chapters 5 and 6). The most famous of Arab philosophers, Muhyiddin Ibn 'Arabi, (known as the 'Sheikh al-Akbar', the 'Greatest Sheikh') held that 'symmetry and correspondence (*mudaha*) and the

Fig. 43. Small area at the Alhambra gardens showing formal box hedges; the hedges are laid out to geometric designs in several places which, although relatively recent (twentieth century), are in keeping with the Islamic ideal of order.

display of beauty (*mubaha*), to be two of the most important premises by which mankind may gain knowledge of the Creator'.[86]

Prominent Figures in Islamic Garden Design History

Cyrus the Great and the Persian Emperors

The aim of this book is not to trace a careful historic and geographic development of the *chahar-bagh* design and its various interpretations. However, the importance of the ancient gardens of the Achaemenid period (500–300BC) including those at Pasargardae, built by Cyrus the Great in the sixth century BC and the *pairidaezas* (hunting-parks) of the Sassanian period (AD200–600) should briefly be mentioned for their role in the *chahar-bagh* layout. These no longer survive but archaeological remains reveal their sophisticated irrigation systems to us. These consisted of long, straight gravity-fed channels, interrupted every so often by basins about a metre square; there were also open ditches for watering plants and an hydraulic system. Besides being aware of the political power that these great gardens represented, especially when attached to a magnificent palace such as Persepolis, the Persian emperors were conscious of a more profound and universal meaning. The mysterious four-fold nature of the universe was reflected in the repeat four-fold geometric design of their irrigation channels. Similar to the later Islamic gardens, practical, aesthetic, political and spiritual needs were all beautifully integrated in these gardens. Cyrus and his descendents had a great love for their gardens and *pairidaezas*, one of the emperors declaring that he never sat down to dinner without first performing some task of gardening.

Ibn al-'Awwam

John Harvey writes that the Moorish twelfth century treatise by Ibn al-'Awwam 'breaks new ground by suggesting here and there principles of design'.[87] According to Harvey, Ibn al-'Awwam recommends cypresses to mark the corners of beds and also to be planted in rows alongside main walks (just as there are in the Generalife gardens today. See Fig. 160). He also recommends other trees for planting in rows such as cedars and pines, as well as citrus and sweet bay. He suggests that pools should be shaded by planting trees nearby (something we are told to be careful about today because of the shedding of leaves onto the water, and in fact he does add a similar warning) such as the pomegranate, elm, poplar or willow. For hedges, box and laurel are recommended, as well as plants for climbing up trellises such as ivy and jasmine, with the grapevine used ornamentally.[88] From a design point of view, it is fascinating that these remarks, written nearly one thousand years ago still, in the main, hold true today. One feels that Rosemary Verey and her 'full stops' to mark the corners of beds would have got on well with Ibn al-'Awwam!

Ibn Luyun

About one hundred years later in 1248, in Almeria in southern Spain, Ibn Luyun wrote his book on the principles of beauty and the purpose of learning. This looks at the basic rules of landscape design and agriculture, and makes recommendations that could well prove helpful when designing your own garden, providing it is a large one.[89] For example, first of all he suggests an elevated site for the house, 'Both for reasons of vigilance and of layout', a southern aspect, the entrance at one side and the water source (cistern or well) on an upper level. He continues, and is worth quoting at some length since his ideas are practical and can be adapted to different sites:

> Or instead of a well have a watercourse where the water runs underneath the shade... Then next to the reservoir plant shrubs whose leaves do not fall and which [therefore] rejoice the sight; And somewhat further off, arrange flowers of different kinds, and further off still, evergreen trees, And around the perimeter climbing vines, and in the centre of the whole enclosure a sufficiency of vines; And under the climbing vines let there be paths which surround the garden to serve as margin. And amongst the fruit trees include the [common] grapevine similar to a slim woman, or wood-producing trees; Afterward arrange the virgin soil for planting whatever you wish should

prosper. In the background let there be trees like the fig or any other which does no harm: and plant any fruit tree which grows big in a confining basin so that its mature growth may serve as protection against the north wind without preventing the sun from reaching [the plants]. In the centre of the garden let there be a pavilion in which to sit, and with vistas on all sides, but of such a form that no one approaching could overhear the conversation within and whereunto none could approach undetected. Clinging to it let there be [rambler] roses and myrtle, likewise all manner of plants with which a garden is adorned. And this last should be longer than it is wide in order that the beholder's gaze may expand in contemplation.[90]

The Patio de la Aceqia, the enclosed garden in the large Generalife Gardens mentioned above, is laid out according to Ibn Luyun's recommendation of being longer than it is wide (Figs. 40 and 52). Instead of a pavilion at the centre, it has pavilions (in fact originally the summer palace of the Sultan) at either end, a wall on the side set against the hill and a wall pierced with arches on the fourth side with wonderful views across to the Alhambra. Interestingly, Ibn Luyun is obviously keen on cultivating vines for the production of wine as well as for eating the grapes. The Muslim rulers of the Spanish 'statelets', the *taifa* kings,[91] were evidently flexible in their interpretation of the Quranic injunctions regarding alcohol. Al-Mutamid, the ruler of Seville and overlord of Cordoba in the eleventh century, made a trip to the legendary ruined splendour of Madinat az-Zahra where, with his courtiers, 'they wandered from palace to palace, hacking away at the branches and brambles… exchanging cups of wine on those high terraces… In the garden they settled themselves on springtime carpets striped with white flowers and bordered with streams and water-channels… All the while they drank cups of wine and wandered about, both enjoying themselves and yet pausing for reflection'.[92] This is a far cry from a traveller in Iran recently who, when driving along roads lined with vineyards near Shiraz (the home of the well-known variety of grape) was fiercely assured by his guide that the grapes were only for eating.

Emperor Babur

Ibn Luyun's description is similar to that of the Emperor Babur (d. 1530). He was the first Mughal emperor of India, (the word *mughal* being a corruption of 'mongol', the people from whom he was descended) and his memoirs make clear his notion of an ideal garden. Babur ruled Kabul for twenty-two years before going to India. In his memoirs he describes how he wanted his Garden of Fidelity (*Bagh-I Wafa*) to be laid out near the city saying that it should be set on a high position on rising ground, facing south with running water nearby. When Babur invaded India, or Hindustan as it was called then, he wanted to create gardens similar to the ones he had visited in Herat in western Afghanistan as a young man. Here in the fifteenth century the ruler, Husayn Bayqara, had constructed a vast *chahar-bagh* garden around the city, as well as smaller gardens such as the romantic-sounding Heart-Expanding Garden (*Bagh-I Dilkusha*). But the land of Hindustan was a challenge, even for someone of Babur's skill and determination:

> One of the great defects of Hindustan being its lack of running waters, it kept coming to my mind that waters should be made to flow by means of wheels erected wherever I might settle down, also that grounds should be laid out in an orderly and symmetrical way. With this object in view, we crossed the Jun-water to look at garden-grounds a few days after entering Agra; these grounds were so bad and unattractive that we traversed them with a hundred disgusts and repulsions. So ugly and displeasing were they that the idea of making a *chahar-bagh* in them passed from my mind, but needs must! As there was no other land near Agra, that same ground was taken in hand a few days later.[93]

Evidently the layout that Ibn Luyun and Babur are referring to are for larger rural gardens, open to vistas, not the inward-looking courtyard gardens. However, the principles are similar in that water and ordered layout are uppermost in both their minds (shade is mentioned by Ibn Luyun in the first sentence but Babur was more concerned with how to achieve running water and symmetry). Writing during the reign of the Emperor Akbar (1556–1605), Babur's grandson, Abu al-Fazl, observed that 'Gardens and flower-beds are everywhere to be found. Formerly people used to plant their gardens without any order, but since the time of the arrival in India of the Emperor Babur, a more methodical arrangement of the gardens has obtained; and travellers nowadays admire the beauty of the palaces and their murmuring fountains.'[94]

Babur himself is laid to rest back in his homeland, Afghanistan, in a pavilion originally built by his grandson, Shah Jahan, in 1640 and restored in the late-nineteenth and the mid-twentieth century. In around 1970 a traveller wrote of Babur's tomb, 'The site is an old and disused garden out of sight of the city, on a hillside above the Kabul river with mulberry trees and one or two enormous planes of such a girth and with such limbs they may have stood here since Babur's death. The mulberries probably date from 1640'.[95] Today (2003-2004), since the recent war, the surrounding garden is undergoing major repair and restoration and it is beginning to return to its former beauty. The tomb is inside a mosque built from Kandahar marble and there is a marvellous inscription to this garden-loving emperor over the main entrance:

Only this mosque of beauty, this temple of nobility, constructed for the prayer of saints and the epiphany of cherubs, was fit to stand in so venerable a sanctuary as this highway of archangels, this theatre of heaven, the light garden of the God-forgiven angel king whose rest is in the garden of heaven, Zahiruddin Muhammad Babur the Conqueror.[96]

Names of Gardens

We seem to have lost the poetic art of naming gardens. Babur's many beautifully named gardens in Kabul are famous, such as his 'Garden of Fidelity', 'Heart-Expanding Garden', 'Moonlight Garden' and 'City-Adorning Garden', (which had a stream eight feet wide running down its centre, which he and his courtiers tried to jump but failed).[96A] In Isphahan there is the 'Garden of the Eight Paradises' and in Turkey, especially the imperial seat of Istanbul, the

Ottomans' created a multitude of gardens, both palace gardens – one with 'jasmine banisters' – and private ones;[96B] these latter were often known after the owner-gardener, such as 'Enthusiastic Suleyman's Garden', 'Nurseryman Abdullah's Garden' and 'Hothouse Ali's Garden'. Further afield, the Chinese surpass everyone in their inventive and romantic names. In *A Record of Famous Gardens of Luoyang* written by LI Gefei in AD1095 he describes many gardens all of which have enchanting names such as 'Appreciation of Seclusion Terrace', the 'Double Wave Balcony', 'The Garden of Gathered Springtime', and the 'Back to Benevolence Garden'. The Chinese also give their pavilions and arbours names such as 'Content with what One Has' or 'Purified by Flowers'.[96C] It may seem pretentious to name one's urban courtyard garden but perhaps, after creating your own Islamic garden, you will be inspired by the Mughals, the Persians, the Ottoman Turks or the Chinese!

European and Islamic Garden Design

The power of the garden as a symbol to awaken in the visitor an awareness of the spiritual essence that the natural world both veils and reveals, is by no means confined to Islam. It is also very much a part of the Western Christian tradition, in particular the enclosed quadripartite garden, the *hortus conclusus*. There is no doubt that there is a tremendous similarity in outlook between the mentality that gave rise to the traditional Islamic *chahar-bagh* and the outlook of medieval Europe, which gave rise to a variety of monastic gardens, primarily based on a similar four-fold plan. In both cases there was a fundamental understanding that this temporary lower world was a preparation for the eternal afterlife, an understanding that was to change in Europe during the Renaissance. In both these worlds, Islamic and Christian, gardening was both a physical necessity – producing food to eat and herbs for medicinal purposes – while at the same time it glorified God through the ordering and tending of His creation. Benedictine as well as Cistercian monastic life was centred on order: a well-ordered spiritual life meant a well-ordered everyday life and this principle permeated every activity including

Fig. 44. Salisbury Cathedral Cloisters.

since not only did it symbolize rebirth and everlasting life but also it was considered restful for the eyes – just as the desert Arabs experienced. Hugh of Fouilloy observed, 'The green turf which is in the middle of the material cloister refreshes encloistered eyes and their desire to study returns. It is truly the nature of the colour green that it nourishes the eyes and preserves their vision.'[99] Monasteries also sometimes possessed an enclosed space called a 'paradise garden', perhaps partly in remembrance of Christ's words to one of the thieves who was crucified with him, 'Today thou shalt be with me in Paradise.'[100] This 'paradise garden' was possibly attached to, or in some cases the same as, the cemetery orchard; as early as the ninth and tenth centuries there are documents recording flowering trees and orchards in graveyards around churches, echoing the Islamic concept of the paradise gardens full of fruit trees.[101] Other gardens attached to monasteries were herb gardens (herbariums) and the cellarer's garden which mainly consisted of vegetables.

The great European botanical gardens of the sixteenth and seventeenth centuries, such as Padua (founded 1545) and Oxford (founded 1621, originally the Physic Garden), were also laid out to a square or rectangular plan, divided into four quarters and then quarters again to separate the plant genera and species. In fact the Islamic world had already founded botanic gardens far earlier: for example, the eleventh-century garden at Toledo founded by Ibn Wafid, and a little later in the same century, the royal garden at Seville became a scientific and botanic garden under Ibn Bassal. The European botanic gardens were partly constructed to literally recreate the Garden of Eden. The founders of botanical gardens thought that by exploring every corner of the world and bringing back a specimen of every plant in

agriculture and gardening. This is very similar to Islam, where the order of five prayers a day with ablutions before prayers means that the day is not only structured from beginning to end but is punctuated regularly by the remembrance of God. This lack of differentiation between the sacred and secular continues to this day in most Islamic countries, and is remarked upon elsewhere in the book, since it is of fundamental importance in understanding Islamic culture and civilization.[97]

Similarities between the Islamic garden and the medieval European garden can be seen, for example, in cloisters or the 'cloister garth' as it was originally called. These were attached to all the great monasteries and cathedrals and consisted of covered, arcaded walks surrounding an open grass quadrangle, for example, the Little Cloisters at Westminster Abbey and those at Salisbury Cathedral. They were primarily for walking meditation and prayer and, like the quadrangles of many of the early Oxford and Cambridge colleges,[98] are based on an enclosed square, or approximately square, plan. As far as we know these squares were always lawn with perhaps a cedar of Lebanon planted in the centre, as at Salisbury Cathedral, to remind the faithful of the Holy Land. As in a mosque, there was always some form of water for washing, either a fountain or perhaps rainwater collected in a pool. Interestingly, similar to Islam, the colour green was important, existence they would thereby represent the many faces of the Creator. Jacob Bobart (1599–1679) was the first gardener of the Oxford Botanic garden who, 'By his care and his industry replenish'd the walls with all manner of good fruits our clime would ripen, and bedeck the earth with a great variety of trees, plants and exotic flowers, dayly augmented by the Botanists, who bring them hither from remote Quarters of ye world.'[102]

In the Islamic world, the four-fold design was not only apparent in gardens but also in the layout of mosques, *madrasas* (the theological schools) and caravanserais. The great mosques of Egypt or Safavid mosques of Persia (Fig. 37) or mosques of Morocco are all constructed around large courtyards with central ablution fountains or pools. Other examples are the Bou Inaniyya *madrasas* in Fes and Meknes, and the khans and caravanserais in Damascus. Similarly, in Europe, medieval and renaissance manor houses were often built around a central courtyard or several courtyards.

Before the development of the monastery gardens in northern Europe there was little distinction between pleasure gardens, kitchen gardens, orchards and farmland – indeed, there were no gardens as we would recognize them. It has been observed many times that in the early Middle Ages, Britain and northern Europe were horticulturally backward compared to southern Europe, the Near East and Persia. They were 'far behind the sophisticated sunnier courtyards surrounding the Mediterranean where the influence of the Arabic and Near-Eastern worlds was beginning to unfold and where everything grew in sumptuous splendour'.[103] However, monastic gardens developed fairly quickly after AD1000 with pilgrims, monks and crusaders bringing back seeds from the Near East; but they were still not in the same league as the early Muslims who, after all, had built the great palace of Madinat az-Zahra outside Cordoba in the tenth century. From the archaeological remains, the splendour of this palace has been described by many an historian: its profusion of gardens, water-channels and fountains was an extraordinary accomplishment, especially when the complex irrigation system that was required is taken into account (see Chapter 4).[104]

In the larger Islamic gardens, similar to the medieval European gardens, there was no large-scale separation between orchard, garden and kitchen garden. It seems that fruit-trees, flowers and vegetables were grown within the same area but neatly divided into plots, separated by geometric paths or irrigation channels. One of the reasons for everything being grown in close proximity is possibly the descriptions of the paradise gardens in the Quran, which include fruit trees of all kinds and delicious foods to eat, as well as trees, shrubs and scented flowers. There are a few sayings of the Prophet Muhammad that emphasize the importance of cultivating edible plants as a form of charity: 'No Muslim who plants trees and from their fruits the human beings or the beasts or birds eat, but that would be taken as an act of charity on the Day of Resurrection.'[105] Some English friends who lived in

Fig. 45. Fountain, Bou Inaniya Madrasa, Fes.

Egypt in the 1940s and 1950s, at Giza near the Pyramids, made a beautiful garden full of roses and other colourful and scented flowers. They were modestly pleased with their achievement and thought their neighbours might like to see it but their reaction was to gasp in dismay because none of the plants and flowers were edible!

The combination of monks and pilgrims travelling from the Holy Land, as well as soldiers returning from the Crusades, meant a steady improvement in horticultural knowledge in northern Europe. In addition to this were the increasing number of Greek scientific, philosophical and horticultural manuscripts introduced into Europe by the Arabs. These were first translated from Greek into Arabic and subsequently from Arabic into Latin, the *lingua franca* of the 'educated classes' of north-western Europe. The most famous of the Greek works was a book of plant descriptions called *De Materia Medica* written by a physician in the Roman army called Pedanius Dioscorides. It was written in the first century AD but only copies of it survive, the earliest dating from the sixth century AD. This became the primary source of horticultural knowledge in the Islamic world, although the Arabs themselves were fast to learn and soon began writing up their own observations. A well-known saying of the Prophet Muhammad is 'Seek knowledge, even unto China' and this meant there was (and still is) a great emphasis on learning for all Muslims, for whom it is a responsibility to seek knowledge and study the natural world. One of the earliest of the Arab horticultural treatise to be imported to Muslim Spain was the *Book of Plants* by the 'Father of Arab Botany' as he was known, Abu Hanifah al-Dinawari (c. AD820–895). It was taken there by Yunus ibn Ahmed al-Harrani in about AD880. Soon after this, Ibn al-Wahshiyya al-Kaldani compiled a treatise on agriculture called *Nabataean Agriculture*, which became 'one of the most widely quoted of all source-books in the Arabic-speaking world'.[106]

In Chapters 5 and 6, the plant lists of other Muslim gardeners and writers on horticulture, such as the famous Ibn Wafid (AD999–1075) and Ibn Bassal, his successor, will be looked at. For the moment it is enough to note that, while the Islamic sciences and horticulture flourished, Europe was just emerging from the Dark Ages (see Chapter 3).

Mediterranean Gardens and Islamic Gardens: Comparing and Contrasting

There is no doubt that Spanish cities formerly under Muslim rule, such as Granada, Cordoba or Seville, are deeply penetrated by a Muslim sensibility. The famous cobbled courtyard next to the great mosque of Cordoba, planted with rows of orange trees set in regular irrigation-channels, is the perfect preparation for prayer for Muslim and Christian alike; giving shade, water and fruit it is a kind of paradise garden itself. The whole ambience, like the gardens of the Alcazar in the same city, in spite of being under Christian rule for several centuries, is quintessentially Islamic. The gardens of the Cordoba Alcazar are large and varied but there are two in particular that are laid out on a *chahar-bagh* plan, both with central fountains. The smaller garden is enclosed on three sides by Hispano-Mauresque architecture (Fig. 36) and the larger one is more open with much more planting – informal planting, mainly large flowering shrubs enclosed within a box-hedge formal geometric plan (Fig. 47). Paradoxically, despite the original patrons of these gardens being Catholic kings, they seem to me to be two of the most enchanting *chahar-baghs* in existence, retaining everything that the Muslims held sacred: not only luxuriant planting, fragrant flowers

Fig. 46. The Orange-tree courtyard, Cordoba Mosque.

Fig. 47. The Alcazar, Cordoba, larger chahar-bagh *with raised central fountain.*

beds which are discussed a little later in the chapter. In the fifteenth century the King of Castille's palace-castle of Olite in Navarre was transformed into an eastern paradise with a 'hanging garden' on a wall supported by arcades. There was also a garden laid out on a geometric plan with straight walks, canals, fountains and aviaries filled with singing birds.

However, over the centuries, apart from certain royal palaces, the Moorish garden has given way to the typical Iberian/Mediterranean garden. It is a delightful experience to walk along the narrow back streets of Cordoba looking through iron gates into whitewashed courtyards filled with a profusion of pots of geraniums and pelargoniums, often the window-sills and doors painted in bright colours. They are pure Mediterranean and very lovely indeed – but they are not Islamic, and why not? These courtyard gardens certainly have elements of the Islamic garden, such as the enclosed area filled with brightly coloured flowers, many scented. However, unlike an Islamic garden, water is not the unifying factor, easily visible in the form of a central pool or fountain, providing the quintessential fulcrum of order and contemplation.[107] (Often there was a tap for watering in one corner but this was purely functional.) Also, on closer inspection one felt there was something fundamental missing; it was hard to pin down at first, since the scene was very charming and tempting, but it soon became

and water but order and harmony – a true manifestation of divine unity on earth. The Spanish Catholic rulers evidently realized that the Muslims knew how to design gardens and adopted Moorish gardens as their model. After all, the idea behind them, that of an earthly reflection of the heavenly gardens, was in no way contradictory to their own beliefs. Indeed, based as they were on an ancient universal archetype, described in the Book of Genesis no less, the Islamic gardens could be embraced by the Christians with equanimity.

It was Pedro el Justiciero or King Peter the Cruel (1334–69) who was especially taken with the Moorish gardens and had several laid out by Muslim designers and craftsmen at the Alcazar in Seville. These include two beautiful examples with sunken

Fig. 48. Courtyard of private house, Cordoba; although very attractive and with a fountain in the centre, the fountain is almost obscured by plants and is not the unifying factor and contemplative centre that it is in an Islamic garden.

clear that it was a sense of order and an overall vision that was lacking – that profound sense of unity so crucial to all Islamic design.

Looking at these courtyards was a practical, visible lesson that an accumulation of several component parts (as mentioned earlier), such as whitewashed walls, scented flowers and some colourful tiles, do not an Islamic garden make. An interesting garden to visit with these thoughts in mind is the Jardin Majorelle in Marrakech, begun in the 1920s by the French painter, Jacques Majorelle (1886–1962). This is a wonderful garden, full of exotic plants including bamboo groves, palms and agaves, as well as plenty of water in the form of channels, pools and fountains. There are many paths occasionally interspersed with arbours and everywhere there is a marvellous profusion of bright bougainvilleas of every possible colour. There is a museum with elegant Moroccan ironwork (Fig. 2; see Chapter 3) and the walls of the garden are painted in a strong blue, which gives the garden its distinctive tone and one tends to think of it as 'the Blue Garden'. The combination of this blue with the plants such as bamboo and agave, not normally associated with a traditional Islamic garden, is striking and different, and, with its lush planting of trees, plants and flowers, combined with pools, fountains and arbours, it is unquestionably a beautiful garden in its

own way. However, to me it lacked that fundamental underlying unity that is vital in a traditional Islamic garden; clarity, simplicity and a centre drawing the whole composition together in an harmonious way was not in evidence. To be fair, Majorelle himself, the original designer, did not have the intention of making this kind of garden and so the result in a sense proves the case.

Mystery

Since, as mentioned before, it is in the nature of paradise to be hidden, the notions of secrecy and the mysterious are important elements of Islamic garden design, just as they are of Islamic architecture. There is already a sense of mystery in the fact that the garden is usually within a walled enclosure, especially in the city where the high walls shut out the world, providing protection and seclusion. They also keep the world within a secret to all but the residents and invited guests, retaining the mystery of the heart of the house: the courtyard – which opens, not horizontally but vertically, to the sky above. The heart of the house corresponds to the heart of the believer, echoing the words of God as pronounced by the Prophet Muhammad: 'My earth hath not room for Me, neither hath My Heaven, but the Heart of My believing slave hath room for Me.'[108] The architecture of the mosque is similar to the Arab-Islamic house in that the 'bent axis' is a typical feature of both. It protects the privacy, mystery and beauty of the inward and also provides a sense of anticipation for the visitor who is forced to approach slowly, in semi-darkness, to prepare for the light and beauty that is to come. At the Sultan Hassan mosque

Fig. 49. Jardin Majorelle, Marrakech; lush, exotic and colourful but not Islamic.

Fig. 50. The Dismounting Yard with its beautiful simple central fountain, Generalife.

in Cairo the worshipper or visitor walks along a very high-ceilinged dark corridor then around one or two corners to suddenly emerge from the darkness into a vast bright open courtyard. It is an awe-inspiring experience and the impact on our senses is all the greater because of the preparation. The Alhambra Palaces are jewels of this kind of architecture: between the Cuarto Dorado and the Court of Myrtles there is a dark and angled passage, as if the heart and soul are contracting in order to expand again; the same thing happens on a smaller scale between the Court of Myrtles and the Court of Lions; and again in the Generalife, walking from the Dismounting Yard up the dark steps to the Patio de la Acequia. As Burckhardt writes:

> At the ends of elusive corridors one finds oneself in hidden courtyards around which rooms are grouped as though by chance. One might never suspect what other worlds may be concealed behind the walls. It is somewhat like the oriental tale of a traveller who is thrown into a salt quarry and finds there an underground palace replete with orchards and maidens, where he lives happily for twelve years, until one day he opens a secret doorway which leads him into an even more magnificent palace.[109]

So a true Islamic garden is hidden and mysterious, like the true gardens of paradise, *jannat al-firdaws*. This is in its very nature; this garden should not be

Fig. 51. The Dark Steps leading to the Patio de la Acequia, giving a sense a mystery and expectation as one climbs towards the light.

easy to access,[110] rather, it has to be earned since ultimately it is only offered to sincere and righteous believers and 'people who reflect'.

Despite the planting dating mainly from the twentieth century, the Generalife gardens of the Alhambra retain the Islamic ambience in many ways, one of which is the feeling of anticipation as one penetrates further into the gardens. On a more practical level, once inside an Islamic garden, then the opportunities for further mystery depend on the garden's size. If it is a small urban garden, the opportunities are limited. But a larger one may well have secluded areas around a still pool or fountain, hidden by vine-covered trellises; or there may be a pergola, pavilion or arbour within which the visitor

Fig. 52. The Patio de la Acequia, Generalife. This garden has recently been undergoing restoration and re-planting (2002–2003).

Fig. 53. Gardens of the Al-Batha Museum, Fes.

may withdraw for more privacy. These are all features of Islamic gardens and are looked at in more detail in the next chapter. In a hot country, or in the summer months in more northern regions, the pavilions are retreats within which the visitor can hide from the sun, as well as from other people; there may be couches and cushions (as mentioned in the Quran) providing comfortable places to sit with views over the garden and cool breezes from the water. The Mughals were masters of this particular art, the Shalimar gardens in Lahore having many pavilions carefully placed between the three large terraces of water (see Chapter 4, Fig. 116).

Elements of Design

Paths

Paths are essential in formal gardens such as the Islamic garden, providing they are an integral part of the order and geometry of the design. In very many cases paths are used as part of the ground-plan of the garden, together with water-channels or as an alternative to them. Paths often provide the actual four-fold layout such as in the garden at the al-Batha Museum in Fes (Fig. 7) or the gardens at the Alcazar in both Cordoba (Figs. 36 and 47) and Seville. Winding or meandering paths are definitely not part of a *chahar-bagh*, nor are 'organic' pools such as those favoured by designers such as R. Burle Marx (see Chapter 4). Careful attention needs to be paid to the material of the paths: natural materials such as stone, slate, brick (hand-made if possible), cobbles, granite setts and terracotta tiles are recommended – or a combination of two of these, such as stone and cobbles; also *zellij* (Moroccan ceramic-tile pieces), when carefully placed, can be used to great effect and blend in well in an Islamic courtyard garden in northern Europe or North America (see Chapter 3). Less expensive alternatives for paths are the wide variety of concrete setts available today; the ones made in imitation of faded pink bricks are quite natural-looking and can be laid in geometric patterns as well as fitting in well with brick architecture. Coloured marble and pastework (plaster and colour mixed) is also used to good effect in geometric and

Fig. 54. Front walled garden designed by the author of a house in west London showing combination of stone and zellij (Moroccan ceramic tile-work).

Fig. 55. Damascus, colourful patterned pastework (mixture of plaster and colour) decorating wall.

arabesque patterns in courtyards in Damascus and Cairo but would look out of place in all but the grandest of courtyards in our Islamic garden of the north. Paths provide wonderful opportunities for geometric patterns and these are looked at in the next chapter. The important point from the initial design perspective is that the paths should be formal, in keeping with the garden layout and the overall structure. Like the geometric water-rills, the paths can provide the rigour within which more informal planting can be cultivated.

Sunken Beds

It is interesting to consider the concept of the sunken flower-bed when thinking about the design of your garden. Although it initially came about as a contributing factor in the irrigation of plants and

Fig. 56. Patio de la Acequia from the opposite direction, showing central channel with the fountains turned off.

Fig. 57. One quarter of the Court of Lions showing orange tree in tub.

been undergoing restoration and repair (2002) and so hopefully we shall see a return to the sunken flower-beds. A similar discovery was made when excavating the Court of Lions in the Alhambra and it was found that the former level of the four flower-beds was 80cm below the present one.[111] Today, the four quarters of the Court of Lions only have one citrus tree in each quarter, the rest of the beds being gravelled over. This is necessary because the roots of the plants and dampness of soil were adversely affecting the surrounding architecture; even the citrus trees are planted in pots below ground level with their own separate drainage.

As with many Islamic gardens in other parts of the world, imagination needs to be exercised in order to picture the Court of Lions as it undoubtedly was for many centuries: a beautifully balanced composition of architecture, planting and water. Now there is no avoiding the fact that the court is somewhat stark without the softening effect of the vegetation. However, it is interesting from a design point of view as one can observe the result when one of the second of the two primary components of an Islamic garden mentioned earlier – tree or shrub-planting for shade – is absent. There is no doubt that the architecture is of exceptional ethereal beauty but there is also no doubt that some planting would soften and complement its crystalline elegance to give a more harmonious unified picture.

The most obvious and practical reason for these sunken beds was the need for irrigation, so that when the rain did eventually fall it would collect in the beds and not drain away or evaporate. In more temperate climates, for example, in England where the raised herbaceous border is the norm, and where in many areas there is a predominance of water-retaining clay soil, the desire is for the flower-beds to be more free-draining. So one needs to take this into account before thinking about sinking the flower-beds in

shrubs in a hot country, the sunken bed could still be employed as a design element even if your garden is in a region of lower temperatures and higher rainfall. To a lesser extent it was used in the Patio de la Acequia, the famous enclosed garden in the Generalife gardens. When they were excavating this garden in the late 1950s they discovered the original level of the Arab parterres – 50cm below the pathways – as well as holes pierced in the watercourse for irrigation. They covered these over to make the beds the same height as the paths instead of returning them to their original depth. However, this garden has

Fig. 58. Drawing of twelfth century sunken garden, Alcazar (Qasr al-Mubarak) Seville.

response to Islamic design. If your soil is fairly heavy you will probably need to add some sharp sand or grit to make sure the roots of your plants are not forever soaking – unless you choose plants which enjoy these conditions. It is interesting to read one author and gardener who lived in India at the turn of the nineteenth and twentieth centuries. She relates, when she first arrived in the country, that she clung to the English plan of flat paths and raised herbaceous borders, but the *mali* (gardener) 'won the day' and made her realize that 'the walks in an irrigated garden must be necessarily raised for the water to pass under them'.[112]

The result of the sunken beds was not only to accentuate the geometry of the design but was also to create the impression of walking on a floral carpet (see Chapter 7), which must have been a wonderful aesthetic and sensuous experience. As the visitor walked along the paths with feet and ankles brushing through lavender, rosemary, thyme, roses and other herbs and flowers, sweet scents would be released into the air to both uplift and soothe at the same time. In one part of the Alcazar in Seville, the patio of the Qasr al-Mubarak, the beds were sunk in a four-fold design, reproduced in a drawing here (Fig. 58). In another courtyard, the beds were sunk to 5m (approximately16ft), so trees could be planted and

the tops of them would be at the level of the paths. This was the eleventh-century courtyard garden called El Crucero, named after its cruciform plan. It is, or rather was, a classic *chahar-bagh* design, but was mostly destroyed by an earthquake in the eighteenth century. The cross-axes were formed by paths rather than by water-channels and the paths are rather like bridges supported by arches over the four deep quarter-beds. Like other surviving sunken beds the side walls are composed of blind arches, one traveller writing in the seventeenth century that:

Below it [the ground level of the courtyard] lies a subterranean garden of orange trees, divided into four quarters; and it is so deep, in relation to the courtyard that the tops of the trees almost reach the level [of the paths]... this courtyard, with the expanse of sky visible from it, its extraordinary scale and vistas in the subterranean garden, is very cheerful and grandiose and with the shade in its lower part is, during the summer, the shadiest and coolest of places.[113]

Few gardeners will want to dig out sunken beds as deep as El Crucero but it would be interesting to create a proper sunken quadripartite garden with more realistic dimensions, perhaps more along the lines of another twelfth-century courtyard garden in the Seville Alcazar, now known as the Casas de Contratacion. The four flower-beds of this twelfth-century garden are about 2m (6ft 6in) in depth and are constructed around a central circular pool. Like El Crucero, the walls of the sunk beds have blind arches in brick. Originally, these walls were stuccoed and painted – perhaps, as one author suggests, this was to provide some colour in the winter months.

Fig. 59. *Drawing of Casas de Contratacion, Alcazar, Seville.*

Fig. 60. Zellij *border, garden, west London.*

Practical Suggestions

Two metres is still a substantial depth to dig, so maybe up to one metre is more realistic. I myself have only experimented with shallow sunken beds of half a metre or less, which is sufficient for the purpose of hiding the lower stems of rose bushes or small shrubs such as lavender. However, if you are able to go down as far as a metre or more with your sunken beds then you will need to make provision for the inside 'walls'. These will probably be of cement 'bricks' rendered, unless you are fortunate enough to live in an area where local stone is plentiful and not prohibitively expensive. If you are rendering, then the best colour would probably be a neutral shade of off-white or perhaps you may wish to be a bit more ambitious and mix a colour into the render or apply ceramic tiles. Either way, this needs to be thought about carefully, as you do not want to clash with, or detract from, the colour of the plants. If you prefer to avoid cream or off-white then an 'earthy' natural colour would probably be the best for the wall, such as terracotta or a washed-out green – not a bright colour, which only looks good when the sun is shining on it. The tiles, too, should be of similar colours, not more than two or three colours at one time: perhaps mid-green with ochre or off-white, or an earthy red or deep blue – all very much depending on the planting. Strong bright colours may look wonderful in sunny climates but look sad and drab when there are grey skies overhead.

If you are fortunate enough to have the time and means, then it would be an interesting project to construct some blind arches in the sides of the sunken beds. If the beds are next to a path of stone or brick then this hard material (including the mortar on which it is laid) should provide a sufficiently strong edge; if they are constructed next to a lawn then a narrow hard edge – brick or stone again – surmounting the arches will be required to prevent the lawn sinking.

How to Put the Design Into Practice

First, consider the architecture of your house or flat, both the period in which it was built and the materials with which it is made, as this will influence the materials employed in your garden. If your house is Victorian brick, then this gives you plenty of opportunity for geometric patterns in brick and another material, perhaps some ceramic tiles – both of which were used in Moorish Spain (see Chapter 3). Second, consider very carefully the size and shape of your garden; as many a garden design manual has

Fig. 61. Water-channel, Hestercombe, Somerset.

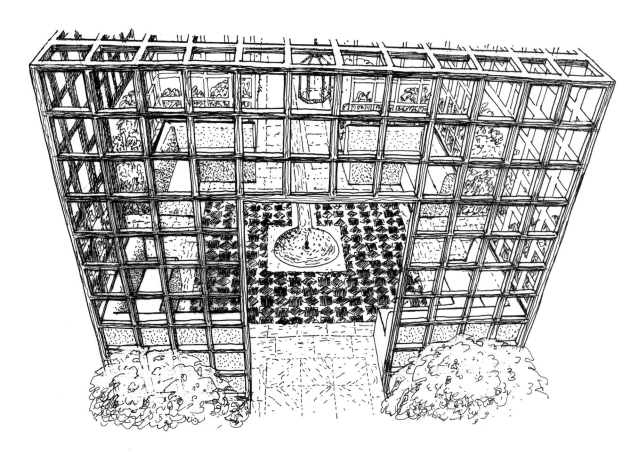

Fig. 62. Drawing of contemporary Islamic courtyard surrounded by mashrabbiyya *(turned or slatted wood) screen.*

suggested, if you have a long, narrow back garden (remember Ibn Luyun's recommendation that it is better to be longer than wide), between ten and twenty metres long and the width about half that much or less, then in order to achieve a good proportion you could divide it up into equal thirds according to a proportional rectangle.[114] Perhaps in the central third or the last third, farthest from the house depending on the aspect and surroundings, the formal *chahar-bagh* could be laid out. Paths can be used, as suggested above, as an alternative to water-channels. However small the *chahar-bagh* is there must always be water in it, and, bearing in mind the weather of northern climes, one small pool or fountain in the centre should be sufficient. Unless the garden is fairly large, it is unlikely that garden lovers from northern Europe will want too many open channels of cool rushing water, however beautiful and inviting they are in the summer months. In larger gardens in England, such as Hestercombe in Somerset, Coleton Fishacre in Devon or Shute

House in Dorset, Islamic-style water-channels have been created to great effect and blend in beautifully with their surroundings. However, there is no doubt that on a grey, rainy day they are not seen to their best advantage.

To give your Islamic garden some sense of seclusion it should be carefully sectioned off from the other parts by a hedge or a trellis with a climbing rose or vine or *Trachelospermum jasminoides*, if there is plenty of sun. An alternative would be to erect a *mashrabbiyya*, a turned or slatted wood screen composed of geometric patterns seen in many parts of the Islamic world (see Chapter 3) – but make sure the wood has been treated properly to survive the rigours of northern winters. A central pool or fountain with four paths, or water-channels if possible, leading from the centre to the perimeter would give you the initial layout (Fig. 30). Depending on the size of the area and the shape of the site, the position of the flower-beds will be made clear as your plan progresses. This may sound rather unhelpful but in fact this is what happens when you start dividing up a space: the central idea determines the rest of the plan and there is not necessarily a clear answer for the more detailed areas to be imposed theoretically. You need to be on the site and, as with all design-work, when problems arise you ponder and consider them and the best solution eventually arrives (*insha 'Allah*); but sometimes it is not easy, as many designers will understand all too well: there is no short cut.[115] Thought and concentration, as well as intention, is fundamental to all design and craft. The inspiration that will hopefully result, will not only help to solve problems as they arise but will also link the practical matters with universal principles. As emphasized earlier, Islamic garden design is about order, proportion, harmony and, most of all, unity. These are the principles that need to be kept in mind as you think through your design and find practical, technical and aesthetic solutions to a given situation: use, beauty and symbolism are all integrally linked (Figs. 36, 47 and 52).

Ibn Luyun's recommendation quoted earlier is useful for those with long narrow back gardens, since it turns what could be a negative point into something positive, namely that being 'longer than it is wide' is a support for contemplation. Thus an urban garden of approximately twenty metres long by ten metres wide, as an alternative to being divided into thirds suggested above, could be divided just once for a *chahar-bagh* layout, divided by paths or rills with a central fountain (the Patio de la Acequia being the classic example of this; see Fig. 52). Or, if desired, the plot could be divided once more again for greater variety, as well as adding a sense of mystery. The two areas may be separated by an evergreen hedge or *mashrabbiyya*, the second area either divided into a *chahar-bagh* also, with different planting and a still pool rather than a 'murmuring' fountain; or it may not be an Islamic garden at all, but a more English style 'cottage' garden. The hedge between the two should be fairly formal, possibly clipped into an arch in the centre inviting the visitor through to the back garden. The hedge could be one of several choices depending on the aspect of the garden. If you are fortunate enough

to have a south-facing or south-west facing garden then I would recommend a myrtle hedge, *Myrtus communis* subsp. 'Tarentina' is one of the best ones to choose, as it has a compact habit with small leaves and can be clipped into shape well. For a higher hedge, sweet bay (*Laurus nobilis*) could be used. In both cases, the aromatic leaves immediately conjure up a Mediterranean atmosphere (not to mention visions of the Court of Myrtles at the Alhambra if planting myrtle) and myrtle produces scented white flowers in the late spring which continue flowering all summer. There are many other shrubs for hedging which both suit northern locations as well as being appropriate to an Islamic style garden, and these are expanded on in Chapter 5.

Discipline Directs Creativity

Within the geometric and disciplined form of a *chahar-bagh* there is enormous scope for variation in the design – from hard landscaping materials and geometric patterns to the planting of trees, shrubs and flowers, to the water, which may take whatever form is most suitable. It would be a mistake to think that the quadripartite plan was some form of straitjacket that prevented creative planting and innovative design. Rather, it provides a framework or language within which the thoughtful gardener can implement a great variety of interpretations – witness the number and range of Islamic gardens centred on the *chahar-bagh* design across the world and spanning several centuries. In gardening there is also the nature and limitations of the site, which in fact are not limitations but rather provide a discipline within which to work. The details of the site – aspect, soil, climate and so on – may confine your choice of planting but this is something to be very thankful for as it focuses you on the possibilities that are on offer within the given criteria. So between the discipline of the geometric plan and the 'limitations' of the site, the garden designer has the bare bones of an Islamic garden already. The creative energy can then be directed towards the designing of patterns for paths as well as, perhaps, walls, fountains, *chadors* (carved stone slabs for water to travel down), tile decoration and so on, not forgetting the trees and plants themselves.

Genius Loci

'Choice of site and the genius of the place are the first consideration of the garden-maker everywhere,' Constance Villiers Stuart writes in her marvellous book on Mughal gardens.[116] The *genius loci*, a term often used in Western gardening, is more often translated as the 'spirit of the place' rather than the 'genius of the place'. Either way, the term means the same thing: first of all, on the most obvious level, it refers to the surroundings together with the special atmosphere or quality of a particular place. However, at the highest level, the phrase indicates the hidden spiritual power, the grace of God (*barakah* in Arabic) which informs all sacred and traditional art. This power is invisible and intangible and is only perceivable intuitively, requiring time and contemplation on the part of the visitor to be open to it and absorb its mysterious, quiet and subtle presence. Etymologically, 'genius' is related to the Arabic word *jinn*. The *jinn* are the inhabitants of the subtle world and can only become visible if they take on a material form – the *genie* or *jinnie* of the Arabian tales.

So it is worth taking time at the beginning of your design project to meditate upon and absorb the *genius loci* in order not to impose a plan that would be out of keeping with it. This recommendation is more applicable with larger country gardens than the small urban garden but is nevertheless worth keeping in mind.

Outdoor 'Rooms'

Hidcote and Sissinghurst[117] are held up as early examples of gardens laid out according to a plan of outdoor 'rooms'. However, it could be said, in a more literal sense, that the Muslims were, after the Romans and their *atrium*, the first to develop the concept of the outdoor 'room' – that is, the interior courtyard garden. This really was, and still is, a living space in many parts of the Islamic world. Families eat, talk, pray, sit, and make their ablutions in the central courtyard. Indeed, the garden designer George Dillistone at Castle Drogo in Devon, who was employed in 1922 after Edwin Luytens' designs were considered too ambitious,[118]

wrote a book in which he echoes the Islamic view: 'The garden is an artificial creation for a specific purpose. It is the room of the house that is out of doors. As man's handiwork it should bear the indelible stamp of man's art and craft.'[119]

Stimulating the Senses

Psychological research has established the importance to health and well-being of the balance between the stimulation of the senses. If some senses are over-stimulated while others are neglected, this may have a negative effect psychologically. Today, we tend to overdo certain senses – sight and sound principally – and under-stimulate others, principally the senses of smell and touch. It is often written that the Islamic garden was to be enjoyed by all the senses, and this is very true. First and foremost, the ordered layout together with the lush planting and the water is delightful and pleasing to the eyes; second, our sense of smell is rewarded in the form of sweetly scented flowers and herbs; third, the aural sense is stimulated by bird-song, running water, and wind rustling through the leaves; fourth, our sense of touch is provided for in rubbing our fingers on herbs such as mint, rosemary and lavender, on the great pleasure of picking fruit such as an apple, feeling its shape and texture in one's hands or letting the water run through one's fingers; and finally taste – drinking the water and eating the wide choice of fruit and vegetables traditionally grown in an Islamic garden. There is a balance in the animation of the senses here that reflects the balance of the design and is part of the profound mystery of the Islamic garden, contributing towards the awakening of our primordial sense, the sub-conscious intimation of the Heavenly Garden.

What to Avoid

In Europe, the period of the renaissance saw the beginning of a gradual disintegration of the medieval world picture centred on a transcendent principle; in brief, man was fast replacing God as the centre of the world. The medieval Christian outlook was very similar to that of traditional Islam but with the onset

Fig. 63. Detail of Lions, Court of Lions, Alhambra.

of the renaissance, followed by the baroque, rococo and the 'age of enlightenment', the two civilizations diverted. Their different outlooks were reflected in garden design as well as in art and architecture in general. The European gardens of the sixteenth century and later are no longer on an intimate human scale focused on the inward: they look outward to ever-more grandiose vistas such as Le Notre's creation at Versailles. With the classical influence making itself felt across Europe, gardens became filled with ornate statuary, sculpture, fantastic topiary, dripping grottoes and self-conscious, artificial waterworks of every description. (Fountains and pools appropriate for Islamic gardens are considered in Chapter 4.) These are anathema to the traditional Muslim sensibility and garden design, and should be avoided at all costs if you wish to make an authentic Islamic garden of your own.

The avoidance of statuary in gardens is an extension of the avoidance of anthropomorphism and depiction of images in Islamic art as a whole. This is partly because of the fear of idol-worship, so prevalent in pre-Islamic Arabia. Nothing that may become an idol should come between man and the invisible presence of God. Aniconism, as the avoidance of idols is properly called, protects the primordial dignity of man. Made as he is in the image of God, any depiction of man is necessarily limited, and this is the main reason for the prohibition of images of the Divinity: it brings the Absolute down to the level of the relative and the human. Also, depicting humans in a naturalistic, life-like manner, as most European statues – and paintings – do, is imitating God's creation and this is seen to be blasphemous, since we cannot 'breathe life' into these counterfeits.

Divine unity, at the heart of all Islamic art, is an abstract concept and beyond literal representation and can therefore only be intimated through symbolic form, via the order and harmony of geometry and arabesque.[120] In garden design, as in all Islamic art, this means a rigorous adherence to the concepts outlined before, in particular the concept of unity from which emanates simplicity and clarity of design, as well as avoiding 'clutter' in the form of statues and other garden ornaments.

It is true that animals are sometimes depicted in early Islamic art, in particular one thinks of the lions in the Court of Lions, but they are not very life-like; rather, they represent archetypal qualities of majesty, dignity and power – the lion being both an emblem of royalty as well as associated with the sun, the great symbol of the spirit.[120A] However, the presence of the lion statues in the Alhambra are the exception rather than the norm. On the whole it is best to avoid any sculpture if you wish to create a traditional Islamic garden.

Meandering paths, natural-looking streams, lakes and waterfalls with moss-covered rocks and wet-woodland style planting are also to be avoided when laying out an Islamic garden. This is the domain of the Japanese or Chinese landscape garden or the English country garden, but it is not in keeping with the principles of order and clean-cut geometry that mark out a traditional Islamic garden. Curved wooden bridges, wooden pavilions and bamboo groves – so beloved of Chinese gardens[121] – also should not be included in your garden. Water trickling through bamboo into pools is another Japanese speciality which would be quite out of place in an Islamic garden. What to avoid and what to include in the great variety of water devices is included in Chapter 4 on water. For example, the lion's mask fixed to a wall with water trickling out should not be included in your Islamic garden – unless you are fortunate enough to have discovered a twelfth-century stone lion (or a good copy) similar to those in the Court of Lions at the Alhambra.

Cacti and other succulents, although they are now grown fairly widely in North Africa and the Near East, are not plants for a traditional Islamic garden and should be avoided; they are part of the 'wild' and therefore not to be included in the sanctuary of the garden. They are mostly native to Mexico and other parts of the Americas and were not popular in the Islamic world until relatively recently – as fashion and water-conservation begins to direct planting more than tradition. In Morocco, *Agave Americana* is used widely as a barrier against intruders (see Chapter 6) but is not yet generally planted within the interior courtyard garden. Today in northern Europe and North America, the romantic notion of a wild garden with different types of grasses or 'natural' meadows is very popular; so is a garden blending in with the surrounding landscape (a fashion started over two hundred years ago by Lancelot 'Capability' Brown). These are all quite alien to the Islamic perspective – quite under-standably, since the surrounding landscape was what the early Muslims were retreating from. The last thing they wanted was the desert penetrating their inner sanctum of shade and cool and running water. Theirs was an artificially contrived environment made with the express intention of creating an area of the greatest contrast possible to the arid and hostile natural world.

Conclusion

So it is only through considering the underlying principles beforehand, understanding where they come from and something of their meaning that a successful Islamic garden in a potentially 'alien' environment can result. For the final garden to capture the essence of a traditional Islamic garden, the designer should ideally possess a combination of an understanding of the underlying spiritual message and the design principles, together with a knowledge and experience of the climate and growing conditions of the local area; not forgetting to hope and pray for a guiding hand from Heaven.

CHAPTER 3

Geometry, Hard-landscaping and Architectural Ornament

One of the most important aspects of an Islamic garden is its harmonious relationship with architecture. This is especially relevant for the smaller urban garden, which, like the early Islamic garden, is separated – usually by walls – from its adverse surroundings. These walls and hedges, together with plants, water and geometric patterns in the hard landscaping, should all contribute to this harmony. After the initial design has been thought out, it is through the careful application of these elements that the designer can put the idea into practice.

In this chapter we will look at some of the treasure-trove of geometry, hard-landscaping and architectural ornament found across the Islamic world in a wide variety of craft materials. In your own garden you may be tempted to use some *zellij* (Moroccan ceramic tile-work, Fig. 65), carved plaster or *mashrabbiyyas* (geometric-patterned screens in turned or slatted wood; Figs. 66 and 62), or some simple geometric patterns on the ground in brick, stone, slate or other natural material. If you are fortunate enough to have the space to design a large open garden as opposed to a smaller, enclosed one, you may wish to include a small pavilion or 'kiosk' to be placed near a pool or fountain with a good view: the Shalimar gardens in the suburbs of Lahore are a fine – if ambitious – example! (See 'Pavilions and Tents' below and Figs. 116 and 131). Fountains, water-channels and other forms of water are the essential and most well-known elements in an Islamic garden, and are looked at extensively in the next chapter on water. As mentioned previously, what inspires a designer most is to see examples of gardens *in*

Fig. 65. Zellij *(Moroccan ceramic tile-work) on wall, Fes.*

situ; failing that, images of gardens and architecture from around the Islamic world, as well as visiting certain museums,[122] may also give you wonderful ideas. A few examples of simple geometric patterns for paths or small paved areas are included with recommendations of where to look further.

Left: Fig. 64. Terracotta pots lining a path in the Alhambra gardens (containing a species of Euonymus*).*
Right: Fig. 66. Mashrabbiyya *(turned wood screen) in different patterns.*

Geometry and Islamic Art

Why is geometry so important in Islamic art in general and in Islamic gardens in particular? It represents the essence of nature through abstract pattern; this means that every geometric form carries a qualitative symbolic meaning. Therefore, geometry is not just an aesthetically pleasing decorative pattern, it is a pure and objective means of glorifying God's creation of the natural order. Traditional Islamic art, as mentioned earlier, is centred on Divine unity, which is an abstract concept and not possible to represent directly. Nevertheless, through order and harmony, as manifested by geometry and rhythmic interlacement (arabesque) in art, the essential nature of the created world, the underlying unity within the multiplicity of forms, can be made visible.

Order in the traditional Islamic garden is manifested primarily by the geometric formality of the four-fold design, the *chahar-bagh*, and its repetition; there are of course a multiplicity of other geometric patterns, based on six-fold, eight-fold, twelve-fold and other geometric grids but the *chahar-bagh*, as its name suggests is based fundamentally on the four-fold lay-out. As well as being a

Fig. 68. Dome of the Mosque of Qayt Bey, Cairo.

Fig. 67. Carved stone panel on wall of the Bou Inaniya Madrasa, Meknes, showing a balance between geometry and arabesque. The square represents the terrestrial realm while the circle represents the celestial.

demonstration of order, geometry is also symbolic of the crystalline forms in nature, while the arabesque represents the sinuous, undulating forms. These two, geometry and arabesque, are two of the three principle elements of Islamic art, the third being calligraphy. The abstraction of Islamic art has little in common with modern abstract art: the former is objective and is about the remembrance of Divine unity, while the latter, generally speaking, is subjective, usually reflecting the psyche of the individual artist.[123]

Geometric patterns in all their beauty and infinite variety are found right across the Islamic world, from the domes of mosques to carpets and textiles, Quran illuminations, wood-carving and ceramics, not to mention *zellij* (Figs. 65 and 73). It is not exclusive to Islamic art – rather, it is the universal language that underpins the sacred art of all the great world traditions: from the precise rendering of the sculpture of a Buddha, to the placing of the Virgin's head in a medieval icon, to the dance positions of Krishna in an Indian temple hanging.[124]

So, what, you may ask, does this have to do with creating your Islamic garden? Well, everything in fact.

move to the knowledge of the essence of the soul, and that is the root of knowledge.[126]

It was Pythagoras who stated that, 'Four are the foundations of wisdom – arithmetic, music, geometry, astronomy, ordered one, two, three, four.'[127] Every geometric shape, from the triangle and the square to the hexagon, the octagon and the dodecagon, has a qualitative meaning over and above its outward form. It is the same with numbers, and this is explained further on. For the moment it is enough to be aware that there is a close link in Islamic art between the hidden meaning (*batin*) and the outer form (*zahir*), for 'a spiritual vision necessarily finds its expression in a particular formal language'.[128] Thus it is clear that, when designing an Islamic garden, geometry is not just a useful tool to lay out a garden in a symmetrical or well-proportioned way or to draw aesthetically pleasing patterns: of course, in the right hands, it performs these tasks beautifully but over and above this, it is a profound language of sacred art.

Geometry is an essential language of sacred art, being the means of creating order and rigour; and there is no doubt that the Islamic garden is a kind of sacred art – therefore geometry is an integral part of it. An Islamic garden is about the rhythm of nature represented by plants and trees with order imposed upon it in the form of geometry by man in his role of God's representative on earth. This is what might be termed 'true geometry' (rather different from lessons at school) going back to Plato's Academy and further, where geometry was one of the 'Seven Liberal Arts'.[125] They were taught as a means of understanding the universe as well as a means of liberating the soul from the concerns of the world – hence 'Liberal' Arts. The Brotherhood of Purity (*Ikhwan as-Safa*), founded in Iraq in the tenth century, continued Plato's ideas and wrote:

> Know, oh brother... that the study of sensible geometry leads to skill in all practical arts while the study of intelligible geometry leads to skill in the intellectual arts because this science is one of the gates through which we

Fig. 70. Geometric pattern carved in wood with ivory inlay, Cairo.

Geo-metry, the word itself means the 'measure of the earth'. The two essential tools for practising it are the dividers or the compasses for drawing a circle, and a straight edge or ruler for drawing a straight line. The circle is the symbol of unity from which all other geometric figures derive. Tradition says that the tools themselves symbolize, respectively, the circle of the heavens (the sun is one of the great symbols of the spirit) and the straight line of the horizon, the earth. Why is it that even the most sceptical people are drawn to look at a sunset or a sunrise? The perfect beauty of heaven and earth are there before us in all their awe-inspiring majesty and glory.

Geometry and Number

In order to grasp the fundamental ideas behind the *chahar-bagh* it is good to understand a little about the essential nature of number and geometry. As we have seen, these are both universal arts/sciences which the Muslim Arabs assimilated via Pythagoras and Plato. According to the Pythagorean tradition, as well as many other traditions including the Babylonian, Hindu and Hermetic, number is the basic principle of the universe from which the manifest world proceeds. Number, like geometry, has an obvious 'outward' or quantitative meaning that we use in everyday life (two apples, three trees, etc.), as well as an inner qualitative meaning, its 'threeness' or, in the context of the *chahar-bagh*, its 'fourness'. The concept of unity is embodied in the number one or, in geometric terms, by the circle. The number two embodies the notion of duality, expressed geometrically by two points and a line. With duality, separation has taken place and only with the number three, geometrically the triangle, can we return to the beginning again. It is written in the Quran, 'Truly we are from God and to God we shall return' (*Inna li'llahi wa inna ilayhi raji'oon*, II:156). Thus three represents the soul on its journey from separation back to wholeness and is therefore a heavenly number, suggesting balance and harmony.[129] So, it is not just good design when garden designers recommend that three of a particular species of plant look good together; as briefly explained, there is a lot going on behind the scene that tells us *why* this is the case.

Now we reach the number four, already touched upon in the previous chapter, and expressed in geometric terms by the square or cube. Four is arrived at through the addition or multiplication of a number by itself: two plus two or two times two, and it therefore represents 'that which is born'. The word 'nature', means 'that which is born'. So the number four indicates nature and the created world. Whereas the circle is symbolic of undifferentiated unity and the celestial world, the square represents differentiated unity, 'unity in multiplicity' and the material world. The triangle represents the transition from one world to the other. When we think of the number four and everything associated with it, such as the four elements (earth, air, fire, water) and their qualities (heat, cold, wetness and dryness), the four seasons, the four cardinal directions and the four ages of man (childhood, youth, adulthood and old age), it can be seen that all these things are, in a sense, 'earthly'. For Muslims this dimension is symbolized *par excellence* by the Kaaba,[130] which actually means 'cube' and the shape of which is a slightly imperfect cube.

The Number Eight

Titus Burckhardt has written, 'All sacred architecture, whatever the tradition to which it belongs, can be seen as a development of the fundamental theme of the transformation of the circle into the square.'[131] As we have seen above, the circle and square represent heaven and earth,

Fig. 71. Square base with octagon transition to dome, Friday mosque, Isphahan.

respectively, and the *chahar-bagh* form of the traditional Islamic garden represents the earth, while the sky above is itself the dome of heaven. In architecture, the transition between a square base and a domed roof requires the intermediary of the number eight in its geometric form, the octagon, to ensure that they are smoothly joined. In the garden, it will be seen that the central fountain, very often circular, with or without a scalloped edge, is often set into an octagonal base. What is the significance of the number eight? In Islam, eight is associated with paradise, signifying the renewed man after he has travelled through the seven stages or heavens and regained paradise: it is therefore a symbol of renewal and rebirth. In Christianity, the font in a church is usually octagonal, reminding us that baptism is not only a purification but also a symbol of rebirth through anointing with holy water. On the Prophet Muhammad's ascent to heaven, his night journey (*miraj*), he sees the throne (*arsh*) of God supported by eight angels. In Ibn 'Arabi's cosmological diagram, the 'Plain of Assembly' (*Ard al-Hash*),[132] the throne of God is depicted as an eight-pointed star. The poet Saadi divided his poem, *Gulistan* ('The Rose Garden'), into eight parts, each one corresponding to one of the eight paradises.[133] There are gardens in Iran and India called 'Hasht Behesht' meaning 'Eight Paradises' in *farsi*, one for example in Isphahan and another at Agra, designed by the Mughal emperor, Babur.

The octagon is certainly one of the most often employed shapes in geometric patterns across the Islamic world, especially in North Africa and India, some calling it the 'Star of Islam'.[134] However, it must be added that many other numbers with their geometric counterparts – from the hexagon to the dodecagon – are also employed in Islamic geometric patterns. A visit to Fes in Morocco or the Alhambra palaces in Granada, Spain, is to open one's eyes to a spectacular array of colourful geometric patterns made from *zellij* (ceramic tile-work, Figs. 65, 73 and 83). Today, the number of master-craftsmen who truly understand and practise geometry in a variety of craft skills is far fewer than it used to be. Programmes have been initiated for the continuation and renewal of this great art but, as may be imagined, it is an uphill struggle in the industrialized world.[135]

Fig. 72. Fountain in the Cuarto Dorado, Alhambra, showing a scalloped 'lotus' bowl set in an octagonal base.

Simple Geometric Patterns

As mentioned above, you will need a pair of compasses and ruler to start drawing. Simple patterns based on dividing a circle by six to form a hexagon are good ones to start with, since the circle divides equally into six using its own radius. There are several medieval icons which depict God the Creator holding a pair of compasses and, interestingly, an architect or rather master-mason in the Middle Ages was generally known as a 'Master of the Compasses'. Symbolically, the meaning of the number six is the four cardinal directions plus the zenith and the nadir (height and depth). It is also the number of creation, while the number seven represents the day of rest ('And God blessed the seventh day, and sanctified it',

Fig. 73. Zellij, The Alhambra.

Figs. 74a–d. Various geometric patterns for hard-landscaping.

Genesis II:3) amongst other things such as the traditional number of planets. A star hexagon can be made up of two triangles, one overlaying the other 'upside-down', sometimes known as 'Solomon's Seal'. It is beyond the scope of this book to give step-by-step diagrams for drawing geometric patterns, just as it is not possible to enter into the meaning of all the numbers and geometric forms that are used in Islamic art. However, a few patterns for hard-landscaping patio areas, footpaths or small courtyards are shown here and if you are interested in learning to draw more complex geometric patterns, please see footnote and bibliography.[136]

Apprenticeship and Craftsmanship

It is most probable that the traditional Muslim master-craftsmen, including the master-gardeners, would have been aware of the symbolic meanings inherent within the geometric patterns. Some would no doubt have known more than others – we will never know for certain. Incredible patterns are to be seen across the Islamic world such as, to take just two examples, the interior of the dome of the Shah mosque in Isphahan (Fig. 75) and the dome of the mosque of Qayt Bey in Cairo (Fig. 68). They reveal an awe-inspiring knowledge of geometry and mathematics combined with a profound sense of the sacred. It is less likely that apprentices would have been aware of the inner meanings of the designs they were involved in; such esoteric knowledge would probably only have been imparted to them at a certain level, if they were deemed sufficiently responsible, intelligent and humble. These were, as noted in the previous chapter, secret meanings or 'teachings' passed down, primarily orally, from master to apprentice when the master felt that the apprentice was ready. In the past, the master of a craft guild was usually both a master of the craft as well as a spiritual master. The craft guilds were closely allied to the spiritual orders in Islam just as they were in medieval Europe. As the apprentice gradually learnt the discipline of his craft so he also learnt how to discipline his soul.

Fortunately, some of the 'secret teachings' of Japanese gardeners were gathered together in the eleventh-century manuscript, *Sakuteiki* (meaning

'Notes on Garden Making') by Tachibana no Toshitsuna.[137] This is mentioned because no such corresponding work from the Islamic world exists in translation; it is certainly possible that such teachings survive in Arabic, Persian or Turkish manuscripts but as far as is known these have not been researched or made available to a Western readership.[138] Medieval horticultural treatises exist (as has been mentioned and are elaborated upon later) but the inner meaning, passed from master to apprentice by word of mouth and close association through practice, remains alive probably only amongst a few. They are hidden away from the uninitiated but maybe will be revealed one day. Even today, where the crafts still survive in the Islamic world such as in Turkey and Morocco, the masters will not divulge their knowledge to an outsider. A few years ago, a Turkish master-craftsman in *kundekari* (a type of inlay woodwork) visited our department of Islamic and Traditional Art in London[139] and would only teach a certain amount of technical expertise and skill about his craft, maintaining a polite silence when questioned about the underlying meaning. Recently, while designing an Islamic garden in London, the local craftsmen I commissioned to work on it individually expressed reluctance to pass on knowledge until a relationship of trust and understanding had been built up. This is in keeping with the craft tradition and is completely understandable; it is right and honourable to pass on precious, hard-earned knowledge as a teacher or

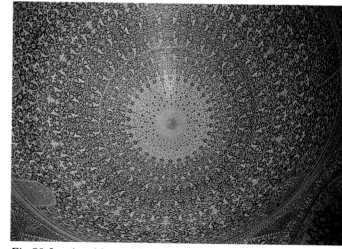

Fig. 75. Interior of dome of the Shah Mosque, Isphahan.

master, indeed it is a responsibility, but the apprentices must first prove themselves worthy of receiving it.

Craftsmanship in the Garden

In view of the above, when thinking of additional 'ornament' in your garden, it is good to have some idea of the careful craftsmanship involved in its execution. Not only is the content or meaning of fundamental importance in traditional art, but so is the method and material with which the work is executed. The hand, heart and mind should be fully involved in a piece of traditional art. It is a contemplative, creative process which reflects the work of the original Creator. Therefore, if you would like everything in your garden to be beautiful in the true sense, in that it reflects the paradisal gardens, then I would recommend you commission skilled craftsmen to carry out most of the art/craftwork. It is tempting, and often necessary, to cut costs but with certain crafts this leads to a cheap and vulgar look. The *zellij*, calligraphy, fountain or carved stone patterns should, as far as possible, be carried out by hand using natural materials. If some calligraphy is desired in the garden (see next section) then a type of stone, slate or wood may be used. If this proves too expensive, then it would be preferable not to include calligraphy in the garden at all. Do not use the less expensive sand-blasted granite lettering, a blight that seems to have taken over the tombstones in our

cemeteries in recent years. The beauty of hand-carved letters in stone can never be equalled by the machine. The care and craftsmanship that are involved can be observed immediately even by an untrained eye, and it is in detail such as this that care and love is revealed. Similarly, stoneware tiles (as well as *zellij* and other ceramic work) and terracotta pots should always be handmade: the very even colouring you get with a factory-produced tile is quite dead compared to the glazes on handmade tiles and pots, just as the shape and colour of a mass-produced pot is dead compared to one turned on the wheel by hand.[140]

Unlike other artists/craftsmen the material that the gardener works with is Nature herself, which is constantly changing. Thus the gardener has to nurture, maintain and constantly renew his work in a way that no other visual artists or craftsmen need to do. Once the work of the non-gardening craftsman is completed – for example designing, executing and laying a geometric-patterned marble floor – he can breathe a sigh of relief, since there should be minimal maintenance thereafter. This is not the case for the gardener!

Fig. 76 (below). Carved stone 'Basmallah' by VITA student, Adam Suleyman (see Endnote 135).
Fig. 77 (right). Simple geometric pattern in stone, in a courtyard in Damascus.

It will be noticed that the terms 'artist' and 'craftsman' are used interchangeably since, in the traditional Islamic world, they were one and the same thing – the root meaning of the word 'art' being skill. The division between so-called 'fine art' and craft is an entirely modern one and very misleading, implying that there is no craft involved in making art and no art involved in making craft. A gardener has always been both an artist and a craftsman – as all traditional artists/craftsman were: making something beautiful and meaningful with great skill and knowledge, love and humility, acquired over years of learning and experience. The skill can never be dispensed with and can only be acquired through dedication, practice and love.

Calligraphy

As mentioned above, the arts and crafts of Islam are centred on three main elements: calligraphy, geometry and arabesque. Calligraphy is the highest of the visual arts of Islam, since it represents a sacred language, the language of classical Arabic as revealed by God through the Angel Gabriel to the Prophet Muhammad, and later transcribed as the Quran. This will be clear to anyone who has visited the Islamic world where calligraphy adorns almost every building, from mosques and *madrasas* (theological schools) to hotels and private houses. Calligraphy in mosques usually depicts the names of God[141] and Blessings upon the Prophet Muhammad, as well as verses from the Quran. They may be carved in stone, marble, plaster, metalwork, ceramic tiles or wood. In

Fig. 78. Ceramic calligraphy, Sokullu Mehmet Pasha mosque, Istanbul.

Fig. 79. Mashrabbiyya, *Gayer-Anderson house, Cairo.*

private homes there will usually be the Name of God in Arabic (*Allah*) and the Prophet Muhammad, painted or printed and mounted in a frame hanging on the wall, as well as the *Shahada*, or a *Basmalah*.[142]

Since calligraphy is such an elevated art in Islam, it was employed with great care in architecture and rarely in gardens. The Alhambra palaces with their succession of courtyard gardens are famous for the repetition of the phrase *Wa la ghaliba illa-Llah*, 'There is no victor besides God!'.[143] It is carved hundreds, if not thousands, of times into the walls, along with the name of God, and verses from the Quran. Although not a usual feature of gardens, fountains were sometimes carved with poems, as on the raised fountain in the Court of Lions at the Alhambra. In your own garden, providing great care is taken, a line from a poem could be carved in slate or stone and set into the wall surrounding the garden; or carved onto a raised fountain, stone bird-bath or sundial – as we often find in gardens in the United Kingdom. Alternatively, calligraphy may be incorporated into a *mashrabbiyya*,[144] as at the Gayer-Anderson house in Cairo (Fig. 79), for example, as well as the more usual geometric patterns. It is important that any calligraphy is high up off the ground at eye-level or above, since in Islam one never walks on sacred text. This is because calligraphy was originally only used to represent the word of God, and to this day is treated with great reverence. Therefore, even if you may wish to carve some poetry or something not specifically religious in your garden, it would be more in keeping with Islamic tradition to place it in an elevated position.[145]

When making your Islamic garden, calligraphy, unlike geometry, is not essential. However, if it is possible, a carefully chosen inscription carved as suggested above could well contribute to the overall contemplative atmosphere. One tends to take more time to read, pause and absorb a short inscription in a garden than when sitting at home reading a whole book. Bearing in mind that one of the principal aims of an Islamic garden is to create a kind of sanctuary, then the content of the inscription is of the utmost importance. If you are a Muslim then you may wish to choose a verse from the Quran such as one of the many that refer to the gardens of paradise:

But such as fears the Station of his Lord,
For them shall be two gardens.[146]

Therein they shall hear no idle talk, no cause of sin,
Only the saying, 'Peace, Peace'.[147]

Another verse from the Quran would be very appropriate inscribed over the entrance or gateway into the garden:

Say: 'O my Lord! Let my entry be by the Gate of Truth and Honour, and likewise, my exit by the Gate of Truth and Honour'.[148]

Another possibility is a saying of the Prophet, such as:

They will enter the Garden of Bliss who have a true, pure and merciful heart.

Ye will not enter Paradise until ye have faith, and ye will not complete your faith until ye love one another.[149]

Non-Muslims may also of course choose something from the Quran or a saying of the Prophet or a poem

expressing a universal message, such as a favourite one of mine found carved into many a garden seat:

The kiss of the sun for pardon
The song of the birds for mirth,
One is nearer God's Heart in a garden
Than anywhere else on earth.[150]

There is also the famous saying attributed to the thirteenth century poet, Amir Khusrau:

If there is a Paradise on earth, it is here, it is here, it is here.[151]

There is such a wealth of contemplative sayings from all the great traditions of the world that the main problem would be in narrowing down your choice. However, since we are concerned with the Islamic garden, my recommendation would be to choose a verse from one of the Quranic passages referring to the gardens of paradise, as suggested above, or from one of the many great Muslim poets of the past.

Rabia al-Adawiyya (d.801), is a famous mystical poet who, when called by her maid to look outside at the beautiful spring flowers, replied that the real gardens and flowers are not outside but are within man's heart.[152] Or Saadi (1184–1292) whose phrase: 'Patience is bitter but its fruit is sweet', is a useful reminder to those frustrated about something not turning out as hoped, who had entered the garden for some solace; or maybe an excerpt from the introduction to his famous poem, *The Gulistan* (The Rose Garden):

The Rose can only bloom an hour:
My garden will forever flow'r.

Saadi is no doubt referring here, like Rabia al-Adawiyya above, to the garden within, the garden of the heart. Jalal ud-Din Rumi (1207–73),[153] often uses gardens, trees, plants and flowers as vivid symbols of divine beauty in his great work, the *Mathnawi*. He refers, like other poets, to the 'garden of the heart', that is, our innermost being where the remembrance of God needs to be constantly nurtured; this is the only garden that lasts forever, since everything in the material world, even beautiful gardens, passes away.

Hard-landscaping Materials

Hard landscaping – not my favourite term but unfortunately it seems to have no synonym – is a large element in Islamic courtyard garden design. This is particularly true of the courts of the grander houses of Syria, Egypt, Jordan, Morocco and elsewhere where a wealth of inspiration is to be found. A wide variety of natural materials are used across the Islamic world, from stone and cobbles to *zellij* (ceramic tile-work) and coloured marble, depending on local resources.[154] Mosaic should be avoided since, although geometric patterns exist in Roman or Byzantine work – such as some at Volubilis in Morocco – the technique itself immediately conjures up a whole different civilization.

> Arab interlacement has a geometrical complexity and rhythmic quality quite lacking in its Roman counterpart... the filled spaces and the empty areas, the design and its ground, are both of strictly equivalent value and balance each other out, in the same way that the lines always flow back on themselves, so that one's attention never halts on a particular element of the décor.[155]

Paths, as suggested in the previous chapter, are a wonderful opportunity for laying patterns within a chahar-bagh design. They can range from the very simple, such as a narrow (7.5cm) *zellij* border either side of a natural stone path (see Fig. 60), to the more elaborate patterns found in Turkey, Syria, Morocco,

Figs. 80 and 81. Patterns in marble floor, Damascus and Cairo.

Fig. 83. Zellij, The Alhambra.

Fig. 82. Roman geometric pattern in mosaic, Volubilis, Morocco. 'Arab interlacement has a geometrical complexity and rhythmic quality quite lacking in its Roman counterpart': Titus Burckhardt (see endnote 155).

Fig. 84. *Geometric patterned glass as architectural feature in a garden (designed and executed by ex-VITA student Martin Moller, see Endnote 135).*

Figs. 85 (top right) and 86 (above). *Two fountains in Shah Jahan's quadrangle, Lahore Fort, showing carved stone geometric star pattern on the ground with arabesque patterns within the fountains – looking lifeless without water.*

Egypt and India (see Figs. 80–1, 85–6 and 88–91). It is unlikely that many of us will have the opportunity to lay out such grandiose schemes as seen here. Nevertheless, it is inspiring to see what has been achieved in the past, as it is always possible to select one particular motif and use that for your own path or other paved area.

It is also instructive to walk around the Victorian areas of London (and other major cities) and look at the paths leading up to the front doors. Some of the geometric tile patterns have quite an Islamic 'look' and yet are, nevertheless, definitely English and a part of the indigenous architectural environment. This is partly because of the architecture itself but also

because of the materials used and the patterns themselves, many of which are based on medieval or more ancient designs. In England, the materials vary between ceramic tiles,[156] brick and a wide variety of stone, slate, flint, gravel or cobbles, depending on the geographical location. In the Islamic world of North Africa and further east, not only are the geometric patterns far more generously applied and more complex but the materials are very often more exotic. Besides brick, stone and cobbles, sea-shells – an Ottoman favourite – different coloured marbles, and stone inlay are intricately and skilfully pieced together, as seen for instance in the courtyards of mosques and houses in Damascus and Cairo.

Careful thought is required when deciding on your hard-landscaping materials: they need to fit in with the locality as well as have the potential to create Islamic patterns and suggest an eastern 'look'. For example, one would probably avoid using Taj Mahal-like *pietra-dura*, since the surrounding architecture is unlikely to be suitable. However, *pietra-dura* could be used very subtly in isolation, on a stone bench for instance. Even then it would depend on its sensitive relationship with the surroundings and the rest of the hard materials used in the garden or nearby architecture. One should be careful when using the colourful ceramic tile-work, *zellij*, in the courtyard

Fig. 87. *Calligraphy, geometry and arabesque in* zellij *and carved plaster: showing balance between the three, Morocco.*

garden of an eighteenth- or nineteenth-century brick house, say, since an excess of it would look out of place. This is elaborated on in the next section.

Tiles, such as those used on the paths of a courtyard garden in Marrakech, with a simple pattern would blend in well with the architecture of a terraced Victorian or Edwardian house; and steps could be similarly treated. Moorish gardens and courtyards

Figs. 88 and 89. *Geometric patterns in marble and stone, Damascus.*

Figs. 90 and 91. Geometric patterns in marble and stone, Damascus.

altogether less harsh and industrial looking, than almost all the mass-produced ones. If funds are available, then these would be far preferable – especially if a large area of patterned brick is desired.

Decking is inappropriate in an Islamic garden as it conjures up quite a different kind of 'look', more Japanese or North American where the 'deck' has been all the rage for some time. Wood was a precious commodity in Arab countries, usually imported from the Indian sub-continent as it still is today, and generally served more important functions than to be walked upon, for example the wooden screens mentioned earlier known as *mashrabbiyyas*.

Zellij

Zellij (Figs. 65, 73, 83 and 99), referred to several times already, is ceramic tile-work based on individual pieces of glazed ceramic cut to different shapes and fitted together to make geometric patterns, arabesque and calligraphy. It is a skill excelled in by the craftsmen of Morocco. With careful choice of colours and design this can be used to great effect in creating Islamic gardens in Europe. A small amount, subtly placed as a border around the flower-beds, besides steps or a path as suggested earlier, or as a kind of 'dado' line could look very effective (Fig. 60). However, large areas of *zellij* as in Morocco, where the lower part of a wall, approximately one metre from the ground, may be entirely applied with it, would not be appropriate in Northern European-type climates. This looks spectacular in its native land as the brighter colours are seen to their best advantage in the strong sunlight but in the predominantly grey light of the North, a large area could easily look rather dull and sad. The colours of the ceramic tiles vary from subtle ochre and deep red to shades of blue and green, and are never too bright or brash but seem to have emerged from the earth naturally – which indeed they have in a manner of speaking. In fact, one piece (roughly 0.5 sq m) of subtle-coloured *zellij* set into a wall in a north-facing back garden would cheer it up no end.

So again, what is important here is to achieve the right balance: between the amount and colour of the *zellij*, the architecture, and the planting. Providing it is all in balance, then the tiles can really transform the space into a Moroccan or Hispano-Mauresque courtyard at the same time as looking quite at home.

used a tremendous amount of brick, which can be seen in certain parts of the Alhambra gardens such as the area surrounding a pool (Fig. 93; and the steps leading up from the Partal Palace pool, Fig. 107). It is interesting to note that the bricks used here are slightly longer and much slimmer than the regular English brick and the resulting herring-bone pattern is therefore more pronounced. It is possible still to obtain handmade bricks that are a softer colour, and

Other practical factors need to be taken into consideration here also – such as what pattern(s) to use and how much sunlight will fall on it at different times of day throughout the year. Recently, I designed an entrance 'courtyard' garden in west London of about 9 sq m and, since there was a wall on three sides (the fourth side being the Victorian rendered gothic revival house), I first thought simple-patterend *zellij* in three colours could be applied on the three walls up to approximately 1.5m high, as seen in several Moroccan courtyard houses. Fortunately, I soon realized that, taking into account the location of the house and the climate, it would look out of place to apply such a great amount of *zellij*. Perhaps if the space had been considerably larger, then the effect would not be so overpowering but in a small area such as this it was eventually decided to install a simple three-colour, 7.5cm border to all the paths and flower-beds, so the effect is subtle but beautiful (modesty has not prevailed!) and decidedly Hispano-Mauresque in feel (Figs. 54 and 60). Because the site is north and east facing, and overshadowed by a leafy London plane tree

Fig. 93. Patterns in brick surrounding pool, Alhambra Gardens.

(*Platanus* x *hispanica*), in the summer there is little sunlight to shine on the *zellij*, so the colours chosen are green, ochre and off-white, a traditional combination which suits the climate here well.

Selecting Materials

Selecting which hard materials to use out of the wealth of exotic ones that are available today can be quite a business – from Indian sandstone, to Italian marble, to Brazilian slate, not to mention the humble brick or reconstituted stone paving. Rigorous discernment should be exercised in the choice of materials, keeping in mind three important points: first, as has been emphasized already, the materials should not be at odds with the architecture of the house and the surroundings; second, they should as far as possible be natural; and third, keeping in mind the other two points, they should, mainly through geometric patterns and a limited combination of materials, evoke the

Fig. 92. Simple pattern of tiles, Marrakech.

Fig. 94. Cobbles and stone, The Alhambra.

hard-landscaping of Islamic gardens. Looking at some of the Hispano-Mauresque gardens in Spain, it is possible to see how much one can do with a simple combination of just two types of material such as stone and cobbles or stone and granite setts. It is best not to use more than two or three different hard materials to execute a design, otherwise it is in danger of becoming fussy and overdone – the total opposite to the order and simplicity of a traditional Islamic garden. Polished York-stone square setts are a beautiful alternative to cobbles or granite setts and could be used in combination with larger paving stones to create some simple patterns in triangles or hexagons.[157] Budget restrictions will also be a determining factor in your final choice of materials but a great deal can be achieved even on a small budget. It is vital that you spend time thinking about the geometric designs and which materials are the optimum choice before embarking on your scheme.

Slate or a combination of slate and cobbles are possible materials for hard-landscaping, which both fit in with the more northern environment as well as suggesting an Islamic influence. There are many possibilities for executing designs with slate and cobbles or brick and cobbles, such as designs based on triangles or diamonds or more complex star patterns involving five-, six-, seven- or eight-pointed stars. This would depend on a certain amount of expertise and experience in drawing up the geometric patterns, as well as a good relationship with your stonemason or other craftsman who is executing the design. For guidance with simple drawings, and if you wish to explore the vast potential of geometry for more complex patterns, there are a few select books to be consulted – although it would be far more rewarding to be taught directly by a master.[158]

For those interested in further research into a combination of Islamic and European – primarily Christian – cultures, it is interesting to look at the *Mudejar* style of architecture and landscaping in Spain. *Mudejar* is the term applied to the culture of the Muslims who lived under Christian rule after the re-conquest of Spain – just as the term *Mozarab* is applied to the Christians who lived under Muslim rule. An example of the *Mudejar* style is the Casa de Pilatos in Seville, a fifteenth-century mansion produced for Christian patrons by Moorish craftsmen. This shows a slightly bizarre mixture of Moorish, Gothic and Renaissance influences. It is interesting as it shows an attempt to combine, not styles exactly, but the skills of the Muslim craftsmen with the form and symbolism of the Christian perspective. However, the result, although aesthetically quite pleasing, does lack the underlying unity essential to the Islamic perspective. The challenge when making your own Islamic garden is to remain in keeping with the surroundings, while at the same time retaining the purity and sense of unity that is the secret key element of the *chahar-bagh*.

Importance of Natural Materials

A word must be said about why natural materials are so important in a traditional Islamic garden; it is not simply nostalgia or sentiment. It has been pointed out several times that every element in the traditional Islamic garden has a deeper significance – and this goes for the materials as well as the design and the planting. Outward forms should always relate to the inner meaning, utility to spiritual significance. The making of a pot on a wheel, in particular, with the whole notion of 'centreing', is highly significant symbolically, since the spiritual life is all about 'centreing' the soul on the

Transcendent. If the pots are replaced by machine-made plastic ones or the modern metal ones, then a whole language of symbolism is lost. The pots are made of the *prima materia*, the earth or clay, from which, as the Quran says, we are created by God, 'It is He who created you of clay';[159] and likewise in the Bible it is written, 'And the Lord God formed man of the dust of the ground, and breathed into his nostrils the breath of life'.[160] Since Islamic art is largely about the ennobling of matter – the breathing into the material of the Divine spirit through the vehicle of the craftsman, then it can be understood that the nature of the material is paramount. This is in effect alchemy, the transformation of base matter into something elevated and noble.[161]

There is no doubt that there is a confusion of art materials in the modern world: we no longer know how to distinguish the cosmic significance of stone, iron or wood. Wood is warm, lively and kind, whereas 'iron is hostile, aggressive and ill-natured' as one commentator observes.[162] It abounds in churches today and the same writer says that it impedes 'the radiation of spiritual forces' and 'gives the impression that Heaven is imprisoned'. Therefore the best way to use it is to counteract its hardness and inflexibility and to lighten it through working it into 'lacework', such as railings and window-grilles (Figs. 2 and 98). Stone may be cold and implacable but its cold is 'neutral and indifferent like that of eternity' and in its raw state it has something ancient and awe-inspiring about it[163] and this could also be said of the noble metals such as silver and gold. The same writer describes concrete, which like iron has invaded the whole world, as 'a base and quantitative sort of counterfeit stone; in it the spiritual aspect of eternity is replaced by an anonymous and brutal heaviness; if stone is implacable like death, concrete is brutal like an overwhelming destruction'. These quotations may seem to make the point rather forcefully but it is worth taking them into account when considering your materials.

Practically speaking, natural materials weather beautifully, stone and terracotta taking on a pleasing patination, going slightly green with the passage of time and the elements. Wood rots eventually in damp weather but it can be broken down and recycled; however, if well treated with oil at the beginning it can last several years. Materials such as steel and galvanised zinc, currently in vogue for containers, do not weather well and, unless maintained carefully can end up

Fig. 95. England, slate and cobbles.

looking scruffy and dirty. Concrete, although not a modern material, needs dyeing or painting regularly to keep looking fresh, otherwise its monotonous 'dead' grey can look drab very quickly. So-called 'cast-stone' is basically a concrete mix with stone powder and tends not to weather well either. However, for the budget-conscious, tremendous improvements have been made with cement in recent years and there are some very nice 'natural-looking' setts available now. These can be laid out in geometric patterns for a quarter of the sum of stone, granite or slate, although this means sacrificing the deeper significance of the material.

Practical Tips

The materials you use for the ground area of your garden will depend on many circumstances, not only the materials of the adjacent buildings or their period and style. How large is the area? Would you like some lawn, however small? How shady is it – do trees overhang the area so will roots be a problem, not to mention lack of moisture? Are there any cables or essential pipes such as water or gas in the way? Is water easily available? Is there room to put in a reservoir for your fountain? Are the neighbours friendly? Remember to allow plenty of time for hiring a skip and, in towns, for suspending a parking bay, which can often involve a bureaucratic nightmare at the local council not to mention a handsome sum; and so on. This is not a definitive design guide so this is just a brief reminder that in an urban situation, more than in the country, many factors need to be taken into account besides the more interesting horticultural ones.

This may sound superfluous but it is really worth taking the time to find good builders or contractors who care about their work, especially stone-masons whose work is heavy and demanding as well as being highly skilled. If you are keen to put some Islamic geometric patterns in your garden, and I would strongly recommend this as it is one of the simplest ways of creating the 'feel' of an Islamic garden, then it is vital to produce some good, clear scale drawings for the craftsmen, and templates if necessary. Cutting the stone to the correct geometric pattern shown on a design requires intelligence, technical skill and physical strength – as anyone who has used a hammer and chisel or an angle-grinder will testify. This may sound very basic but if you are asking the stone-mason to cut out a star octagon design, for example, or something more ambitious, then it is a good idea to mark out the exact dimensions on the ground with old-fashioned pegs and string or marker paint. This will avoid misunderstanding not to mention time and money.

Fig. 96. Mashrabbiyya, house in Jeddah, Saudi Arabia.

Mashrabbiyyas

Mashrabbiyyas are a practical and beautiful way of screening off one area in the garden from another. They are geometrically-patterned turned wood or slatted wood screens used both inside and outside the house. They provide several functions: first, that of separating one area from another – this was probably the original use, as a means of creating privacy for the women's quarters; second, to provide dappled shade from the sun, whilst allowing a cooling breeze to blow through – the sunlight creating beautiful patterns as it shines through (Figs. 62, 66 and 79); and third, a combination of the first and second, providing a screen over windows, which offers both shade to the inhabitants as well as a means of looking out without being seen. Traditionally, in a large house, the women's quarters were on the upper floors and *mashrabbiyyas* were placed along balconies in order that they could look through them onto the courtyard below without inquisitive eyes looking in, an architectural 'veil'. In some parts of the Islamic world, such as Jeddah in Saudi Arabia, the old houses (probably seventeenth or eighteenth century) are not courtyard houses but are tall, single blocks and have balconies looking out onto the street protected by *mashrabbiyyas*.

In the past *mashrabbiyyas* were made from small pieces of wood turned on a lathe and then assembled in such a way that the whole screen is self-supporting, the pieces slotting into each other with no glue. This means that the wood is allowed to shrink and expand without splitting – which would be the case if glue were used. Today, to save time, they are often not made with turned wood but are constructed a bit like trellis with straight pieces of wood slotting into one another. Patterns can still be achieved but nowhere near the same level of refinement and craftsmanship as the traditional *mashrabbiyya*.

Recently, staying in a modern hotel in Amman, Jordan, an outside dining-area was screened off from a dreary car-park and utility zone by a solidly built *mashrabbiyya* in a simple pattern of criss-cross 'dynamic' squares like a trellis. This simple *mashrabbiya* was attractive and gave both shade and privacy to the dining-area, whilst filtering the light and letting a cool breeze blow, as well as screening the ugly area from the diners unless they peered closely through it. It also offered an opportunity for growing climbing plants.

Fig. 97. Carved stone screen, Istanbul.

Although in northern climates we do not often have the problem of too much sun, a *mashrabbiyya* with distinctly Islamic geometric patterns could be employed in a number of ways in a 'northern' Islamic garden. Overhead beams, pergolas and arbours – all favourite elements in gardens where people like to spend time sitting or entertaining out of doors – could be given very effective Islamic treatment through the employment of geometry. In northern climes it is important to use a good and sustainable hardwood such as oak; if they are to be left outside, treating the wood properly with oil and varnish is vital for long-term survival.

Pierced and carved stone screens are another traditional Islamic way of separating one area from another and would be wonderful to use in the garden of a house where the principal material was stone.[164] These are found in various parts of the Islamic world, particularly in India, Pakistan and Turkey. Along with a carved stone *chador* or *chini-khana* (see Chapter 4), it would really transform your garden into a little piece of India. However, it must be said that these are for the garden-maker with means, since the material and the craftsmanship would come at a price and may need to be imported from abroad or commissioned specially here.

Window-Grilles

Window-grilles (Figs. 2 and 98) are decorative scrolled iron 'screens' often placed over windows as an alternative to wooden *mashrabbiyya*s in certain regions of the Islamic world such as Morocco. The function is similar to that of the *mashrabbiyya*, that is, preventing prying eyes from looking in whilst allowing those within to look out at the garden. These would probably not be employed much in an Islamic garden in northern climates, except possibly as decorative security devices. The privacy factor, although highly valued in our over-crowded cities, is not as important as it is in a traditional Islamic home, where separation between male gatherings in the *salamlik* (the 'public' sitting-room for entertaining) and the family gatherings, primarily mothers and children, in the more private rooms, is necessary. As a decorative feature to remind you of visits abroad, a window-grille could be used on the door or window of a summer-house or even a smart garden shed! This would definitely require some weighing-up of different factors, such as the architecture of the house, the garden itself, and so on.

Walls and Colour

'The garden with its buildings and gates, was surrounded by a high wall like a fortress,' wrote a seventeenth-century visitor to a royal Ottoman garden in Istanbul.[165] The traditional Islamic courtyard garden was often enclosed by high walls built of local stone or brick or mud-brick, depending on the geographical region concerned. Hopefully, the walls will not be so high as to make the visitor to the courtyard feel

Fig. 98. Window-grille, Fes.

hemmed-in or claustrophobic, as happened to one observer on a visit to another royal Ottoman garden:

> On entering through a gilded door, I found myself in a garden completely in Turkish style with small flower-beds enclosed by box hedges and paths strewn with seashells. Around a pool with a fountain in which goldfish were swimming were cypresses and orange trees in the shape of pyramids. Behind these rose terraces in the same style with beautiful conservatories and pavilions; however, these were all enclosed by high walls. They were painted green but still gave one a feeling of claustrophobia. The windows on the Bosphorous side each had thickly woven lattices as well as tall bars through which it was possible to look out but not to see in. The harem with its latticed windows was on two floors, but even the windows on the third floor of the palace were tightly covered to the very top.[166]

This is a reminder to achieve a balance between privacy and not feeling hemmed-in. Walls, rendered and painted in pastel or brighter colours are a quick and

Fig. 100. *Jardin Majorelle, Marrakech, showing exotic planting and blue-painted edge of pool.*

Fig. 99. Madrasa *(religous school) courtyard, showing usual height of* zellij.

relatively inexpensive way of capturing something of the atmosphere of a Mediterranean garden – but not necessarily Islamic, as described in the previous chapter. The courtyard garden walls of a Muslim house in say, Fes, Marrakech or Damascus, are not, on the whole, painted in a bright colour; generally it is white or off-white or a natural stone hue. Colour is usually provided by the *zellij* tiles. The deep blue of the painted walls and water-edges of the Jardin Majorelle in Marrakech works well in a climate where the sun is hot and very bright, and it leaves a strong imprint on the visitor's memory. However, if it is an authentic traditional Islamic garden you are aiming for, then it is probably best to avoid painting the walls or fences any strong colour, whether it be blue, red, yellow or green, if your garden is situated in northern climes where the light is much gentler on the eyes. In hot countries bright colours can withstand the intensity of the light but in the north they end up looking dull and dirty and as if they would rather be somewhere else. It seems that in these arid countries bright colours are employed when there is little in the way of greenery or flowing water: they are a kind of substitute for vegetation, just as one finds the poorest Indian women looking like princesses in their beautiful, brightly-coloured flowing saris. In both cases it an expression of joy in a barren landscape.

The walls of the courtyards of Islamic houses need to be neutral so as not to compete with the colourful *zellij* tiles, the marble floor designs, and decorative inlaid pastework that you find in some cities. These provide a mosaic of colour: Damascene houses in particular excel at this latter craft (Fig. 55). The city walls of Marrakech are well known for being a specific terracotta-red colour, the colour of the surrounding earth; but this is not a glaring colour at all – it is in complete harmony with the surrounding countryside. So, the moral is to think carefully before slapping on some bright blue or bright yellow paint to cheer yourself up in the hope that you can transform Maida Vale into Marrakech on a small budget! The more likely outcome is that it will look effective for the first summer but will begin to look out of place as the autumn cloud and drizzle set in. However, there is no doubt that the softer, earthier colours of ochre, green and cream – for example – can look beautiful throughout the year under northern skies. It is a tradition in England to paint seaside houses in different colours and it is interesting to note that these houses are most often painted in pastel colours, not strong, bright ones.

Pavilions and Tents

Pavilions or *kiosks* (from the Turkish word *kosk*) are an integral part of the large gardens of the Indian subcontinent such as the Shalimar Gardens in Lahore, as well as the larger gardens of Persia, Ottoman Turkey, North Africa and elsewhere in the Islamic world. In the Shalimar gardens there are several pavilions, mostly with wide-arched openings in order that those sitting within may enjoy the cool breeze blowing off the water; at the same time as looking out onto the grand vista of water-terraces they are shaded from the hot overhead sun. There are also the grander palace-pavilions which incorporate a large inner protected room or rooms, often with a loggia linking the inside area with the outside such as that of Chehel Sutun ('Forty Columns') in Isphahan. Here, the grand palace-pavilion is set at the head of a vast still pool and the twenty columns (a

Fig. 101. The large pool in front of the palace-pavilion of Chehel Sutun, Isphahan.

reduced number now) of the loggia are reflected in the pool to make forty columns, hence the name.

These are rather grand ideas for your own garden! However, it may give inspiration for a simpler version if you are fortunate enough to have the space and appropriate location. The smaller, delicate Ottoman *kiosks*, such as those in the Topkapi Seray in Istanbul, might well offer more realistic ideas for designing your own 'summer-house'[167] or the one shown in the Persian miniature illustrated over the page (Fig. 102). In northern climates a summer-house, as we would probably refer to a pavilion, will need to be more enclosed to keep out the wind and rain, and to extend its seasonal use. If you have an enclosed Islamic garden that receives sun at least part of the day during the summer, then a small 'pavilion' might be a practical and potentially beautiful solution to sitting within the garden, providing somewhere to read, rest or contemplate, in the shade and in private. However, pavilions will be expensive, even if simple and constructed of wood. A strong possibility as an alternative is a tent in Eastern style. Tents were an obvious source of protection for those almost constantly on the move (with an army or large entourage), such as the Emperor Babur or Sultan Mehmet the Conqueror. They would choose the most pleasant of environments they could find to erect their tents and sometimes lay out gardens around them. Here political and diplomatic meetings would take place, as well as hours of rest and entertainment. A visitor to Istanbul in the early nineteenth century gives an evocative description of one of the royal gardens and tents:

A large silken tent adorned with arabesques formed an extension to the ceiling, and the garden paths, decorated with mosaics of sea-shells and coloured gravel, joined with the flowers arranged in beds in colourful patterns to form a splendid carpet. It was difficult to decide where the room ended and the garden began; whether the fountain was murmuring to you in the room or the long low-seat you were sitting on was in the garden. The cool freshness of the breeze from the Bosphorous wafted through the open latticed windows, filling the room and mingling with the delightful perfumes from the sunlit garden...[168]

There are companies that specialize in beautiful Indian or Ottoman-style tents, which can be put up in the garden for the summer months and taken into store for the winter.[169] These will immediately give your garden an Eastern 'feel' and inspire you to lay out cushions on rugs within it. Then all you need are delicious cold drinks or mint tea and perhaps a *shisha* (water-pipe) and you will be transported to a timeless world, sinking back into a pillow, allowing the ambience of peace and contemplation (and indolence!) to take over.

Parasols

Large parasols could also be used instead of a tent. From miniature paintings we can see that a cross between a tent and a parasol was sometimes used. These parasol/tent affairs were not the simple circular ones on a central pole set into a stand we are familiar with today but were usually rectangular or square, erected on three or four poles like the original open-sided Bedouin tent. However, unlike the coarse goat-hair of the Bedouin tent, these ones were of brightly coloured, patterned and embroidered material, probably a mixture of silk and cotton. In Egypt, colourful appliqué cotton hangings, awnings and tents with calligraphy and geometric patterns, are still widely used, many still made in the Street of the Tent-makers in old Cairo.

Seating

'Costly Persian carpets were spread and there were raised seats covered with gold embroidered velvet cushions,' wrote a seventeenth-century visitor to a palace garden in Instanbul.[170] These will probably not be readily available to most readers; however, it is amazing how good a substitute an Indian cotton bedspread is, with cushions scattered on top. Whenever possible, seating outside in an Islamic garden should consist of low seats or large cushions or, if available, an old rug or kelim on the ground, preferably placed on top of something waterproof, since the ground is always damp in Northern Europe, even during a hot summer spell. When sitting in one of his gardens, the Sultan would be provided with a throne or grand stool placed in a *kiosk*, while his entourage would stand around in respectful attendance.

In a traditional Muslim home there is very little furniture, much of the activities of daily life taking place on the floor: eating, praying and sitting on cushions or low seats, drinking tea or coffee and chatting. The floor, because of prayer, is a sanctified space, and this is the underlying reason for removing

Fig. 102. Persian miniature showing a square open pavilion with octagonal pool in the foreground, cypress and flowering fruit trees in the background, seventeenth century, from the Houghton Shahnamah.

Fig. 103. The Street of the Tentmakers, Old Cairo.

shoes before entering a Muslim house. However, although tables and chairs are contrary to an Islamic ambience, they are obviously far more practical in areas of high rainfall. If you would like a wooden bench in your garden, to create a more Islamic 'feel' you could design a simple geometric pattern for the bench-back and commission a good woodworker to make it.

Arbours, Pergolas and Gazebos

Looking at Mughal, Persian and Ottoman miniature paintings from approximately the fifteenth to the eighteenth centuries, as well as later European paintings and engravings of Islamic gardens, it seems that the pavilion, kiosk, tent or loggia was more popular than the arbour or pergola entwined with climbing plants, so prized by Europeans.[171] In England, similar to Islamic countries, shade was important in Tudor and Elizabethan gardens and indeed, right up until the mid-twentieth century, ladies liked to retain their pale complexion; a 'tan' was considered rather vulgar and indicated that one may have been labouring outside – horror of horrors! The sought-after all-year-round tan only became fashionable in the second half of the last century.

Tunnel arbours or pergolas covered with vines or roses are to be seen in early European illustrations, such as a Flemish fifteenth-century depiction of a Boccaccio tale in which an elaborate tunnel arbour is shown covered in a fruiting vine.[172] Perhaps the Islamic garden, in hotter climes as it is, demanded stronger protection from the sun in the form a pavilion built of stone. However, pergolas and arbours did exist in eastern gardens, as Jahangir describes one in his Memoirs: 'On entering the garden I found myself immediately in a covered avenue [pergola] planted on each side with scarlet roses and beyond them arose groves of cypress, fir, plane, and evergreens variously disposed.'[173] Dating from the late-nineteenth or early twentieth century, the oleander tunnel in the Generalife gardens fits in well to the primary need for shade in an Islamic garden, especially as this garden is built on the side of a hill exposed to the sun for much of the day (Fig. 104).

For your own Islamic garden in Northern Europe, a pergola extending from the house covered in an ornamental vine such as *Vitis coignetiae* or *V. vinifera* 'Brant', would answer to the Islamic garden's craving for shade as well as blending well into the traditions of Europe. Few of us can afford, or have space for, a Mughal-style stone pavilion, but a vine-, jasmine- or rose-covered pergola, arbour or gazebo (old roses such as one of the *Rosa gallicas* originally from Near East, or a *Rosa damascena* should be used if possible – see Chapter 6), would be a good alternative. The climbers could be entwined around a framework of simple geometric-patterned willow or hazel poles making a happy blending of Eastern and Western tradition.

Although we are mainly concerned with the enclosed courtyard garden, it is worth mentioning that, whenever possible in the larger Islamic gardens, a view was sought after as well as seclusion – the Alhambra offers one of the supreme examples of this. As one wanders from one courtyard to another one comes across beautiful arched-shaped belvederes, gazebos or 'miradors', from where there are spectacular views of the Generalife gardens and the Sierra Nevada mountains beyond; but no-one can peer within (see Chapter 4; Fig. 121) In the Western gardening tradition, a gazebo is usually a structure separate from the house, placed somewhere in the garden with the best view but also providing a certain seclusion. A more humble means is the *clair-voyée*, a simple aperture in a wall or hedge providing a 'look-out'. As Villiers Stuart wrote, 'if the lie of the land

Fig. 104. Oleander tunnel, Generalife gardens.

allowed it, the Indian gardens would often succeed in the 'double charm of complete seclusion and a wide prospect over the world without walls'.[174]

Conservatories

In a Northern European climate, glass conservatories are very popular and have been since at least the middle of the nineteenth century. In Islamic countries, because of the heat, they are far less popular. In order to extend the flowering time and enjoyment of your more tender plants, then a conservatory, if you have the space and the means, is very tempting. It could be argued that, besides the summer-house and the arbour for the warmer months, the conservatory is a northern substitute for the Islamic pavilion in the winter months. There is no doubt that a conservatory extending from the house, with bougainvillea, jasmine, citrus and pomegranate, as well as a small, gentle fountain set in some geometric tiles, would be a welcome addition to any house. Its use would extend over a far longer period than the summer house or arbour. Sitting on comfortable cushions, listening to the fountain with the smell of jasmine scenting the air, a very pleasant Islamic garden ambience could well be conjured up – albeit enclosed rather than open to the sky.

Pots, Urns, Planters, Containers...

...or whatever you like to call them, are all very appropriate in an Islamic garden. They are also exceptionally useful, not just because the pots themselves look beautiful, but, providing they are not too large, they can be moved around to follow the sun. In the traditional Arab-Islamic house, the courtyard would be designed so that it received maximum shade in the summer months and maximum sun in the winter months, and the inhabitants could rearrange their accommodation and meals accordingly. So pots in a cooler, wetter climate can be moved throughout the day in order that those containing sun-loving flowers and herbs such as rosemary, sage, lavender and lilies can receive the maximum amount of warm rays.

In an Islamic garden, in my view it is best that only terracotta (Fig. 64), stone or ceramic pots[175] should be used, not the steel or zinc ones fashionable at the moment. These suit a modern, perhaps minimalist garden, but not a traditional Islamic one. The glazed ceramic ones should not predominate and the colour should be subtle, not bright or standing out garishly, competing with the flowers. Wooden half-barrels are fine too, especially large ones for the citrus trees or pomegranates that need to be moved indoors before the frosts arrive. In fact it may be a good idea to save the half-barrels for the tender plants since, as they will be indoors during the worst weather they will not rot and collapse as quickly. For reasons explained earlier, the terracotta pots should be hand-turned and not the factory-made ones found in large garden-centres. It is in fact possible, with a little research, to track down handmade pots that are not prohibitively expensive. Not only do they contribute something of true beauty to your garden but in so doing you will be supporting the individual craftsman or small workshop who are in need of patrons in a world dominated by market giants.

Lighting

This is a large and important subject, which I do not have the space to do justice to in this book. However, briefly, it is very important to choose the right lighting in your Islamic garden as this contributes so much to the atmosphere at night. As with all aspects of the Islamic garden, lighting should be subtle and discreet, contributing to the overall contemplative atmosphere. Ideally, I would recommend only using candles, night-lights or paraffin lamps, since no modern lighting equals the beauty and romance of a flickering flame in a garden at night.[176] Kanahaya Lal, the nineteenth-century engineer-historian, described a gathering at the Shalimar Bagh (the gardens on the outskirts of Lahore built by Shah Jahan in the seventeenth century): 'the garden was so well illuminated that during the night the effect of daylight was produced. At each tree pots were hung and in each pot fifty lamps were placed. The walls appeared red with light'. Another historian describing the Shalimar gardens, writes of the 'chirags', 'the little open earthenware oil lamp of the country, whose tiny speck of soft light is a means of illumination the most effective in the world'.[177] Today this soft light can easily be replicated with candles or night-lights in jam-jars, providing the most beautiful and one of the least expensive options. Of course they take time and trouble, and if you have children or animals there is the safety aspect to consider. I read a charming description recently about boys flying their kites at night in a village in late-Victorian England. They tied lighted candle-ends to the ends of their kites: 'The little lights floated and flickered like fireflies against the dusk of the sky and the darker tree-tops.'[178] However, you may not be very popular if you suggested children doing this to give your garden the right atmosphere!

There is a huge range of lamps for holding night-lights or candles, but the most appropriate for an Islamic garden would be the Moroccan, Indian or Egyptian metal or pottery lamps or lanterns pierced with geometric shapes. If possible, these may be brought back from a trip abroad: they are widely available in the souks of Marrakech, Fes, Cairo, Damascus, Istanbul and elsewhere. Failing this there are several places in the United Kingdom, Europe and North America that import them from abroad.[179] The lamps themselves can be fixed permanently to the walls and night-lights or candles replaced whenever necessary. However, if you prefer the convenience and safety of electricity then you need an experienced electrician to put these in for you. In this case I would recommend the lamps just mentioned with low-voltage, candle-shaped bulbs. The low-voltage bulbs result in a far more subtle and discreet light radiating from the lamps or lanterns; they cast a beautiful patterned light onto the garden, conjuring up something of an Eastern-Islamic atmosphere despite the lack of flickering candles. Small lanterns could be hung

in the trees in a more sophisticated and subtle variation of the Christmas-tree fairy-lights theme – as in the Shalimar gardens.[180] Another alternative are fibre optics, lighting devices created by a single source located remotely in a light-box; a special reflector focuses the light down individual glass fibres enabling it to radiate without emitting heat or ultra-violet rays. Fibre optics can be used to great effect lighting water-rills and fountains at a low level.[181]

The more one reads contemporary accounts of the early Islamic gardens and their incredibly glamorous lighting and entertaining schemes, the more one realizes that modern technology – for all its conveniences – rarely comes close to the beauty and romance of former times. The many extracts that Nurhan Atasoy has included in her fascinating book on Ottoman gardens clearly demonstrate this and make one long to have been present at such magical extravagances. Not only were thousands of candles kept burning by hundreds of gardeners for the night-time festivities, but there were nightingales and canaries whose singing 'can be heard by those sitting everywhere in the garden', peacocks wandering freely, pure white rabbits (only white ones allowed) let loose to hop about, swings to ride in on moonlit nights, delicious feasts, musicians playing, poetry recitation and singing songs – usually on the subject of flowers – and strolling amongst the flowers, blossoming trees and fruit, picking and eating as you desired: a paradise garden indeed![182]

Finally, one may be inspired to use coloured glass for lighting by the following description of the Shalimar Bagh, Lahore, by a Russian prince in 1842.

> I went to take leave of Sher Singh at the garden of Shalamar, where he had been staying for several days and he gave us magnificent entertainment. The whole garden was illuminated from the edges of the fountains and water channels to the branches of the orange trees. Globes of coloured glass placed behind these candles tinged the sparkling water green or red. Add to all of this continuous fireworks, the magnificent warlike courtiers, the garden with its walks covered with Kashmiri shawls with the horses trampling upon them, the intoxicating smell of the orange blossom, and the even more intoxicating movements of the dancing girls. One felt inclined to say like Poor Tom in King Lear, 'God keep us in our five senses'.[183]

CHAPTER 4

Water

The spirit of the garden-paradises of Europe hides in the flowers, the grass, the trees, but the soul of the Eastern garden lies in none of these; it is centred on the running water which alone makes its other beauties possible.[183A]

There is no question that water is the supreme element in the Islamic garden, both on a physical and metaphysical level. Even if your garden is only 5 sq m or smaller, then a stone or ceramic bowl of water for a bird-bath, measuring as little as half a metre in diameter, is better than no water at all. It can easily be cleaned out and refreshed every week and the birds will be very grateful – and you will be grateful for the birds! There is a Muslim saying that every time a bird drinks a drop of water it lifts its eyes in gratitude toward Heaven.[184]

This chapter is primarily to throw some light on why water is so important in an Islamic garden, both practically and symbolically. Secondly, the different ways in which it is used across certain parts of the Islamic world will be touched upon. Then finally, we will look at how some of these ideas may be borrowed for your own garden. Differences in climate and environment are two all-important factors to weigh up when interpreting these ideas for your own specific site. The practical aspects of excavating the ground to make a pool, or water-channels, or a rill or installing a fountain are not dealt with in this book, since there are already several good publications on these subjects.[185]

Water in an Islamic garden is formal. This means that it does not try to imitate nature with meandering streams through woodland or 'natural' ponds. Water may vary from one simple circular fountain in the centre of a small courtyard, to a great diversity of water-channels, pools and fountains. However, as with the design of the garden as a whole, straight lines and

geometry always predominate. In the larger, royal gardens, such as the Shalimar gardens in Kashmir and Lahore, there are more elaborate ways of directing water: over cascades between one level and the next, over carved stone slabs (*chador* in Persian and *salsabil* in Arabic) or over stone niches set in rows (*chini-khanas*, see below). In the gardens of the Alhambra and Generalife, water is channelled down steps, on each side or down the centre (Fig. 107). There are fountains and pools in many different shapes and forms, but always formal, geometric shapes such as rectangles, 'lobulated' or in circles, never the 'organic' kidney-shaped type (Fig. 108–9). These formal shapes are examined later in the chapter. However, there is one notable exception to prove the rule of geometry and formality in the water of an Islamic garden, and this is the spectacular water stairway above the Garden of the Sultana in the Generalife. Here the water rushes down the hollowed-out tops of the stone walls that are moulded in a flowing, organic manner, reminiscent of climbing tendrils in nature (Fig. 110).

One author has written, 'It was upon irrigation that the existence of gardens depended in Arabia, Persia and India, and it was the irrigation system that gave

Fig. 105. Water channel and pools above the Partal Palace, Alhambra.

Fig. 106. Fountain in centre of Dismounting Yard, Generalife.

Fig. 107. Water travelling down centre of steps, Alhambra.

Fig. 108. Formal 'lobulated' fountain, Generalife.

the garden its form';[186] to a certain extent this is true. The most practical and effective form of irrigation is to use straight lines; but in traditional Islamic culture, as stated many times because of its importance in the making of an Islamic garden, the practical and the spiritual go hand-in-hand. There is no doubt also that besides the practical uses of the geometric lay-out and the symbolic qualities described later, running water in a hot climate also possesses health-giving and healing properties. The air that surrounds clean running water is always clearer and cooler, especially in an enclosed space, and this is extremely pleasant and invigorating in a hot and sultry environment. The sound of water in fountains, when carefully controlled to be gentle and melodious rather than loud and gushing, can have a soothing and uplifting effect. On a more prosaic note, in countries where water is a cherished 'commodity', to ostentatiously employ it in gardens with fountains and pools was, and still is, one way of demonstrating wealth and power.[187]

Our own view of water is largely determined by the climate in which we were brought up. This book is mainly directed towards readers in northern Europe and countries with a similar temperate climate. This means, as those who live in the United Kingdom know only too well, a generous amount of rain, approximately 100cm (40in) per year. Water does not mean the same to inhabitants of such temperate climates, as to the inhabitants of the sun-baked lands of many Islamic countries.[187A] A Bedouin friend told me recently, for example, that water is so precious to them that their vocabulary developed accordingly with a great number of special terms for every intricate movement that water makes. Hassan Fathy, the great Egyptian reviver of traditional Islamic architecture, suggested that the fountain in a hot country was equivalent in importance to the open fire in a cold country – in terms of both practical use and symbolic significance. There is much to be said for this analogy as it brings home the crucial necessity of water to those of us who complain about the rain and take water for granted. Living in such relatively easy conditions, we are unfamiliar with an existence where avoiding the sun is the norm instead of rushing out and basking in it, as we sun-starved inhabitants of northern Europe like to do.

Therefore, both imagination and caution should be exercised when selecting what form your water will take: imagination, since one needs to be able to see beyond the literal veil of mist caused by rain and perceive that there still is potential for water in the garden; and caution, since one does not want to overdo it and find oneself ending up living in something approaching a dank cave, far from the

Fig. 109. Formal octagonal fountain, Generalife.

Islamic ideal hoped for. As many readers know who enjoy going for walks or visiting gardens in the winter, coming across a flowing fountain increases that unpleasant cold and damp feeling and one walks on as quickly as possible, particularly if the wind blows the water towards you. It is altogether a miserable experience, the opposite of the original aim. So, in cooler climates, fountains are definitely for the summer months and should be turned off in winter, leaving only enough water for the birds.[188]

Symbolism

Water is present in most gardening traditions, from the Japanese and Chinese to the medieval Christian and the Italian Renaissance, all emphasizing one aspect or other. Why is it that we are so drawn to water? In spite of our rain-soaked climate, it seems more popular than ever to include a 'water-feature'. The answer is very profound and lies beyond both the practical requirements of irrigation, ablutions and drinking, and the sensuous pleasure of dipping your hand in a fountain and feeling the water running through your fingers. There is a beauty and mystery that draws us towards water in a garden, in whatever form it may take, whether it be a fountain, a large still pool, a cascade or a narrow rill. The Arabs and pre-Islamic Persians understood this very well and there seems little doubt that it is only in the tradition of gardening born from a religion revealed in a desert land that the full meaning of water becomes apparent.

Fig. 110. Water Stairway, Generalife.

Since the Arabs were used to a harsh environment they already considered water and shade as sacred, long before the Quran was revealed. It is interesting that the Bedouin have a multitude of words for water, not because there is so much of it (like the Inuit and their words for snow or the Laplanders and their words for reindeer) but because there is so little of it and it is so precious. As we know there is no life on earth without water; it is written in Genesis that nothing was created, not even light, until 'the spirit of God moved upon the face of the waters',[189] and in the Quran it is written, 'The heavens and the earth were of one piece, then We parted them, and We made every living thing of water'.[190] Profoundly, we are all connected through this element, human beings consisting largely – approximately 70% – of water. There are many references to water throughout the Quran – it is, along with all the wonders of nature such as 'heaven and the earth', 'night and the day', the 'sun and the moon', one of the 'signs' or 'similitudes' of God, and the Quran is constantly reminding us whence water comes and not to take it for granted: 'Hast thou not seen how that God sends down out of heaven water?';[191] 'We sent down out of

Fig. 111. Stone fountain, Generalife.

Heaven water and caused to grow in it of every generous kind'.[192] Water is seen as a gift and a blessing from God and is considered a sign of God's mercy: 'And of His signs is that thou seest the earth humble: then, when We send down water upon it, it quivers and swells. Surely He who quickens it is He who quickens the dead'.[193] When the Virgin Mary (*Sayyidatna Maryam* in Arabic) gave birth to the infant Jesus beneath a palm-tree, she was comforted in her distress by dates to eat from the palm and a voice saying, 'Thy Lord has set below thee a rivulet' so that she could drink.[194] No doubt this has contributed towards the sanctity of running water and the importance of a 'rivulet' or water-channel in the Islamic garden. These are just a fraction of the verses about water in the Quran; they are important to quote here to give the non-Muslim reader some idea of how much water means, on a deeper level than the purely physical, to the perceptive Muslim.

The lack of division between practical daily life and spiritual needs is summed up most powerfully by the dual role of water, which is both life-giving and cleansing in the obvious senses, as well as being spiritually rejuvenating and purifying.[195] Water is used not just to cleanse ourselves of physical dirt but also to 'wash away sins', as in Christian baptism. There is a similar attitude in Islam. Not only are Muslims required to make careful ablutions before their five daily prayers but these ablutions are symbolically a cleansing of the soul as well as the body, a returning to a state of purity in preparation for the ritual prayer (*salat*).[196] 'Cleanliness is, indeed, next to Godliness' could well be an Islamic saying.[197] On a more profound level, water is symbolic of the soul, a concept that appears in Christian, Hindu, Japanese and many other cultures, as well as Islamic. This is no doubt one of the primary reasons, albeit often unconscious, that we are so drawn to it.[198] When walking around a garden, it is near water where we end up sitting because near water there is a feeling of rest and calm, of being at home, so to speak. It is something for the eye, the heart and the soul to completely engage upon and never be bored.

The fountain in the centre of an Islamic garden, as in the courtyard of a mosque, is used for ablutions and for drinking, and represents one of the fountains in the gardens of paradise. It also symbolizes the source of the ever-flowing waters of the spirit, continually replenishing and purifying the soul, just as spring water is constantly purified at its source. The human soul has much to withstand in the modern world, and is often very agitated and in need of balm and renewal. The presence of water in a garden, as well as mirroring the soul's fluctuations, acts as a soothing balm, helping to put troubles into perspective and reminding us that the trials of life, like life itself, are as transient as a reflection in water. In Sufi[199] terms equilibrium and peace of soul is restored by the sincere and concentrated remembrance of God (*dhikr 'Allah*). There is an inscription in one of the palaces of the Alhambra that reads, 'The fountain in my midst is like the soul of a believer, immersed in the remembrance of God'.[200]

This purifying quality of water is a powerful symbol for Hindus also, for whom the water of life flows in the river Ganges, its source being the Himalayas, the mountains of the Gods:[201]

Whoever, with repentant mind, bathes in the Ganges, is freed from all his sins: inner purification here finds its symbolic support in the outward purification that comes from the water of the sacred river. It is as if the purifying water came from Heaven, for its origin in the eternal ice of the roof of the world is like a symbol of the heavenly origin of divine grace which, as 'living water', springs from timeless and immutable Peace.[202]

The Japanese also hold water sacred; profoundly aware of its purifying powers they make pilgrimages to waterfalls and spend hours gazing into temple pools. There is a story, too, that when the Chinese sage, Hsuyu, dreamt that the Emperor wanted to give him his kingdom, he fled to the mountains to wash his ears in a waterfall.[203]

The different manifestations of water in an Islamic garden are reflections of the subtle fluidity of the soul, changing as it does from one moment to the next – from alert activity to rest and renewal and many variations between. The water trickles gently, cascades down small waterfalls, sprays from fountains, falls over carved stone slabs (*chadors*, Fig. 139), runs along channels and rills or remains still in pools, reflecting the sky above. The characteristics of movement and stillness, as well as reflections in water, combine to create an harmonious environment, which both attracts and soothes the onlooker. One moment the reflection is crystal clear in a perfectly still pool; then in a second, a breath of wind can shatter the image. We are reminded of an idea central to Islam – that this world is an illusion, an ephemeral reflection of the eternal Heavenly realm. St. Paul wrote that the spiritual person will always look beyond the visible to the invisible: 'We look not at the things which are seen but at the things which are not seen, for the things which are seen are temporal; but the things which are not seen are eternal';[204] one of the principal roles of water and reflections in an Islamic garden is to remind us of this. When a tree – or anything else – is reflected in water it is inverted, it is in fact an image of an image,

Fig. 113. Pool in front of Court of Myrtles, Alhambra.

in that the earthly tree is already a faint image of the 'real tree', the archetypal tree in heaven. 'An intelligent man, seeing the image of a tree in a pond will look up to see the tree itself. A wise man, seeing the tree will look beyond it to the archetypal tree standing inverted at the centre of the universe.'[205]

In Sufi poetry, such as that of Jalal ud-din Rumi, there is also an emphasis on the invisible and the 'garden within' – the visible object we perceive with the eye is as fleeting as a reflection in water:

The real orchards and verdure are in the very essence of the soul: the reflection thereof upon that which is without is as the reflection in running water.
In the water there is only the phantom of the orchard, which quivers on account of the subtle quality of the water.
The real orchards and fruits are within the heart: the reflection of their beauty
Is falling upon this water and earth.[206]

In Islam, art and contemplation go hand-in-hand, and the art of the garden is no exception. In order to soak up the ambience of an Islamic garden, it is important to take time to experience it, not to walk through quickly, glancing at the plants, making passing remarks on the design or the fountains. The visitor should, if possible, take time to sit and ponder, allowing the reflections in the water to stir his or her soul. When approached in a receptive frame of mind,

Fig. 112. Circular fountain, Generalife.

the beauty of this garden may open our hearts and souls to grace from above. There seems no doubt that it is this focus on the heavenly qualities in an Islamic garden that, often unconsciously, attracts garden-lovers from Western backgrounds.

Fountains

The fountain or fountains in an Islamic garden are not just for coolness and beauty but are themselves reminders of their archetype described in the paradise gardens in the Quran. In the first pair of gardens, described in Chapter LV, The All-Merciful (*Surat al-Rahman*) there are 'two fountains of running water' and in the second, higher pair of gardens there are 'two fountains of gushing water' indicating that this pair is nearer to God Himself. These higher gardens have 'green green pastures' implying great intensity of colour and thus also suggesting nearness to God.[207] Elsewhere in the Quran, the fountains in the paradise gardens are named as *Tasnim*,[208] which means 'exaltation' and *Kauthar*, which means 'abundance', both of which are flavoured with musk; and a fountain called *Salsabil*[209] is also mentioned, which is flavoured with ginger.

When installing your own fountain in your Islamic garden it is important to remember to control the flow of water so that it is always gently overflowing the basin. This is in order to recall the ever-flowing waters of paradise, the 'abundance' of the waters of *Kauthar*. Flavouring the water with musk or ginger may be kept for special occasions! (See Scented Fountains below.) Like the fruits grown in the paradise gardens, these fountains are symbolic of the soul's journey along the spiritual path.[210]

So the presence of movement and stillness in water is an important element in Islamic gardens, reflecting the central idea of the fluidity of the soul as well as the interplay between the changing corporeal world and the unchanging heavenly world. It has

been suggested that the earliest Islamic fountains were probably the *shadirwan-salasabil* type, which encapsulate this concept of movement and stillness. The *shadirwan-salasabil* type of fountain starts as a wall-fountain (*salsabil*), a simple spout with water flowing from it over a sloping, intricately carved marble slab (*shadirwan*, or *chador* in Persian); from here the water travels into a narrow channel where it runs fast, and then the channel opens up into a square or octagonal pool where the water slows down to be quite still; then it may continue to flow down a small cascade and into a larger pool if the site allows it or away underground to irrigate flower or vegetable gardens farther away. One of the earliest examples of this type of fountain that survives can be seen at the twelfth-century La Ziza Palace in Palermo, Sicily (Fig. 114). It is clear that these early patrons and master-craftsmen loved to juxtapose the qualities of energetic movement and tranquil calm which water manifests so beautifully. If the enthusiastic Islamic garden designer today had sufficient funds it would be a wonderful project to commission a stone-carver to build and carve a *shadirwan-salasabil* such as this.[211]

Ibn Jubair, the twelfth-century traveller from Andalucia, remarks on two fountains in Damascus: one in the Madrasa al-Kallasa (built in 1156 and which no longer survives), near the Ummayyed mosque: 'Its courtyard contains a large round pool of marble into which water flows from an octagonal plane located at the head of a pierced column through which the water rises.'[212] The other is at the twelfth-century Madrasa of Nur ad-Din, where

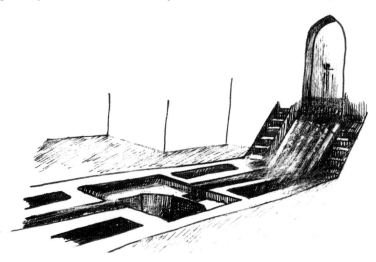

Fig. 114. Drawing of wall-fountain, La Ziza Palace, Palermo, Sicily.

Fig. 115. Courtyard of the Maristan Nur-ad-Din, Damascus.

'Water pours into it from a *shadirwan* into a pool, extends in long channels until it falls into a central pool'. Unfortunately, today this *shadirwan-salsabil* has been paved over but it is still a beautiful, peaceful courtyard with a large central pool (Fig. 115).

The fluidity of water and its seemingly infinite variations of movement in a garden were often contrasted to the stillness of stone and compared to the brightness of precious metals and jewels. There are many references to the fountains in royal palaces in the works of Sicily's poet, Ibn Hamdis (d. AD1172). He describes al-Mansur's palace in Bougie as having pools, the waters of which, 'are like ingots of silver which melt on the steps of a *shadirwan*'.[213] In the poem inscribed on the Fountain of Lions in the Court of Lions at the Alhambra it is written:

In appearance water and marble seem to confuse themselves, not knowing which of each is flowing.
Do you not see that water spills into the basin, but its drains hide it immediately?
It is a lover whose eyelids brim with tears, tears which hide in fear of a betrayer.

Scented Fountains

It is written in the Quran that the fountain in paradise, named *Tasnim* (Exaltation), and the supreme river, *Kauthar* (Abundance) are both flavoured with the fragrance of musk. It is partly this, besides the 'scented herbs' (Quran, Chapter LV) that makes sweet-smelling flowers so important in your earthly Islamic garden; the beautiful perfumes will be a foretaste of the perfumes of the heavenly gardens and may arouse a remembrance of the primordial and mysterious Edenic world. Think how powerful a stimulant certain smells are to the memory, often conjuring up long-buried childhood events. Arabian countries have been renowned in Europe at least as far back as the sixteenth century for their marvellous scented oils, Shakespeare referring to them in Macbeth when Lady Macbeth cries: 'All the perfumes of Arabia will not sweeten this little hand';[214] and today it is noticeable that the 'perfumes of Arabia', worn by men from the Gulf region, are usually more potent than those worn by people in the West. Burning incense is also an Eastern tradition since most incense comes from trees and plants grown in this part of the world. The most obvious example is frankincense (*Boswellia sacra*; other species are found in East Africa) the incense generally burned in Orthodox, Coptic and Roman Catholic churches today in remembrance of the gift of one of the three Kings to the infant Jesus, and '*oud* (*Aquilaria* species), the most heavenly incense of all.

Water Used With Restraint

It is important and interesting to look at the early Islamic fountains mentioned above as they underline the notion, earlier touched upon, that water in an Islamic garden is on the whole used with restraint. As Russell Page comments, 'Water is always in place where it is used to enhance the harmony of a garden or to relate it to its surroundings. I do not like the artificial forcing of a landscape and there is often a temptation to use water out of context.'[215] This sentiment is particularly true in connection with water in an Islamic garden where it should never be used as a means of showing off brilliance of technique. This has become very fashionable in cities all over the world today, where many an urban roundabout or public square has been disfigured by overblown water 'creations'. The fashion dates back to the later Renaissance and Baroque periods. Russell Page describes a garden made by Le Notre outside Paris:

Nothing in this mild and undramatic landscape prepared me for the violence of this garden where an artificial hill at the end of the perspective was used for an arrangement of boiling cascades and innumerable fountains. Water was used in every conceivable way to make a very impressive but disquieting spectacle. One felt that it was detached from, and so ill-accorded with, its surroundings.[216]

This is a very good description of precisely how water is not used in a traditional Islamic garden, and therefore should be avoided at all costs when thinking what form the water will take in your own garden. In Islamic gardens, water is treated with love and reverence, in a sober and dignified way and with a sense of its true beauty and majesty; it is never impressive in a 'disquieting' way but is calming and serene. The fountains are restrained instead of 'boiling cascades', according well with the surrounding landscape. This concept is examined more closely later in the chapter under 'Water in Your Own Garden'.

Shalimar Gardens

You may be thinking, 'What about the cascades of water at the Shalimar Gardens outside Lahore?' not to mention their prototype, the Shalimar Gardens in Kashmir, both of which have three vast terraces of water with fountains and pavilions. But, although spectacular in size and situation, these water terraces and fountains are in no way overdone: they do not jar with their surroundings, which, in the case of the Kashmir gardens, consist of a dramatic backdrop of snow-capped mountains. Here the sublime majesty of the mountains sets off the beauty of the water. The fountains in the Lahore Shalimar gardens are simple fluted spouts with single sprays of water arranged in orderly lines across the great terraces. Not only is the balance between stillness and movement of water maintained but also there is harmony between the water, the architecture (the stone and sandstone pavilions) and the landscape. For all its royal grandeur an atmosphere of great tranquillity reigns.

Fig. 116. Shalimar Gardens, Lahore.

Fig. 117. Cypress with circular channel dug around the base to ensure minimum waste of water.

Fig. 118. Detail of orange trees and irrigation channels at the Cordoba mosque.

The Lahore Shalimar Gardens were built in less than eighteen months by Shah Jahan between 1641 and 1642, and the Kashmir Shalimar Gardens were built a little earlier by his father Jahangir, starting in 1620. These large gardens are the exception,[217] not the norm, since they were built for the royal family and their vast entourage to entertain in. They are not the private, intimate spaces that are typical of traditional urban Islamic architecture and which contain the Islamic garden-type focused on here, the *chahar-bagh*. Nevertheless, it is fascinating to read descriptions of these Mughal gardens, since they conjure up beautifully the combination of luxury and delight with intimations of paradise that is the distinguishing feature of all true Islamic gardens. Ahmed Nabi Khan writes how delighted the Emperor was when he visited the newly created garden at Lahore in 1642:

Wonderstruck, Shah Jahan was overjoyed to see the serene beauty of the place, the sweet-scented atmosphere, and never-ending flow of rippling water, while the atmosphere was pulsating with soft and serene music being played by colourfully attired damsels standing alone here and there, or seated in groups in the pavilion among the jutting and shooting fountains. They were chanting love songs and panegyrics in praise of the Emperor.[218]

No wonder that he was delighted! Shah-Jahan's governor in Lahore and master-designer of the gardens, Ali Mardan Khan, was a Persian nobleman who understood well both the practical aspects of water and its sacred significance. The gardens are a great celebration of the beauty and delights of water, as well as its majestic qualities and profound spiritual

Fig. 119. Stream rushing down from the Sierra Nevada mountains into the Generalife Gardens.

symbolism. The name 'Shalimar' itself has been variously interpreted as the 'Abode of Love' or the 'Abode of Bliss and Beauty'. Visiting them today, one feels a little love in the form of maintenance would not go amiss.

History and Geography

As discussed in Chapter 1, the phrase most often repeated in the Quranic descriptions of the *jannat al-firdaws* (gardens of paradise) is *jannat tajri min tahtiha al-anhar* (meaning 'Gardens underneath which rivers flow').[219] This concept of water flowing underneath is almost literally reproduced in many gardens across the Islamic world, where water runs in channels below the paths so that the visitor may walk over it. As well as echoing the Quranic descriptions of the

paradise gardens, it is a practical solution to the problems of irrigation in countries where the climate is predominantly hot and dry. When observing these gardens, one often sees small circular channels dug around the base of individual trees or large shrubs, lower than ground-level. This is to retain as much water as possible for the plant and not allow it to seep away. Depending on the irrigation method and size of the garden, these individual channels are sometimes, but not always, linked to other channels and back to the main artery. This is generally if the garden is fairly large, perhaps an acre, and the narrow water-channels branch off from the main flow to reach the different areas of the garden. This gives rise naturally to a geometric design, described at the beginning of this chapter and Chapter 2.

Outside the garden, irrigation in a hot country was often conducted completely underground to avoid evaporation by the sun. For example, in the past in Persia and Afghanistan (and still in use today in certain places), the only source of water for much of the year was from underground oases or irrigation systems such as the *qanats*. These rely on water from the melting snow, which rushes down from the mountains to be collected at their foot in deep wells below ground. The water then travels underground in an ingenious network of water-channels, relying entirely on gravity for movement away from the mountains towards the villages and towns. In Tehran today it is a marvellous sight to see the ice-cold clear water flowing along the open channels bordering the streets, after the snow has melted in the spring.

A description of a garden 'renowned for its beauty and fruitfulness' at Khoi in Iran from the late-eighteenth century reveals the use of the *qanats*: 'It consists of a fine alley of chenar trees, which lead up to a pleasure house... built on the elevation of six terraces, from each of which falls a beautiful cascade conducted by Kanauts [*qanats*] from the neighbouring mountains. On the right and left is a wood of fruit trees of every sort and description, with a fine crop of grass at their roots.'[220]

A brief description of how water is used in various parts of the Islamic world is now included. Some examples will hopefully prove inspiring for the would-be Islamic garden designer.

Spain

The Acequia System

This is similar to the *qanats*, although generally speaking not underground. It is an ancient and ingenious system of irrigation channels or aqueducts still in use in parts of Southern Spain today, determining the lives of many villages and remote farming communities. In order to understand just what a skilled craft the *acequia* system is, and its continuing importance in rural Spain, it is fascinating to read the observations of an Englishman who settled in the Alpujarras (bordering on Andalucia, the home of Granada) in the last ten years or so:

> There are literally hundreds of miles of *acequias* in the Alpujarras, and the paths along their banks, lined with grasses and a rich variety of alpine flowers – gentians, campanula, digitalis, saxifrage – make wonderful walking with occasional heart-stopping views... high in the mountains, way above the villages, the channels are wide streams of clear rushing water, ice-cold and lying far above any possible source of contamination, delicious to drink.... Hundreds of small farmers depend on these *acequias* and so an organised social system has grown up to ensure an equitable supply. Each *acequia* has its president, elected each year, its treasurer, and its *acequero*... If your land has water rights from a certain *acequia*, you are allotted a certain time and a certain quantity of water. You may be unlucky (or out of favour with the water president) and come up with, say seventeen minutes of one-third of the *acequia* at ten past three on Thursday mornings. Accordingly you plod out to your orange grove and your vegetables with your torch stuck in your mouth and your mattock over your shoulder. At ten past three – not nine minutes or eleven minutes past – you pull the hatch and let the great body of water tumble through onto your land.[221]

This extract gives a vivid impression of just how vital the *acequias* still are, and how water represents something unimaginably precious. It is easy to believe that in countries where water 'has a price beyond

Fig. 120. Aqueduct at the water tower, Alhambra.

rubies', that many disputes, violent ones too, occur over water rights. In Egypt, recently, I was told of one that almost led to murder in the oasis of Fayoum, about two hours drive south of Cairo.

The Alhambra and Generalife

The majority of these *acequias* in southern Spain were constructed by the Arab Muslims from the eighth century onwards, and were maintained by the Catholics as they re-conquered the country. However, certainly in some areas, the Romans had also introduced water systems, but it is generally agreed that it was the Arabs who developed the *acequia* system to an extraordinary high level of sophistication. One visit to the Alhambra in southern Spain is enough to see how ingenious they were; here, in the thirteenth-century, the Muslim Nasrid dynasty harnessed the tremendous fall of water from the melting snow of the Sierra Nevada. When the Muslim Arabs first arrived in

Fig. 121. View through oriel window of the Alhambra to the Generalife Palace, within which is the enclosed garden known as the Patio de la Acequia (aqueduct).

Fig. 122. View of the cultivated area, facing the Alhambra, on the side of the Hill of the Sun on which the Generalife is situated.

Granada, with its combination of mountain and Mediterranean climate, they believed they had found their earthly gardens of paradise. They saw the potential of the mountain water and devised an intricate and skilful system of aqueducts and reservoirs on the Hill of the Sun above the Alhambra.[222] These came to water and nourish all the gardens of the Generalife. From here the water was, and still is, directed over the aqueduct where the water tower still stands, and into the royal canal to bring it flowing into the courtyards and gardens of the Alhambra. Nowhere is water more in evidence and more soothing – to the eye and to the ear and, above all, to the soul, than here.

The gardens and pavilion of the Generalife were built as a convenient country retreat for the Nasrid sultans, very close by, so that they could easily retire there from the crowded and busy Alhambra city-palace. According to most scholars, the name 'Generalife' derives from the Arabic *jannat*, meaning both 'garden' and 'paradise', and *al-arif* meaning master-builder or architect. Thus the name has usually been translated as 'Garden of the Architect'. However, *al-arif* also means the 'One who Knows', or the Gnostic, and this seems very appropriate. When considering the extraordinary beauty of the Moorish palaces of the Alhambra, the unity of the design linking one palace courtyard to the next, as well as the summer retreat of the Generalife, it seems unarguable that they were conceived by rulers and master-craftsmen who possessed knowledge of a scholarly and esoteric nature. The Generalife gardens, now mainly dating from Francisco Prieto Moreno's re-design and re-planting from 1930 to 1950, have been in cultivation since the thirteenth century. They consisted of orchards, fruit and vegetables as well as ornamental trees and flowers – all the produce required for the entire population of the Alhambra was grown here. The same area is still in cultivation and can be seen from the Alhambra palaces today (Fig. 122).

A Walk Through the Palaces and Gardens of the Alhambra and Generalife

Titus Burckhardt writes that:

> The architecture of the Alhambra does not permit the visitor to enter with dramatic mien; it doesn't magnify the experience of power beyond

Fig. 123. The Cuarto Dorado, Alhambra.

Fig. 125. The Court of Myrtles, Alhambra: side view showing perfectly balanced composition of water, hedge and decorated wall.

the human scale; it is completely indifferent, limpid and serene, like geometry, of which Plato says that no-one should enter into the mansion of wisdom without it.[223]

This observation of the 'human scale' is good to remember when considering water in the Alhambra:

Fig. 124. The Court of Myrtles, Alhambra: abstracted key-shaped fountain, one at each end of the pool.

not only is water the secret life of this palace-city-garden but the manner in which it is used, like the architecture, is always on a human scale. When visiting the Alhambra palaces today, the first experience of water on a human and intimate scale is on entering the first courtyard, the Cuarto Dorado (The Golden Courtyard). The fountain in its centre is a perfect example of balanced, understated Islamic design: it is a large low scalloped basin of pale marble, between one and a half and two metres in diameter. The rim is carved with sixty scallops, a multiple of the number twelve, the solar number linking this court with the Court of Lions. Water very gently bubbles up from a simple 'lotus-bud' spout in the centre, making just the right amount of 'murmuring' sound. It is always just over-flowing, like the eternal waters of Paradise, into the octagon recess in which it sits (Fig. 123).

The next courtyard is the Court of Myrtles (Fig. 42) in which there is a large still rectangular pool with simplified 'Yale key-shaped' fountains at either end, both with water trickling very gently. Around the two myrtle hedges are narrow, straight rills running in symmetry opposite each other. This courtyard is a fine example of harmony between architecture, water and vegetation, and is highly conducive to quiet contemplation.[224] Despite the thousands of visitors who pass through the Alhambra (approximately 6,000 per day) it is still possible, if you stay there a while, to soak up the peace and harmony that reigns in this magical place.

Then we come to the Court of Lions, where the central fountain is a large basin supported by twelve lions with four channels of water streaming from four fountains, one on each side of the courtyard, towards the centre (Figs. 6, 31–2 and 63). It is a remarkable evocation of the four rivers of the Garden of Eden described in Genesis and the four rivers of Paradise described in the Quran, as well as in the Sayings of the Prophet Muhammad. This has already been described in Chapter 2 by Titus Burckhardt but it is also entertaining to read the romantic Washington Irving who writes:[225]

> In the centre stands the fountain famous in song and story. The alabaster basins still shed their diamond drops, and the twelve lions that support them cast forth their crystal streams as in the days of Boabdil. The court is laid out in flower-beds and surrounded by light Arabian arcades of open filigree-work, supported by slender pillars of white marble.

It is interesting that Irving mentions 'flower-beds' since, as observed in Chapter 2, without them there is a certain starkness about this courtyard.

From the courtyards of the Alhambra palaces the visitor walks through the courtyard gardens of the Grille and Lindaraja (probably a derivation of *ain-dar-Aisha*, 'the eyes of the house of Aisha'), both with

Fig. 127. The Partal Palace and pool, Alhambra.

fountains in the centre. The Lindaraja courtyard, although laid out by the Catholics about thirty years after the demise of Boabdil, the last Moorish sultan, is a good example of an essentially Islamic composition of architecture, water and planting. The planting is very simple formal box hedging with tall conifers and smaller citrus trees. There is an elegant pillared arcade

Fig. 126. The Garden of the Lindaraja, Alhambra.

Fig. 128. Fountain, Alhambra gardens.

on three sides and sitting here for some time, drinking in the subdued atmosphere, listening to the murmuring of the fountain, is a profoundly peaceful experience. The sense of enclosure is almost too much as the palace on one side is very high and imposing, and it is interesting to learn that before the Christian conquest, the arcade on one side was open so one could look out onto the Arab quarter of the city below, called al-Baicin. The planting seems to have changed little since Irving's time who describes the Lindaraja, 'the secluded little patio or garden with its alabaster fountain, its thickets of roses and myrtles, of citrons and oranges' (Fig. 126).[226]

Emerging from the palaces, the visitor comes upon the large still pool in front of the Partal pavilion and the Tower of the Ladies. Like the pool in the Court of the Myrtles there is a small, similar, 'Yale key-shaped' fountain at each end with a trickling stream of water making just the right amount of sound. There are gardens beyond here with formal pools, water-channels and magnificent views across to the Generalife (Fig. 121). Although mainly dating from the nineteenth and twentieth centuries and with rather uninspiring planting, they still retain an essentially peaceful Islamic ambience, a powerful *genius loci* (see Chapter 3). The visitor walks through these, crossing a bridge next to the aqueduct and water-tower, to the Generalife gardens. There are many beautiful formal fountains and pools in these gardens offering a wealth of ideas for one's own garden (Figs. 106, 108–9, 111–2, 128).

The jewel at the heart of the Generalife is the Patio de la Acequia, meaning literally 'of the Aqueduct'. This garden is up on the side of the hill. It is approached through a small courtyard called the Dismounting Yard, which has a perfect small, scalloped, circular fountain in the centre (Fig. 106). Then the visitor walks up a few steps, turns left and walks up narrow dark stairs and through a small arch. There is a great sense of anticipation and mystery. Then suddenly, the small dark archway opens up into a true earthly paradise. Here we experience a taste of what the Quran promises to the God-fearing, a 'garden underneath which rivers flow'. To sit in this garden for any length of time, slowly absorbing the serenity contained there, allows the sound of the water to gradually drown out all pre-occupations of the soul; an overwhelming sense of peace descends and the visitor cannot help but be drawn into a contemplative and serene state (Figs. 40, 50, 51, 52 and 56).

Despite the great changes that the Alhambra and Generalife gardens have undergone over the centuries since their foundation in the thirteenth century, they do still unquestionably retain a powerful Islamic resonance. Although the Catholic monarchs, Ferdinand and Isabella, realized they had captured a treasure of a palace-city and gardens in 1492, subsequent generations were not so careful. The Alhambra palaces and gardens famously suffered destruction and neglect until the late-nineteenth century when restoration began. Washington Irving described what happened after it was deserted by its royal residents in the eighteenth-century:

Its beautiful halls became desolate and some of them fell to ruin, the gardens were destroyed and some of the fountains ceased to play. By degrees the dwellings became filled up with a loose and lawless population.[227]

Nevertheless, throughout the centuries, right up until now, despite the thousands of tourists who visit it each day, a very special atmosphere is retained throughout the Alhambra and Generalife. The longer one stays, the more its peace and beauty penetrate one's soul. There is no question that this ambience is due in large part to the existence of water, present in almost every conceivable form everywhere one walks. The last word here belongs to Irving:

An abundant supply of water, brought from the mountains by old Moorish aqueducts, circulates throughout the palace, supplying its baths and fish-pools, sparkling in jets within its halls or murmuring in channels along the marble pavements. When it has paid tribute to the royal pile and visited its gardens and pastures, it flows down the long avenue leading to the city, tinkling in rills, gushing in fountains and maintaining a perpetual verdure in those groves that embower and beautify the whole hill of the Alhambra.[228]

Madinat al-Zahra

Apart from the Alhambra, one of the best examples of the Muslims' expertise with water was in the construction of Madinat al-Zahra, the long-ruined palace-city with extensive gardens outside Cordoba.

Fig. 129. 'Star' garden, Fes: the combination of brightly coloured zellij, *lack of water and insufficient foliage gives this garden a rather unbalanced composition.*

This was founded in AD936 by Abd al-Rahman III and was only possible because of the skilful introduction of water from the hills above. The water had to travel along a vast aqueduct composed of bridges and tunnels in order to cross the uneven land until it reached the city. Built on Roman foundations, it was nevertheless a great feat – especially since the city, spectacular by all accounts, was so short-lived. It fell victim to weak government, rebellion and plundering mercenaries, and was burned in AD1010, less than one hundred years after it was founded. It contained everything from government offices, mosques, markets and residential areas to a zoo with lions, camels, gazelles and enormous fishponds, the fish apparently eating twelve thousand loaves of bread every day.[229] There were several gardens and orchards as well. From excavations it can be seen that the gardens were divided by water-channels into halves or quarters: the 'Small Garden', an intimate garden,

was divided into imprecise halves, while the 'Upper Garden' was larger and more open, and divided by a quadripartite plan. It is interesting that the geometric division by water-channels was made adaptable, at an early period, to both the inward-looking garden and the outward-looking garden.

Smaller Houses

The courtyard house was a typical feature in Granada, Cordoba, Seville and other towns in Islamic Spain before the final re-conquest in 1492 with the fall of Granada. Similar to the traditional Arab-Islamic house in North Africa and further east, such as the *haveli* house in North India, this courtyard was itself a kind of miniature garden of paradise, the essential ingredient being, not trees, plants and flowers, but running water. The Venetian traveller, Andrea Navagero (1483-1529), observing the houses in the old Arab district of Granada, al-Baicin, wrote: 'Although often hidden between the trees in their garden, gathered all together would constitute another city such as Granada; it is true they are small, but they all have water and roses, eglantyne and myrtle, and are very peaceful.'[230]

After the re-conquest of Spain, the Catholic monarchs realized how proficient the Muslims (or Moriscos as they were called by the Spanish) were at irrigation. In the sixteenth century, Philip II's secretary wrote, 'There was no corner or plot of land that should not have been turned over to the Moriscos because they alone were sufficient to bring about fertility and abundance in all the land, because they knew how to cultivate it so well.'[231]

Morocco

Like the Shalimar Gardens outside Lahore, the two large public gardens on the edge of Marrakech, the Jardin Agdal (Fig. 11) and the Jardin Menara (Fig. 10) consist primarily of water. The former is focused on a vast pool called the Sahraj el Hana, the Tank of Health, approximately 500 sq m, with several smaller irrigation pools. (It does not look healthy at all! Indeed, Sultan Sidi Mohammed met his end in this pool when his launch capsized in 1873, his epitaph recording that he 'departed this life in a water-tank, in the hope of something better to come'.)[232] The Jardin Menara has a raised central basin, approximately 30 sq m. Both these gardens are not gardens in the traditional sense, in that they do not have flower-beds, shrubs and seasonal planting; rather, they concentrate on fruit trees and olives. The perimeter of the Jardin Agdal pool is planted with orange, lemon, fig, apricot, pomegranate and olive trees, all regularly divided into square plots by irrigation channels with raised paths. The water arrives at this garden via a similar system as that in Persia and Spain: from the melted snow of the Atlas mountains, fifty miles south of the city, it is gathered in wells in the Ourika valley and travels in underground channels to the Jardin Agdal. This system probably dates back to the founding of Marrakech in the eleventh century, and it continues to be used although with much repair and restoration. This garden has a rather unloved and abandoned feel to it unlike the Jardin Menara. Here, the smaller raised central pool has families walking around it while the olive groves below provide plenty of space and shade for the local people to picnic or stroll amongst the trees (Fig. 12, see Introduction).

The smaller gardens in the towns of Morocco, such as Marrakech and Fes, are mostly the traditional courtyard-type with a central fountain and perhaps a few shrubs and plants in pots. There is a larger, unusual nineteenth-century one in Fes, part of a palace built in 1860 by Pasha Abd al-Kari, where the fountains no longer work. Despite the colourful *zellij* tiles, the strong geometric pattern composed of octagonal stars, and some planting – without water it is a desolate place (Fig. 129). Also, it is a lesson in not overdoing the *zellij* and providing enough planting to create a balance between the rigour of geometry and the flow of nature. Here, the slightly raised geometric beds have narrow rills between them, perhaps originally for overflowing water; however, there is no water and one is naturally drawn to walking along the rills but this is almost impossible due to their narrow width. Walking was evidently not the idea; the idea was to look down on the ordered pattern

Fig. 130. Main courtyard, Azem Palace, Damascus.

and colour from one or two stories up where the observer has a bird's-eye view.

Syria

It is fascinating and informative to read accounts by travellers from the past of cities such as Damascus, Isphahan and Granada. An outsider's observations show just how important water was in the gardens, physically, aesthetically and spiritually. Brigid Keenan makes very clear in her wonderful book on the old city of Damascus that water is its life-blood.[233] The city grew up in the lush oasis called the Ghuta, created by the Barada river rushing down from the mountains. This green and fertile area is about fifty kilometres wide and is in sharp contrast to the surrounding desert. From early on the Arameans, Greeks and Romans channelled the river into canals and streams to water the gardens and the houses. The Arab geographer, al-Maqdisi, wrote in AD985, 'Damascus is a city intersected with streams and begirt with trees. Here prices are moderate, fruits and snow abound and the products of both hot and cold climes abound. Nowhere else will be seen such magnificent hot baths, nor such beautiful fountains'.[234] Nine hundred years later the English traveller, Alexander Kinglake, expresses the exact same sentiments, remarking,

> The juice of her city is the gushing and ice-cold torrent that tumbles from the snowy sides of Anti-Lebanon. Close along on the river's edge

through seven sweet miles of rustling boughs and deepest shade, the city spreads out her whole length.[235]

The French poet, de Lamartine, on coming across Damascus from the hill above the city saw,

the strangest and most fantastic sight which man has ever seen; it was Damascus… a forest of minarets of all shapes, watered by the seven branches of its river, and streams without number, until the view is lost in a labyrinth of flower gardens and trees.[236]

Today, old Damascus is still a beautiful city but the 'labyrinth of flower gardens and trees' has diminished considerably in face of the onslaught of modern city life. However, if you penetrate behind the imposing high walls and often dilapidated exteriors, the courtyards within reveal lush oases, gardens filled with trees, shrubs, flowers, pools and fountains, hidden paradises offering sanctuary in the busy city as well as inspiring ideas for your own garden (Figs. 15, 16 and 130).

Persia

Russell Page remembers his view of central Iran when he flew over it in the early 1960s:

In the endless haze of pinks and yellows and greys of sky, mountain and desert, I saw a thread of milky blue water edged with the yellow green of poplars. The thread soon became a river, the line of trees widened into groves and woods and soon this oasis flowered into the fantastic opal and turquoise domes of Isphahan. Here on the western edge of the high Asian plateau water is queen. Every house had a shady garden of plane trees, poplars, quinces and hazelnuts which shade great bushes of single yellow, orange, and scarlet sweetly-scented roses.[237]

He goes on to describe the Avenue of the *Chahar-Bagh* (mentioned in Chapter 2) in Isphahan where, 'a tiny stepped canal runs down the middle of the plane-shaded Chaharbagh, perhaps the world's loveliest processional way, and almost every garden is set symmetrically round a central pool whose four subsidiary rills carry water into each quarter of the garden and then to the roots of every tree and plant'.

His description is enough to make one weep since the present-day traffic-choked street is a far cry from the enchanting scene he conjures up for us.

Three hundred years before Russell Page, Sir Thomas Herbert, attached to the British embassy in Iran in the seventeenth-century, has an interesting description of the water in a garden near Isphahan:

Fig. 131. Pavilion and chador, *Shalimar Gardens, Lahore.*

In the centre or middle of the Garden is a spacious Tank, formed into twelve equal sides, each side being five foot, set round with pipes of lead, which spout the liquid element in a variety of conceits: and that sort of pastime continues to the North Gate, where is raised a pile for prospect and other sort of pleasure, antickly garnished without, and within divided into six rooms. The lower part is adorned with tanks of white marble, which fume out a cool breeze by quaffing so much crystalline water as makes it bubble there by a constrained motion; the Aquaduct being brought by extraordinary charge and toil thither from the Coronian Mountain.[238]

Herbert's description of the 'Tank' with the size specified is fascinating, as well as the 'pile' (some kind of pavilion) obviously quite generously proportioned as it had six rooms; and the cool breeze from the water bubbles 'by a constrained motion' – no boiling cascades here!

Water in Your Own Garden

The precise form that water will take in your own Islamic garden depends on many factors, first of all taking into account those considered in the initial design for the garden in Chapter 2; and secondly, factors such as its size and location, whether you are in an urban or rural situation or somewhere in between. As with planting, when deciding where a fountain will be placed you need to observe the aspect and how much sun or shade there will be, whether a tree overhangs it, and where the pump and reservoir will be placed. We are so used to electric pumps now that it is quite awe-inspiring to think that the water for the Alhambra palaces and city, for example, relied entirely on gravity. If you are planning either water-channels with flowing water or pools with still water, then the lie of the land needs careful analysis: you may need to level it for the pool and then make a slight gradient for the flowing water. This may sound ludicrously obvious but such practicalities are of the utmost importance when making the initial decisions about water in your garden.[239]

To a certain extent, since water is always formal in an Islamic garden, the form it will take in your own

Figs. 132, 133 and 134 (top to bottom). Various fountains from the Alhambra and Generalife Gardens, which may serve as inspiring models for your own garden.

garden is already decided upon. It is founded on clean, ordered lines and has a kind of purity which contemporary 'minimalist' gardeners have gained much inspiration from. There are no mossy rocks or 'naturalistically' placed informal plants at the edge; likewise, waterfalls are not falling from a great height of rocky cliffs such as one might find in Japanese or Chinese gardens, but in a clear and ordered fashion, from one terrace to another.

Fig. 136. Indian fountain spouts (after drawings included in Architecture and Landscape *by Sajjad Kausar, see endnote 177).*

Fountains in Your Own Garden

The travellers' descriptions included above, as well as giving fascinating insights into how the gardens looked centuries ago, may also offer ideas for one's own garden. The water-tanks referred to in some accounts, such as the one above of a garden near Isphahan by Thomas Herbert, usually seem to be raised up and geometric in shape – twelve-sided or eight-sided or circular. Something similar would be a handsome centre-piece for your own Islamic garden, bearing in mind that the cost would be fairly high if made of marble, less if made of local stone but still not inexpensive. The central fountain, tank or pool with all the plumbing involved – installing a reservoir and pump with the appropriate electrics, laying pipes, as well as earth-moving, is most likely going to be the costliest item in your garden. This should be taken into consideration at the beginning, since the fountain is also the most important element in your Islamic garden. The practical aspect of a fountain – cooling the air and providing water for ablutions – is

not a primary consideration in northern climes since only during a few months of the year does the weather reach a high enough temperature to make the fountain a truly pleasant experience.

For inspiration, the next best thing after travelling abroad and visiting Islamic gardens, is to leaf through books with good photographs. Of all the places I have visited, the greatest diversity of beautiful and simple fountains in one place are in the palaces and gardens of the Alhambra and Generalife. These have definitely been the most inspiring fountains for me, partly because on the whole they are not too grand or ambitious. They are usually made of a plain marble or stone, and you can see from the photographs here how understated and exquisite they are. Russell Page's dictum, 'How little can I do?' could well have been a Moorish motto since simplicity and beauty go hand-in-hand in all of these fountains (Figs. 105–6, 108–9, 111–2, 123–4, 128, 132–5).

A fountain similar to one of these, even a small, circular one, perhaps half a metre in diameter, with a scalloped edge, set into a circular or octagon base, would immediately lend your garden a taste of Moorish Spain or Morocco (Fig. 135; and see Chapter 7, where illustrations of the Carpet Garden at Highgrove show the central Moroccan or Hispano-Mauresque style scalloped fountain). To have any of these fountains carved for you in the West would most likely be more expensive than buying one from one of the countries mentioned already such as India, Pakistan or Morocco, even taking into account travel and transport expenses. However, if you can find a good stone carver in your own country, and you or your clients have the financial means, then it would be very rewarding to commission a local craftsman. It is advisable to draw up a clear, large-scale plan or template of the design and discuss the material and

Fig. 135. Detail of fountain, Cuarto Dorado, Alhambra.

Fig. 137. Fountain spout, Shalimar Gardens, Lahore.

be.[240] Before the use of electric pumps the pressure of water was usually fairly low and tanks were raised in order to provide a sufficient 'head' of water in order that a fountain would flow successfully. Thus, to a large extent, practical circumstances dictated the aesthetic outcome. This is similar to traditional Islamic architecture where, before the advent of the wide use of reinforced concrete, the size of a dome was determined by the size and strength of the square walls on which it was based. Traditional Islamic architecture and garden design is not about showing off technical prowess: it is about human scale and respect for the materials and for the element of water itself. There should be no extremes in your Islamic garden, and this applies to the water as to everything else, no disproportion and no jarring of the elements: balance and harmony between them all as well as with the site itself is of paramount importance. The water-flow of most of the fountains in the Alhambra and Generalife gardens are a lesson in how to achieve the perfect 'murmur'.

Pools in Your Own Garden

One idea for a small garden is a simple square or rectangular pool of approximately 1m by 1m or 1m by 2m. The water may be almost still with a barely perceptible trickle in at one end and out at the other – like a smaller version of the pool above the Partal Palace in the Alhambra gardens, for example (Fig. 93). It need only be half a metre deep or less, since you are not going to place many plants in it; perhaps a few select lilies such as *Nymphaea alba* if the pool is large enough; or, if your garden is in a more Mediterranean climate and the pool is in full sun, then you may wish to try growing the beautiful lotus, *Nelumbo nucifera*. As is well-known, lilies and lotus do not like moving water so a still pool is perfect for them. The border surrounding the pool should be of stone or marble or some other natural material, approximately 20cm in width for a small pool. If the pool is more ambitious, up to 5m say, then the border should be a little larger, at least 30cm. A narrow border will look mean and out of proportion. It is a good idea to place the stone or brick at the edge and look at it on site yourself to confirm the precise width.

A raised pool (or 'tank', see above) is also a possibility. This could be an octagon, perhaps 50cm

details, transport and installation – and the all-important fee, with the craftsman beforehand. There are also a few companies specializing in importing architectural art and craft from Eastern and Islamic countries, and these would definitely be worth researching (see List of Useful Adresses).

It is important to consider the design of the nozzle or spout in the centre of the fountain. These can vary from elaborate carved stone ones to the more usual simple and elegant 'lotus-bud' type, also usually of carved stone or marble. Remember to take into account how far the spout emerges from the water. It is worth observing other fountains carefully before deciding how high yours should be. For a more accentuated flow, then a higher nozzle should be chosen (Fig. 116); however, for the gentle, murmuring 'Islamic' flow, the spout needs only to protrude about 2cm above the level of the water and then the pump can be adjusted to achieve the correct 'bubbling' effect.

In most instances, when the flow of water is 'natural', that is, the speed with which it travels is determined by the gradient and the volume of water, then the 'jets' of a fountain should never be too violent; this is, obviously, if your fountain is not at the foot of a mountain, which in most cases it will not high or more, made of marble with some Syrian or Indian-style inlay work (Fig. 55). One would need to be careful here about the surroundings, since this emphatically Islamic-style fountain would look out of place near a Victorian brick house. However, if it were placed within an enclosed area surrounded by a substantial evergreen hedge, such as yew (*Taxus baccata*) or the more Mediterranean myrtle (*Myrtus communis* ssp. *Tarentina*), it could look very effective (see Chapter 5 for more ideas for evergreen and deciduous hedges to create enclosed spaces). This kind of raised tank would be an expensive item. It could possibly be found at auction or an antique shop, or it may be possible to find a craftsman who could carry out your own design; otherwise it would probably need to be imported from Egypt, Syria, India or Morocco.

Natural materials should be used as they complement the water and blend with the surrounding nature in a more soothing, natural and tranquil way. Today, some designers choose zinc, steel or aluminium and this is fine for a consciously modern garden. Glass, hardly a new material, is also

Fig. 139. *A carved* chador *takes water from beneath a seating platform (*chabutra*) to a pool with fountains, Nishat Bagh, Kashmir.*

sometimes used today for more 'modern-looking' water designs. This can look good too. However, here we are going for the more authentic traditional Islamic garden, where self-consciously modern materials would be jarring and out of place. Natural stone, marble, cobbles, brick or slate should predominate. The combination of a still pool in the centre of a small garden with a natural stone surround, not only reflects the changing skies and the trees but can act as a strong unifying factor. It can integrate the other elements of the garden such as the paths and the planting as well as the whole composition within its setting.

Chadors, Chini-Khanas, Chabutras

Islamic gardeners thought up a great range of ingenious devices for channelling water, allowing it to spray, trickle, bubble, murmur, meander, rush, letting it fall to create patterns, keeping it still or coaxing it into narrow or wide rills – every way imaginable from the simplest of plain circular fountains to the more elaborate, grand terraces of the Kashmir or Lahore Shalimar gardens (Figs. 131 and 138).

Fig. 138. Chador, *Shalimar Gardens, Lahore.*

Fig. 141. Chabutra.

Apart from the different styles of fountains, these three devices, the *chador*, the *chini-khana* and the *chabutra*, are probably the most effective ways that a small amount of water could be used to maximum benefit – as well as allowing the Muslim rulers and gardeners to indulge their great love of water and the joy that it offered. They have been mentioned before briefly but just to recap: a *chador* (sometimes spelt *chadar*) is a Persian word meaning 'shawl' or 'veil' and is the term now used for the all-enveloping robe, often black, worn by many Iranian women today. In the garden it refers to a stone or marble slab or water shute, usually carved with a geometric design so that the water breaks up into patterns as it falls into a pool or channel below. It is a truly wonderful sight to observe sunlight sparkling on the intricately-patterned water as it runs over the *chador*, fundamentally a variation on a waterfall. The idea of a 'veil' of water is a beautiful one and echoes the profound Muslim belief that the created world both 'veils' and reveals the Almighty: He is both hidden and manifest, invisible and visible. It is up to us to penetrate the visible 'veil' (or thousands of veils as the mystics would say) to move closer to God.

If your garden is sloped, then *chadors* are a gift, as terraces can be created with one or more *chadors* set into the slope(s) of the terrace(s). They vary in size and richness of design: at the Shalimar gardens in Lahore there are four *chadors*, ranging from a small (25cm high) sandstone one carved with a zig-zag design – the abstracted geometric wave pattern – to a grand white marble *chador* carved with a shell pattern

inlaid with black stone. However, if your garden is not sloping and you would still like a *chador* without going to the trouble and expense of earth-moving then the *shadirwan-salsabil* type (mentioned above, page 92) of wall-fountain, of which a carved stone slab is an integral part, is a good alternative. Indeed, this type was often used in Egypt and other parts of the Muslim world in order to enlarge the surface area of running water. This was to increase the rate of evaporation in hot weather which, in turn, would cool incoming air from carefully placed ventilation shafts. In the traditional

Fig. 140. Water falling over a chini-khana, *Shalimar Bagh, Kashmir.*

Arab-Islamic house built around a central courtyard this provided an highly effective means of natural air-conditioning.

Water as a veil is found not only on *chadors* but also running over the edge of fountains and over *chini-khanas*.[241] A *chini-khana* is a small niche, or rather several small niches, carved in rows into stone behind a water-fall. On special night-time occasions, candles or oil-lamps were placed in each of the niches so that the flickering light of the flames would glow through the veil of falling water – a beautiful and romantic scene. In the daytime, flowers were sometimes placed in jars in the niches. Like the *chadors*, *chini-khanas* can be placed where there is a change of level, the water falling in front of them to a pool below. Apparently they were Shah-Jahan's favourite object in a garden, and you can see why. At the Shalimar gardens in Lahore there is a *chini-khana* between the middle and lower terrace and originally there was one between the upper and middle terrace.

If your garden is large enough and money is no object, then it would be a wonderful opportunity to include either a *chador* or a *chini-khana*, or both, either where there is a change in level or against a wall. These could be commissioned from a good stone-carver or possibly imported from India or Pakistan.[242]

A *chabutra* is a stone or marble platform attached to the edge of a pool or raised up in the middle of it. The sultan or emperor who sat on it would have the impression of being totally surrounded by, and floating on, water. Here he could sit and meditate and not be disturbed. Since in some cases there is no 'causeway' over the water to reach the *chabutra*, the ruler was probably carried in some kind of sedan chair to reach it. Again, if you had the means, it would be a great luxury – as well as conducive to meditation – to construct a *chabutra*, your own little island, in the middle of a large still pool. Here you could bring rugs, sit and contemplate or bring friends to talk, eat and drink, and generally pass many a pleasant and soothing hour in the midst of water. The only problem being to persuade someone else to wade backwards and forwards with provisions!

Interestingly, these three features, the *chador*, *chini-khana* and *chabutra*, seem to be specifically Islamic ways of using water in gardens. Fountains on the other hand, are common to all gardening traditions in some form or other; they are seen throughout European gardens, although not so much in the northern countries for obvious climatic reasons. They are also not so typical of Japanese and Chinese gardens, which on the whole concentrate on waterfalls and streams, the Japanese version of a fountain being the beautiful and understated hollow bamboo.[243]

Islamic-Style Water in European Gardens

It is interesting to look at gardens in Europe where Islamic-style water has been employed. In England there are several: for example, Hestercombe in

Fig. 142. Islamic-style rill at a garden in Devon, the west of England.

Somerset (Fig. 61) designed by Jekyll and Luytens, is very inspiring with its 'East and West rills'. These are two long, straight, narrow canals with wide stone borders. They frame a large sunken parterre laid out in a four-fold geometric design with generous planting. The rills are planted with water-loving plants such as iris and arum lilies (*Zantedeschia aethiopica*). The two elements together, the ordered rill and the planting, show a very interesting combination of apparently Islamic-inspired formal water-channels with English-style planting. It works very well, although the planting diminishes the strictly Islamic 'look'; however, it achieves something more important – a successful fusion of styles. If you wish to present a more 'authentic' Islamic style, then you would avoid such planting, allowing the water itself to predominate. In the warmer climates of the East where water is so precious, the desire is to see and enjoy the water itself, not to obscure it with planting. Lutyens may well have been inspired by the rills in the gardens he saw while working in India, while Gertrude Jekyll probably saw these rills mainly as opportunities for planting. Hestercombe is a fine example of a marriage of two gardening styles and an inspiration for those wishing to adapt the Islamic aesthetic to an English setting.[244]

Other interesting gardens to visit in England are Coleton Fishacre in Devon, which is perhaps more strongly Islamic than Hestercombe with its one narrow rill stepping down a natural slope, and Sezincote in Gloucestershire. Arrow Cottage Garden in Herefordshire has a long straight rill, very Islamic in design, bordered with slate and enclosed by tall yew hedges; and some friends in Devon recently made a narrow rill, edged with local stone, lying on a slight gradient to lead away from a summer-house to a small change in level, allowing the water to fall to the terrace below (Fig. 142).

All of these gardens have borrowed the formal rill concept from the Islamic garden. This rill, in temperate climates, is usually purely aesthetic and does not serve any vital irrigation function as it did in ancient Persia and Mesopotamia (present-day Iraq). It is interesting to learn that similar irrigation systems were used in the Amazon rainforest. In this case, the land was subject to annual flooding by the river and so the crops were sown on raised beds to avoid flooding, and the repeat four-fold pattern of water-channels was the same.[245]

Conclusion

After one of the hottest summers on record (2003) in the United Kingdom and the rest of Europe, the value of water to the Northern European began to hit home, particularly to gardeners used to regular rainfall. The following vivid portrayal of the effect of water upon desert life did not, for a short time, seem so wildly distant from our green and pleasant land. The author, Muhammad Asad, was a German Jew who converted to Islam in the 1920s and wrote about his travels and experiences in his book, *The Road to Makkah*:

We had stopped for our noon prayer. As I washed my hands, face and feet from a water-skin, a few drops spilled over a dried-up tuft of grass at my feet, a miserable little plant, yellow and withered and lifeless under the harsh rays of the sun. But as the water trickled over it, a shiver went through the shrivelled blades, and I saw how they slowly, tremblingly, unfolded. A few more drops, and the little blades moved and curled and then straightened themselves slowly, hesitatingly, trembling.... I held my breath as I poured more water over the grass tuft. It moved more quickly, more violently, as if some hidden force were pushing it out of its dream of death. Its blades – what a delight to behold! – contracted and expanded like the arms of a starfish, seemingly overwhelmed by a shy but irrepressible delirium, a real little orgy of sensual joy: and thus life re-entered victoriously what a moment ago had been as dead, entered it visibly, passionately, overpowering and beyond in its majesty.

Life in its majesty... You always feel it in the desert. Because it is so difficult to keep and so hard, it is always like a gift, a treasure, and a surprise. For the desert is always surprising, even though you may have known it for years. Sometimes when you think you can see it in all its rigidity and emptiness, it awakens from its dream, sends forth its breath – and tender, pale-green grass stands suddenly where only yesterday there was nothing but sand and splintery pebbles.[247]

CHAPTER 5

Trees and Shrubs

To the eye of a discerning man, every leaf upon a growing tree is a book imparting knowledge of our Creator.[248]

Saadi (AD1184–1292)

Five trees and shrubs that always spring to mind when thinking of Middle Eastern, Mediterranean or North African gardens – not only Islamic ones – are those with the most wonderful evocative names: jacaranda, bougainvillea (more a climber than a shrub) plumbago, oleander and hibiscus. Then, with Persian miniatures in mind, there is the cypress tree, *chenar* tree (the oriental plane tree, *Platanus orientalis*, Fig. 144) and spring-flowering fruit and nut trees, not forgetting the graceful pale-leaved olive.[249] For fragrance one should add jasmine, gardenia, many species of citrus, frangipani and roses. Just saying them out loud makes one think of warm evenings sitting with friends by a fountain in a scent-filled garden, drinking mint tea and perhaps smoking *argile* (water-pipe). Writing this in February in England with the snow falling outside and the temperatures at freezing, it is hard to see how one can create a similar atmosphere here. In our attempts to create an Islamic garden in a non-Islamic environment – if one can say such a thing – we should not get too carried away and plant the exotic-sounding, heat-loving shrubs mentioned above only to find that they are struck down in their first winter. Compromises will have to be made, not only with fountains and water, as described in the previous chapter, but also with planting. So, generally speaking, when pondering which shrubs and trees to choose for an Islamic-inspired garden in a northern climate, one needs to be realistic and pragmatic rather than idealistic and romantic – sorry to sound really boring. Although in many areas of the Islamic world such as parts of Jordan, Syria, Lebanon, Turkey and Iran,

Fig. 144. Canopy of chenar *trees* (Platanus orientalis) *providing shade near Tehran.*

temperatures drop to well below freezing in winter, there is no avoiding the fact that in the summer these countries also experience many more hours of sunshine and far higher temperatures than in northern Europe.

Such trees and shrubs mentioned above may well survive if the temperature does not drop to below approximately –6°C and, generally speaking today, the temperature stays above this in the United Kingdom – in the southern counties at least. But will they flourish and contribute towards that longed-for Eastern atmosphere of sweet-smelling delight and quiet serenity? Well, there is no doubt that to flourish outside, such plants (and more will be suggested later) demand that most sought-after of positions – the sheltered and well-drained south-facing or south-west facing one (as Ibn Luyan recommended, see Chapter 3), preferably against a nice warm wall. Even then it is touch and go whether they will survive the odd hard frost and the anxiety may not be worth it. Covering a climbing shrub such as a Bougainvillea (*Bougainvillea spectabilis*, more details in next chapter

Fig. 143. Garden of the Lindaraja, Alhambra, *viewed through an arch of the arcade.*

Fig. 145. Bougainvillea spectabilis, *living up to its name, Marrakech.*

Fig. 145) or a Plumbago (*Plumbago auriculata*, syn. *P. capensis*) with fleece is not really an option unless you are really desperate to grow these and do not mind tottering on ladders. Having said this you may be one of the lucky ones and find that your Plumbago does thrive; for example, there is a marvellous specimen climbing up a south-facing wall in the Chelsea Physic Garden in London.

As is well-known, citrus and olive trees bear abundant crops of fruit in Near-Eastern and Mediterranean countries but in northern Europe this will be the exception rather than the norm. Citrus species in particular, so evocative of Islamic gardens, will need much tender loving care and most likely require over-wintering indoors. However, the great benefit we have, which in part makes up for our lack of sun, is a plentiful supply of water, both from the household supply and from rain, and for some fortunate people living in the country, from natural springs or old wells.

As every gardener knows there can be significant differences of temperature within a reasonably small area, especially when there is a change in altitude. For example, a garden on one of the hills surrounding Amman in Jordan experiences several more degrees of frost than one in the plains below, and again in the south of the country at Aqaba there is no frost at all. There may also be subtle alterations in plant-growing conditions in almost every corner of one's garden – soil texture and aspect as well as

temperature. Through trial and error and much patience,[250] one discovers the optimum growing conditions for a variety of plants. If you are one of the fortunate ones to have a south or south-west facing garden, sheltered from chilly north and east winds, then you will have the chance to grow some of the heat-loving shrubs and trees typical of Islamic gardens without necessarily having to bring them indoors for the winter. With so much talk of 'global warming' recently, and indeed evidence of it (see below), this seems to be an increasing possibility. However, if your site is mainly shady, facing north and east, then there is little chance of any Mediterranean plants being happy. The only way to really succeed with an Islamic garden if this is your aspect is to concentrate primarily on the formal geometric plan and the hard-landscaping with a small fountain or *chador* ('shawl' of water, see Chapter 4), which can be turned off when the weather is cold and damp. Although planting will be restricted to those shrubs and flowers that tolerate shade, the Islamic atmosphere can still be suggested through beautiful geometric patterns in stone, brick or ceramic (see Chapter 3 for further suggestions and Fig. 54) around a formal *chahar-bagh* plan.

Changing Climate

Much is written and spoken now about the changing climate world-wide, and certainly it is the case that here in the United Kingdom our winters, in particular, have become gradually warmer in the past thirty to forty years. We do not seem to experience significantly more hours of sunshine in the summer but we certainly have less snow and fewer frosts in winter, and more rain, one report going so far as to say that, 'The UK's whole reputation as a green and pleasant land is under threat'.[251] This sounds dramatic and rather alarming but there is evidence that the average temperature will gradually increase, approximately 2–5°C in the summer and 2–3°C in the winter, over the next fifty years. From the perspective of making an Islamic garden in northern latitudes, this is all to the good since, with less severe frosts, an increasing number of the plants and trees typical of Islamic gardens will survive outside – such as the olive, pomegranate, citrus, date-palm, oleander, and even bougainvillea in London's warmer microclimate. However, plants that require colder winters, such as some fruiting bushes like blackcurrant, and flowers that dislike too much heat like delphiniums, will no longer grow happily in the south of the United Kingdom.

Sources

So, what shrubs and trees can we grow in our more northern climates that will speak to us of Islamic gardens and more exotic lands, but not require too much molly-coddling? To give you what I hope will be a useful brief guide – for flowers in the next chapter as well as shrubs and trees in this chapter – I have considered six main sources: first of all, the Quran itself. For the more pious or spiritually-minded Muslim gardener, the trees and plants mentioned by name in the Holy Book are especially important, since nurturing them and watching them bloom, fade and die is both a reminder of our own short sojourn on earth, and a taste of the eternal beauty and joy of the paradise garden that is to come.

Second, the plant lists of the early Muslim botanists such as Ibn Wafid (d. 1075), Ibn Bassal (c. 1080) and Ibn al-Awwam (c. 1180)[252] who were active in Spain, as well as other earlier Greek and Oriental philosophical and scientific works. One of these is the well-known *Materia Medica* of Dioscorides (a Roman physician born in the first century AD, see Chapter 1), one of the most important books in the medieval Islamic world for the study of plants and their properties. Another is the thirteenth-century Arabic *Kitab al-Diryaq*, which was derived partly from earlier Greek studies and depicts beautiful miniatures of herbs and plants for medicinal use. Ibn al-Baitar of Malaga (d. 1248) is another important horticulturist

and botanist who described around fourteen hundred plants in his Pharmacopoeia, as well as the 'Father of Arab Botany', Abn Hanifah al-Dinawari (c. 820–895). There is no doubt that Muslim Spain led the way at this period (c. 1000–1400) in matters of horticulture, agriculture, science and botany.

Third, accounts of ambassadors, travellers and native chroniclers – such as Sir John Chardin (d. 1713), de Busbecq (seventeenth century) and the Turk, Evliya Celebi (seventeenth century)[253] – as well as the memoirs of garden-loving Muslim rulers, such as the Mughal emperor, Babur (d. 1530) and the Ottoman Sultan, Mehmet II. Mehmet was known as 'Fatih', 'the Conqueror' (d. 1481), since he achieved what had long been considered impossible, the conquest of Constantinople in 1453, renaming it Istanbul. He was also a garden-lover and is said to have employed one thousand gardeners at his new palace, which came to be known as the 'Abode of Bliss'. A contemporary chronicler observed, 'On every side extended very vast and very beautiful gardens, in which grew every imaginable kind of plants and fruits; water, fresh and clear, and drinkable, flowed in abundance on every side; flocks of birds, both of the edible and of the singing variety, chattered and warbled; herds of both domestic and wild animals browsed there'.[254]

The fourth source is the poetry of numerous poets, scholars and mystics, such as Jalal ad-Din Rumi (1207–73), Saadi (1184–1292), Firdawsi (940 to c. 1020) and Nizami (died c. 1209). Saadi was born and died in Shiraz in Persia and his most famous works are the *Bustan* ('The Fruit Garden') and the *Gulistan* ('The Rose Garden'). Firdawsi's real name was Abul-Qasim Mansur but was called Firdawsi by the Sultan because he said that the poet's writings transformed the court into a paradise, *firdaws*. He wrote the famous *Shahnameh* ('Book of Kings') and *Yusuf and Zulaykha*. Nizami's *Khamsa* ('Five Poems') includes the famous legend of Layla and Majnun in which plants and flowers are used to convey hidden meaning (see Chapter 6). Rumi's works are too numerous to mention and are referred to several times in this book. One of the central themes running throughout his writings is that the beauty of the individual trees and flowers is a glorious reflection of the profound truth that penetrates all of creation. Allegorical association between nature and the human soul is a constant feature of Persian and other Eastern poets, reminding us that all true art, including the art of the garden, is about knowledge of ourselves and praising our Maker. Rumi writes:

The trees are engaged in ritual prayer and the birds in singing litany,
the violet is bent down in prostration.[255]

The poetry of all these great poets (and there are many others besides those named here) although often very romantic and containing symbolic spiritual meaning, is nevertheless frequently precise in its descriptions of trees, shrubs and flowers grown across the Muslim world. It offers the reader a fascinating insight into the plants grown in early Islamic gardens.

Fig. 146. Persian miniature with cypresses, a flowering fruit tree, a willow, and a mulberry entwined with a vine bearing an abundance of bunches of grapes, and several flowering plants. From a sixteenth-century Shahnamah.

The fifth source is Persian, Ottoman and Indian miniature paintings: not only do these enchant the viewer with their other-worldly atmosphere but, on a more prosaic note, they are interesting for us since many of them depict gardens in which identifiable trees and plants are grown.

The sixth and final source for selecting which trees and plants to grow in an 'Islamic garden of the North' are, of course, the gardens that exist in the Islamic world today; those which, as stated earlier, were constructed approximately from the tenth until the end of the seventeenth centuries. After this time western European gardens started influencing eastern Islamic gardens in a more noticeable way, so it is preferable to look, as far as possible at these earlier gardens. Also, few people would argue that the greatest Islamic gardens were created before the eighteenth century. Looking at these gardens may seem to be the most obvious source and perhaps the one to start with. However, because in most cases the planting has changed so much over the centuries, and has often been mistakenly re-planted, their principle function today is as examples of lay-out, water-flow and, in some cases, tree-planting, rather than for smaller shrubs and flower-planting ideas. Having said this, when considering which are the most appropriate trees to choose in your creation of an Islamic garden, it is helpful to look at gardens such as the Bagh-i-Fin in Iran, which have not essentially changed much, or indeed the Taj Mahal gardens. In both cases the detailed planting (by which I mean the smaller shrubs and flowering plants) is not important in comparison to the formal design, trees and water.

Information taken from these sources, together with observations made on travels in Islamic lands, and practical notes about site opportunities and limitations, will hopefully offer the reader ideas to work with, as well as fairly specific criteria for selecting plants for your garden. In many of the gardens that are maintained or have been restored today there seems to be little or no regard for the original planting.[257] I am not suggesting that one should slavishly try to grow only those plants that were originally grown, but it is fascinating and worthwhile to consider the early plants lists and other sources, as we are doing here. Taking note of the genera and, in some cases, the species that were planted and nurtured in the early Islamic gardens, gives one a certain guide and inspiration for one's own ideas, which can be adhered to more or less strictly according to personal taste. After all, it is not as if the choice were limited: it is large and varied, as will be seen in both this chapter and the next. Your resulting garden will hopefully conjure up images of Islamic miniature paintings and poetry, as well as passages from the Quran, but will nevertheless also thrive in a cooler, damper climate. In the following pages we will look at suggestions as to which trees and shrubs mentioned in the above sources may be grown under less sunny skies and also make recommendations for appropriate alternatives.

A Brief Guide to Trees and Shrubs

There is no doubt that planting is secondary to form in an Islamic garden. Providing that your fundamental ground-plan is correct and the central fountain or pool is installed and working smoothly, the planting should not present too many difficulties. After these two have been established, the trees and larger shrubs, structural and boundary planting – as in planning all gardens – come next. Indeed, as we have seen in earlier chapters, a traditional Arab-Islamic courtyard with a simple fountain in the centre, and perhaps an orange tree or two, could be said to constitute an Islamic garden. So, despite all the trees and shrubs on offer in the Islamic sources, the layout, the practical circumstances and context will dictate to a large extent which ones to plant where (genera at least, if not species or cultivars) and which ones need substitutes due to the difference in climate. For example, there is much mention in Persian poetry of the intoxicating fragrance of the plants in Islamic gardens, and the Quran speaks of 'sweet-smelling plants' or 'fragrant herbs'.[258] So, besides all the scented spring and summer flowers (see next chapter), in the winter and early spring months why not plant as many of those marvellous scented shrubs or trees that thrive in the northern hemisphere? Shrubs such as the amazing-smelling wintersweet (*Chimonanthus praecox*), the evergreen *Drimys winteri*, which bears creamy-white, sweetly-scented flowers in spring, several Daphnes including the lovely evergreen *Daphne bholua* 'Jaqueline Postill', *Azara microphylla*, which bears vanilla-scented flowers in late winter, wych-hazel (e.g. *Hamamelis mollis* 'Pallida'), *Osmanthus delavayi*, several viburnums such as the popular and deliciously scented *V. x bodnantense* 'Dawn' or *V. farreri*, Christmas box (*Sarcococca* spp.) and the unusual, highly fragrant Chinese shrub, *Edgworthia chrysantha*, used for making paper. The two species of Clerodendrum which survive in milder areas, *C. bungii* and *C. trichotomum* are wonderful sweet-smelling flowering shrubs for late summer into autumn; I particularly like the latter which bears star-shaped white flowers. There are many others of course; I have just mentioned a few of my favourites, none of which, as far as I know, are mentioned in the Arab lists, but nevertheless would fit well in an Islamic garden. You can be pretty certain that if a Moorish gardener in Spain in the Middle Ages had been offered these shrubs he would have seized them with alacrity.

So, this brief guide is just that – a guide to trees, shrubs and, in the next chapter, other plants including flowers, herbs, climbers and vegetables, for a 'northern' Islamic garden; it is not a strict blueprint dictating that only such and such a plant may be grown otherwise the garden's authenticity will be in question. The planting is not about rigid historical, geographical or cultural correctness. It should be based as far as possible on what we know of plants in Islamic gardens but after that there should be flexibility combined with understanding: flexibility, due to the geographical and climatic differences; and understanding, that is, keeping in mind the fundamental theme of the Islamic garden: a transient earthly reflection of the eternal Heavenly gardens.

The Quran, The Sayings of the Prophet[259] and the Symbolism of the Tree

In the early years of Islam, the companion and close friend of the Prophet Muhammad, Abu Bakr, who also became the first Caliph after the death of the Prophet, codified the rules of war. Included in these rules was that the Muslim armies were not only forbidden to attack monks, nuns, women and children, the old and the infirm, but also they were to avoid cutting down trees.[260] As mentioned in Chapter 2, there are Sayings of the Prophet

Fig. 147. Cedar tree (Cedrus libani) *in the cloisters of Salisbury Cathedral.*

cemetery or around a mosque, it is important to know something of the trees held in particular reverence in the Quran and other writings of Muslim saints and scholars. Planting a cedar (*Cedrus libani*) – providing there is space – would be both spiritually appropriate for an Islamic garden as well as beautiful and majestic. The cedar of Lebanon was once known as the 'king of forests' and, mentioned several times in the Bible, is also a tree held in special reverence by Christians. In the book of Psalms it is written: 'The trees of the Lord are full of sap; the cedars of Lebanon which he hath planted.'[265]

Muhammad emphasizing the idea that to nurture plants or trees that produce food is an act of charity.[261] There is another Saying of the Prophet that if you are planting a tree and you see the Hour (of Judgment) coming, then you should continue with your planting, since even at this time, only God knows when that hour will come.

One author has written that the Tree of Knowledge of the Old Testament, the Tree of Immortality and the Lote-Tree of the 'Uttermost Boundary' of the Quran 'eventually become one with the Tree of Bliss'.[262] There is the very important Sidr tree of the Quran, which many have suggested is the Cedar tree (*Cedrus libani*) while some say it is the Lote-tree mentioned in Chapter LIII (verses 13–18):

And verily he saw him at another revelation, beside the Lote-tree of the uttermost boundary, whereby is the Garden of Refuge. When there enshroudeth the lote-tree That Which enshroudeth, the sight wavered not, nor did it transgress. Verily he saw of the signs of his Lord, the Greatest.

Some say this Lote-tree is the Jujube tree (*Ziziphus mauritiana* or *Ziziphus spina-christi*).[263] It is not possible to study in depth the esoteric interpretations of the Quranic verses referring to the Sidr tree and the Lote-tree here.[264] However, for the serious Muslim planting a garden, or perhaps landscaping a

Also very important in Islamic thought is the *Shajarat al-Tuba*, the Tuba tree, known as the Tree of Bliss, not mentioned in the Quran but known as the paradisal tree of the *Hadith*. There is a tradition that a Bedouin asked the Prophet Muhammad, 'What is bliss (*tuba*)?' and the Prophet answered:

Bliss is a tree in Paradise, a tree of a hundred years' walk, and those under the tree are clothed in clothes from the sleeves (i.e. flower calixes) of the tree.[266]

Another tradition relates that when a Bedouin asked the Prophet about the fountains and fruits of Paradise and he asked 'What is bliss?' the Prophet replied, 'It is a tree in Paradise, wherein is a tree called Bliss [*tuba*]'. Then the Bedouin asked, 'Which tree of our earth does it resemble?' The Prophet replied, 'It does not resemble any tree of your earth'.[267]

It is written in the Quran:

Seest thou not how God citeth a symbol? A good word is as a good tree, its roots set firm and its branches in heaven, giving its fruit at every season by the leave of its Lord. God citeth symbols for men that they may remember.[268]

Remembrance (*dhikr*) in Islam, is fundamental to the purification of the heart and the approach to God. Concerning the Quranic passage above it is enlightening to read Dr Martin Lings' penetrating and profound explanation:

> The best example of a good word is a Divine Name uttered as a *dhikr* in upward aspiration towards the Truth. The firm-set root of the tree is the *dhikr* itself uttered with firm-set purpose; the Heaven-reaching branches represent the tremendous impact of the *dhikr* as it passes upwards throughout the whole universe; and the fruit of the tree is the Reality in Whose memory the *dhikr* is performed.[269]

In contrast is a bad word, a profane book, 'A bad word is as a bad tree which lies uprooted on the surface of the earth'.[270]

As can be gathered from this brief sketch of tree symbolism in Islam, there are many layers of meaning attached to trees, which it is not within the scope of this book to go into. But it is a reminder to us that everything planted in the Islamic garden is not only there to stimulate the senses and soothe the soul but it also carries an invisible message for those 'who have eyes to see'.

Many other trees and plants are mentioned in the Quran, which, unlike the mysterious *Tuba* tree, exist on earth and may well serve as a guide to Muslims and non-Muslims alike as to which species to grow in your garden. Some understanding of this can add tremendously to your enjoyment of it. Below I will mention the most important ones as well as those most likely to thrive and look beautiful in gardens located in cooler climates.[271]

Important Trees in an Islamic Garden

From the religious point of view, the most important trees to grow in an Islamic garden – climate permitting – are the four trees mentioned in Chapter 55 of the Quran (*Surat al-Rahman*, 'The All-Merciful', in which the longest description of the gardens of paradise in the Quran is to be found; see Chapter 1). These are: the date palm (*Phoenix dactylifera*), the fig tree (*Ficus carica*), the olive tree (*Olea europea*) and the pomegranate (*Punica granatum*). Of course, in cold and wet climates these four trees will not be happy, so once again exercise

caution before attempting to grow them in your Islamic garden.

The Date-Palm

The date-palm (*Phoenix dactylifera, nekla* in Arabic, Fig. 148), said to be the King of the Oasis, is mentioned many times in the Quran (as well as the Bible) and according to an old Arab saying its uses are as many as the number of days in a year – nutritional, medicinal and as building material. It is particularly revered in Islam because of its association with the Virgin Mary (*Sayyidatna* Maryam) and the birth of Jesus (*Sayyidna* Isa). When Mary was about to give birth she was in 'a distant place' and 'the birth-pangs surprised her by the trunk of a palm-tree'. She was in distress and she heard a voice saying, 'Thy Lord has set below thee a rivulet. Shake also to thee the palm-trunk, and there shall come tumbling upon thee dates fresh and ripe. Eat therefore and drink and be comforted'.[272] So the palm-tree, already revered because of its importance as sustenance in the desert, now took on an even more sacred dimension.

*Fig. 148. Date-palm (*Phoenix dactylifera*).*

The date-palm is a tall and majestic tree, reaching to 30m high when grown in Egypt and other parts of the Islamic world, in particular Saudi Arabia, Iran and Iraq. Interestingly, in spite of its height, the date-palm's roots only penetrate about 1.5m into the ground. Therefore, compared to other desert-surviving plants, such as the tamarisk tree, it is not strong. In northern Europe it can only be grown in a few sheltered areas such as the south-west of England or Ireland, and even here it is not very happy, the damp climate not being to its taste. The archetypal tree of the East, the date-palm (or the canary palm, *Phoenix canariensis*) always looks rather uncomfortable to me when grown under gloomy skies. However, if you are determined to grow a date-palm – it is, after all, one of the most important trees in the Quranic paradise gardens – then there are a couple of reasonably handsome hardy substitutes. First, there is the Chusan palm (*Trachycarpus fortunei*), which has been growing in England since the nineteenth century and tolerates temperatures down to –9°C or lower when mature; and second, there is the European fan palm (*Chamaerops humilis*), which can also tolerate –9°C.

But these are poor substitutes for the graceful date-palm. They are nowhere near as magnificent or evocative as the real thing, even if they do have the advantage of actually surviving in your Islamic garden of the North. I myself would sacrifice the palm in my Islamic garden in England. They never seem to look at home in our lush green landscape, even though the two mentioned above, along with the smaller cabbage palm (*Cordyline australis*) have become fairly common-place in the southern half of the United Kingdom.

The Fig Tree

The species of fig we are referring to (*Ficus carica, al-Teen* in Arabic) is the only one that can be widely grown in the United Kingdom. It must be in a sheltered warm site, where it should bear fruit. It is likely that this fig has been cultivated here since the Romans, although the earliest written reference to it is in 1525 when several trees were brought back from Italy and planted by the Archbishop at Lambeth Palace, one or two of which still survive. So, if you have a south- or west-facing garden, then plant a fig

against the hottest wall and maybe it will grow as tall as one of these first ones at Lambeth Palace, 16m high (about 50ft).[273] *Ficus carica* is native to the eastern Mediterranean countries and then became naturalized in southern Europe, especially Greece and Italy. Apparently Plato loved figs so much he was nicknamed 'Philosokos', meaning lover (*philo*) of figs (*sokos*).[274]

There are many other more exotic species of fig found in the Near East and Asia, such as the papal/peepul or bo-tree (*Ficus religiosa*) and the banyan tree (*Ficus benghalensis*).[275] These two species of fig are more associated with Buddhism and Hinduism than Islam, particularly the peepul tree, said to be the one under which the Buddha was sitting when he attained enlightenment. *Ficus retusa* and *Ficus elastica* are planted as street trees all over North Africa and the Middle East from Marrakech and Cairo to Damascus and Amman, and seem to thrive in spite of increasing traffic pollution. However, these require more warmth than *Ficus carica*, popularly claimed to be the tree growing in the Garden of Eden from which Adam and Eve 'sewed fig leaves together, and made themselves aprons'.[276] So, providing you have the space, a fig tree is a must in your Islamic garden, since not only is it one of the important trees in the gardens of paradise in the Quran, but it looks at home further north, having been tried and tested in the United Kingdom for centuries.

There is one powerful reference to the fig in the Quran and this is in one of the last chapters, Chapter XCV, called by that name, 'The Fig'. The opening words are: 'By the fig and the olive and the Mount Sinai and this land secure! We indeed created Man in the fairest stature'. The fig has a multiplicity of uses, both nutritious and medicinal and when the Prophet Muhammad was offered a tray of them he said, 'Eat', and he ate and said, 'If I were to say that any fruit descended from Paradise, I should say these. For the fruit of Paradise has no stones. So eat from them…'[277]

The Olive Tree

Of the four trees mentioned in Chapter LV of the Quran, after the fig, the olive (*Olea europea, al-Zaitun* in Arabic; see Fig. 9) is the next tree most likely to thrive in northern climates. Increasingly, owing to our milder winters, olives seem to be growing reasonably happily in the south of England. As may be expected, like the fig and other Mediterranean plants, they need a good, sunny, well-drained position, preferably with a wall behind acting as a radiator. The olive tree in the Chelsea Physic Garden in London is a vast (about 10m/33ft high), mature and wonderful specimen, probably planted in the late-nineteenth century.

The olive has tremendous symbolic meaning for Muslims due to its mention in what is known as the Verse of Light in the Quran:

> God is the Light of the heavens and the earth;
> The likeness of His Light is as a niche
> wherein is a lamp
> (the lamp in a glass,
> the glass as it were a glittering star)
> kindled from a Blessed Tree,
> an olive that is neither of the East nor of the West
> whose oil well nigh would shine, even if no fire
> touched it.[278]

Here, the fact that the olive tree is 'neither of the East nor of the West' has been interpreted as meaning that it grows all over the world, from Europe and Africa in the West to Afghanistan and Iran in the East.[279] More profoundly, this verse implies the tree's centrality and is 'therefore open to being interpreted as the Tree of Bliss' discussed above.[280] There are many other meanings attributed to the olive tree, the most famous being the olive branch symbolizing peace in memory of the dove that the Prophet Noah (Nuh in Arabic) sent forth from the ark who returned 'and lo, in her mouth was an olive leaf pluckt off'.[281] So then Noah knew that the waters were abating from the earth and this signified that God's wrath had also abated. From this time on the olive and the dove have both represented peace and unity.

In the Old Testament, olive oil is used for anointing objects (the Tabernacle and its contents by Moses) and people (both priests and monarchs) as a means of consecration, of making holy and sanctifying.[282] There is a Saying of the Prophet Muhammad: 'Eat olive oil and anoint yourselves with it, for it is from a blessed tree'.[283] In Islam, partly because of the verse of the Quran quoted above, the distinguishing feature of a prayer-rug is the niche (*mihrab*), sometimes woven with a lamp hanging within it and sometimes woven with an abstracted tree. It is usually impossible to identify this tree, since it is a symbol of an archetypal tree, not one observed from Nature. However, despite this, it is sometimes suggested that it represents the olive-tree in the verse of Light. A tree in the *mihrab* of a prayer-rug also carries the suggestion of the *mihrab* being the doorway to the gardens of paradise.

Mature olives are reasonably cold-hardy and recent research claims that they are almost as tolerant of frost as the fig, providing they are in a sheltered site. If you are not blessed with this sunny, protected site, then the alternative is to grow an olive tree in a container, which can then be brought inside in the winter (again, this is assuming you have the space inside). Cultivars of *Olea europea* recommended for

*Fig. 149. Pomegranate (*Punica granatum*).*

pots are 'Aglandau', which is compact and slow-growing, reaching about 2m (6.5ft), 'Bouteillan', 'Cipressino' or 'El Greco'.[284] Pruning an olive simply means removing a few branches when they grow too dense or tall. Apparently 'a perfectly pruned olive is one through which a swallow can fly without its wings brushing the branches'.[285]

The Pomegranate

The deciduous pomegranate (*Punica granata*, *Rumman* in Arabic; Fig. 149) can, in fact, tolerate temperatures down to −7°C of frost but it dislikes damp, and therefore in Northern Europe it needs extra favourable conditions: warm, sunny, sheltered and well-drained. As with citrus (see below) it is probably best to play safe and keep your shrub or small tree (they reach up to 5m) in a large pot and bring it inside during the winter. The dwarf pomegranate, *Punica granatum* var. 'Nana', is the one to choose and will certainly bring a taste of the East to your garden.[286] As with the olive, it is unlikely that your plant will bear fruit unless kept in a greenhouse; but it has many other qualities to recommend it, not least its red-bronze spring foliage followed by brilliant red flowers in early summer,

Fig. 150. Pomegranate in cobbles, Generalife gardens.

and its informal habit blends well into a northern European garden.

The pomegranate is referred to three times in the Quran, one reference being in the descriptions of the gardens of paradise in Chapter LV, (see Chapter 1).[287] Symbolically, the primary significance of the pomegranate is that it represents diversity in unity and unity in diversity – arising from its multiple seeds within its one roughly circular shape; this is also the reason for its being associated with fertility. Since the central message of the Quran is the Oneness of God and the unity of the cosmos, it is not surprising that the pomegranate is considered by the esoterists to be the highest of the fruits in the Quranic gardens of paradise.[288] There is also a Saying of the Prophet: 'There is not a pomegranate which does not have a pip from one of the pomegranates of the Garden in it'.[289] So if you have the facilities, then it is certainly worth taking the trouble to grow one. In The Prince of Wales' Carpet Garden in Gloucestershire (see Chapter 7) they experimented leaving the three pomegranates outside over the winter (2002-2003) unprotected, and two of them survived. In subsequent winters they will be given some form of protective covering, probably fleece.

The pomegranate arrived in England as early as the fourteenth century. It is native to parts of Asia including Iran, Afghanistan, India and Syria, and reached Europe via the first Arabs in Spain. Like the other three great trees in the gardens of paradise – the date-palm, the olive and the fig – the pomegranate is full of nutritional and medicinal properties, being a rich source of vitamins. Abd al-Rahman I, who escaped slaughter by the Abbasids in Syria, established Ummayyad rule in Cordoba in AD756. For the rest of his life in Spain he desperately missed his homeland, including its wonderful fruits. One day some pomegranates arrived for him as a present, rather the worse for wear since they had come across land and sea all the way from Syria. The Emir's Spanish gardener was intrigued and took great trouble nurturing the seeds, eventually successfully growing a tree, which bore beautiful and delicious fruit, 'and the people planted groves of them'.[290] Indeed, *granada* is the Spanish word for pomegranate and today, not only are pomegranates grown in abundance in Granada, but the fruit is represented in the cobbles (Fig. 150) and in the bedding-plants in the Generalife gardens.

Observations

Apart from the four trees described above, there are other trees and shrubs referred to in the Quran that can and do thrive in a cooler, damper climate. If we leave aside the more specific trees of the Quran for the moment and concentrate on a more flexible interpretation inspired by the other sources referred to, then we should be able to create an Islamic 'feel' to a garden without necessarily taking risks with more tender, exotic plants. It just needs a bit more thought and planning.

In the transplanting of the Islamic garden to different climes, what Russell Page says, and what no doubt many gardeners have said before and since, is that the plantings should 'have an air of belonging'.[291] So, when making this garden in a more temperate climate than that of the lands ordinarily associated with Islam,[292] one of the most important points to consider is that the planting does not look wildly out of place. This should be kept in mind when selecting trees and shrubs for your own garden.

When looking at miniature paintings, three of the most often depicted trees are the *chenar* or plane tree (*Platanus orientalis*), the Mediterranean cypress (*Cupressus sempervirens*) and a flowering fruit or nut tree such as a cherry or almond (one of the many species of *Prunus*). Providing you have the space, all of these trees can be grown in northern gardens with ease. It is these three we shall look at a little more closely now.

The Chenar or Oriental Plane Tree[293]

In the Quran, and in Persian poetry too, there is often mention of shade-giving trees ('spreading-shade' and 'abounding in branches')[294] in the paradise gardens and it is usually the *chenar* tree (*Platanus orientalis*; Fig. 144) that provides this shade. This oriental plane tree was probably first introduced into England as far back as the fourteenth century. Like its close relative, the London plane tree (*Platanus x hispanica*, a hybrid between the *P. orientalis* and *P. occidentalis*) it has large lobed leaves, which make beautiful patterns on the ground as the sunlight is filtered through. In fact, the distinguishing feature of the oriental plane is that the 'lobes' of its leaves are slightly longer and slimmer than those of the London plane. They are often

compared to human hands and thus, according to Rumi, are the leaders in the ritual prayer of all the plants in the garden.[295] If you have a large enough garden, then some species of plane tree should definitely be included. There are many good alternatives to the oriental plane tree, possessing shade-giving leaves but which grow perhaps more easily on our soil: for example, the mulberry (*Morus nigra*), a favourite tree in Islamic gardens, several of the maples such as the red maple (*Acer rubrum*), providing marvellous deep red foliage in the autumn, the Norway maple (*Acer platanoides*), the sweet gum (*Liquidambar styraciflua*), also giving lovely autumn colour, and of course the majestic London plane itself (*Platanus x hispanica*).

The Cypress and its Alternatives

The cypress (*Cupressus sempervirens*) provides a marvellous dark 'rest for the eyes' when observed soaring out of a dry monotonous desert landscape, or from the hills in southern Spain (Fig. 151). Appearing as it does in so many miniatures and in poetry, as well as in 'real life' in many Islamic countries (North Africa, the Near-East and Iran), it could justifiably be claimed that the cypress is an essential ingredient of an Islamic garden. It first

*Fig. 151. Cypress (*Cupressus sempervirens*), rising majestically out of the Moroccan landscape.*

*Fig. 152. Irish yew (*Taxus baccata*), Clovelly, Devon.*

reason that the Carpet Garden (see Chapter 7) at Highgrove is such a success is because it is entirely within a 'room of its own', secluded behind Mediterranean-style walls and not attempting to be a part of the Gloucestershire countryside in which it is placed.

The tall slim Italian cypress, *Cupressus sempervirens* (the form 'Fastigiata' or 'Stricta' is unknown in the wild state),[296] so typical a feature of the Mediterranean landscape, as well as parts of Asia – and native to both – is most probably the one depicted in Islamic miniature paintings, and thus the one grown in so many of the early Islamic gardens. Now, for one reason or another – a cold east wind, for example – this may not be suitable for your garden in northern Europe. There are a variety of possible alternatives to the Italian cypress for your northern Islamic garden – my favourite probably being the Irish yew, *Taxus baccata* 'Fastigiata'. Although not so slim and elegant as the cypress, its upright, dense, dark green form gives a similar vertical, noble impression but with the great advantage of being stronger and hardier and looking perfectly at home in northern Europe; it does tend to thicken out as it matures but with some careful pruning the fastigiate shape can be maintained. Other possible substitutes for the Mediterranean cypress are: several cultivars of the Lawson cypress, for example, *Chamaecyparis lawsoniana* 'Columnaris', *C. l.* 'Grayswood Pillar' and *C. l.* 'Pottenii'; also, the three cypresses, *Cupressus arizonica* 'Pyramidalis', *C. a.* 'Nevadensis' and *C. abramsiana*; various junipers, for example, *Juniperus communis* 'Hibernica' or *J. c.* 'Pyramidalis'; and the tall, slim 'Incense' cedar, *Calocedrus decurrens*, very popular in Britain in the nineteenth century. All of these are good columnar evergreen conifers which fit well in northern Europe and which, when planted with the correct layout and water, would evoke a traditional Islamic garden.

In addition, there are several possible alternatives to the conifers, such as the deciduous fastigiate hornbeam (*Carpinus betulus* 'Fastigiata'), a good formal tree with a dense habit, often used in the United Kingdom as a street tree or for a short avenue. However, after the first few years, its fastigiate form becomes pear-shaped and, although beautiful, this is not the shape we are aiming for in the Islamic garden. The columnar hornbeam (*C. b.* 'Columnaris'), which

arrived in England as early as the fourteenth century, so by now it should be a part of our landscape. However, despite growing here for several hundred years, there is no doubt that it looks more at home in Mediterranean/Near-Eastern surroundings than further north. Therefore, the cypress needs to be planted very carefully in order to look as though it has 'an air of belonging' and give the effect we want – that is, both sitting comfortably in its situation, while at the same time suggesting an Islamic garden of the East. With this end in view, the nearby architecture and planting should be scrutinized extra diligently, in addition to whether the situation is urban or rural or somewhere in between. To take a specific example, it seems to me that a cypress looks very striking and quite at home when placed with architecture of the twentieth-century Bauhaus type or later 'modernist' architecture, and rather less at home when planted in the garden of a nineteenth-century red-brick terraced house, say. Of course many readers may disagree: there are no absolutes here. I just wanted to emphasize, at the risk of being repetitive the enormous importance of the surroundings. One

*Fig. 153. Hornbeam avenue (*Carpinus betula *'Fastigiata')
in west London.*

retains its vertical shape, is a better alternative. Other deciduous trees with fastigiate forms that could be tried in the northern Islamic garden are the English oak, *Quercus robur* 'Fastigiata', the pear, *Pyrus callyreena* 'Chanticleer', the fastigiate beech, *Fagus sylvatica* 'Dawyck', the maple, *Acer campestre* 'William Coldwell' and the hop-tree, *Ptelea trifoliata* 'Fastigiata'. I am currently considering the evergreen *Eucryphia nymansensis* x 'Nymansay' for a short avenue in an Islamic garden in the south-east of England. Its marvellous, creamy-white, scented, cupped-shaped flowers cover the tall, columnar form in August – a short-cut to the typical scene of a miniature painting depicting a tall evergreen and spring-flowering fruit tree.[297]

The cypress and the spring-flowering trees planted together symbolize, respectively, eternity and transience, as well as representing the masculine and feminine aspects.[298] In her book on Mughal gardens, Villiers-Stuart writes:

> The best known and most beautiful theme of all, the entwined cypress and fruit tree, which appears and reappears on carpets, in tiles, embroideries, and paintings, was taken directly from the garden avenues, where cypress and fruit trees planted alternately were the favourite symbols of life, death and eternity; the solemn background of the deep-toned cypress, emblem of death and eternity, contrasted with the waving

delicate sprays of rosy almond tree or silvery flowering plum, emblems of life and hope.[299]

If you would like to recreate the scene that this author observes so well, then near your cypress or cypress-substitute, should be planted a spring-flowering fruit or nut tree, such as the lightly scented almond (*Prunus dulcis*)[300] or one of the cherries (Fig. 154). I would recommend planting one or both (depending on your space) of the native English ornamental cherries: *Prunus avium*, the wild cherry or *Prunus padus*, the bird cherry. There are several cultivars to choose from, mostly having an informal, rounded habit contrasting with the dense upright form of the cypress. Many cherries grown in the United Kingdom are the Japanese cherries (such as the spectacular *Prunus* 'Tai Haiku', the 'Great White' or my favourites, the beautiful *P. incisa* x *speciosa* 'Umineki' and *P.* x *yedoensis*). These are not usually scented and although very beautiful both in flower and when their leaves start turning in the autumn, will not strike quite the right note for your Islamic garden of the north. For this garden, it is probably better to avoid the Japanese cherries and stick to the native ones or go for another fruit altogether, such as an apple, pear, plum or crab-apple (see below).

Today, in North Africa in particular, one often sees a bright bougainvillea, as opposed to a flowering fruit tree, climbing up a dark cypress, and it is a striking scene, especially against a Mediterranean blue sky. In

*Fig. 154. Wild cherry (*Prunus avium *or* Prunus padus*).*

the few summer months that we enjoy further north, the Eastern magic of this scene may still be achieved, albeit in a more gentle fashion due to our weaker sunlight. One way of coming close to a similar scene is through the meticulous training of delicious-smelling old-fashioned sweet peas (see next chapter) up the elegant cypress – as we did in the Carpet Garden (Fig. 173). Then a miniature painting is really brought to life.

Fruit and Nut Trees

In the paradise gardens described in the Quran, fruit is in abundance, the inhabitants will have 'such fruits as they shall choose'[301] and 'fruits of the gardens nigh to gather'.[302] In the early plant and agricultural treatises of the great horticulturalists mentioned above, Ibn Bassal (c. 1080), Ibn al-'Awwam (c. 1180) and Ibn Wafid (999–1075),[303] many fruit and nut trees are mentioned as being in cultivation. Most of these trees, such as the plum (*Prunus domestica*), the sour cherry (*Prunus cerasus*), the damson (*Prunus damascena*), the sloe (*Prunus spinosa*), the quince (*Chaenomeles*), the pear (*Pyrus communis*), the apple and crab-apple (*Malus spp.*), the medlar (*Mespilus germanica*), the walnut (*Juglans regia*), the mulberry (*Morus nigra*), the strawberry tree (*Arbutus unedo*), the chestnut (*Castanea sativa*) and the hazelnut (*Corylus avellana*), are completely at home in northern locations, and in most cases have been so for centuries.

Of course the modern-day hybrids or cultivars bred in our climate may well be different from those grown hundreds of years ago in southern or eastern lands; there have been a multitude of introductions over the past one thousand years or so. This does not pose too much of a problem, since we are not attempting to design an historically accurate and horticulturally precise traditional Islamic garden. Rather, our main objective is to create a garden inspired by the early Islamic gardens centred on water, shade and contemplation, which will also be at home in a northern European climate. Therefore, as stated earlier in the chapter, the genera of trees and shrubs chosen for your garden need not be exactly the same as those grown in the early Islamic gardens but there should be a good reason, taking into account our main objective, for the selection. Even if you wish

only to choose genera that were originally grown in these gardens, you have a wide choice of species as well as perhaps some carefully selected cultivars. Your final choice of trees and shrubs, and other plants, will be the result of a careful weighing-up of those originally grown, your own preferences, and the local climatic conditions. For instance, previously (see above, A Brief Guide) several shrubs were recommended, not because they were typical of early Islamic gardens, but because they are scented and scented plants were highly valued in these gardens. Your selection will be based upon the dual aim of being integral to the Islamic garden for one reason or another and having 'an air of belonging' in a northern climate.

One important difference between a southern and northern climate, when growing productive trees, is that with the more exotic fruit or nut trees, such as the peach (*Prunus persica*),[304] the pistachio (*Pistacia vera*) and the apricot (*Prunus armeniaca*), in a cooler climate they will not produce much fruit unless grown in a sheltered sun-trap or in a greenhouse. So these may be ornamental rather than productive.

If you prefer your garden to be more productive – which an Islamic garden generally was – then choose the less exotic but nevertheless delicious, apples, pears and plums. These fruit-trees have been well established in England since the Middle Ages and earlier, and may be grown in an open orchard (*bustan*) or trained against a south- or west-facing wall in a

Fig. 155. Espaliered pear tree, Devon.

wide variety of ways, such as espaliered or cordoned in a fan shape. There are numerous cultivars of these and your selection will be based on your own taste, availability and growing conditions.[305] They may also be trained over arches to form enchanting blossom-filled arbours or tunnels in the spring, followed by delicious fruit later in the season.

Like the Muslims, the English have been keen fruit growers for centuries and there are many records from the Middle Ages of apple and pear orchards flourishing in monasteries and the houses of the nobility. Even near London, one writer records that, 'Everywhere without the Houses of the suburbs, the citizens have Gardens and Orchards planted with Trees, large and beautiful, and one joining to another.'[306] This sounds similar to some descriptions of Islamic gardens in which fruit trees are always mentioned, and often depicted in garden-carpets (Fig. 210), as well as miniature paintings.

After the conquest of Istanbul, Mehmet II gave orders for a garden to made with 'kiosks, pools and fountains' on the banks of the Bosphorous in what was formerly a vineyard. Evliya Celebi wrote:

> One could faint from the sweetness of the scent from the twelve thousand cypress trees laid in a chessboard pattern here. The garden was adorned with thousands of fruit trees, plane trees, weeping willows, box and pistachio trees, which shaded it from the sun. Fountains gushed with water night and day like springs in the garden of Eden. The songs of nightingales and birds were food for the soul. Of the fruit, the juicy apricots and peaches were especially praised.[307]

On a more modest scale than the Ottoman sultans, if you have a large enough garden, a mulberry tree (*Morus nigra*), one of the most popular trees in an Islamic garden since its large heart-shaped leaves offer welcome shade, makes a marvellous specimen tree. Not only is it very hardy as well as being tolerant of heat, but it gives delicious fruit even in less sunny climates. An Irish yew (*Taxus baccata* 'Fastigiata') grown not far from a mulberry tree provides contrasting shape and texture. To see these planted in a lawn, a pool in the centre with a natural stone surround and perhaps a very gently bubbling fountain, conjures up the beginnings of an Islamic

Fig. 156. Pittosporum tobira *(sometimes known as 'Mock orange' like* Philadelphus coronarius*).*

garden while simultaneously looking completely at home in an English or other north European environment.

Citrus

Citrus trees, as everyone who has travelled in North Africa and the Near East knows, are an essential feature in the Islamic garden or small courtyard. However, in a cooler, wetter climate, citrus trees are really only possible in containers so that they can be brought in for the winter. In order to achieve this you really need a greenhouse or conservatory to over-winter them, where the temperature does not drop to more than a few degrees below freezing (depending on the species). Your trouble will be amply rewarded, since there is nothing like the heady scent of orange-blossom wafting through the air to conjure up warm Eastern magical nights.[308]

There are many citrus trees to choose from, the first suggestion being the sweet orange tree, *Citrus sinensis*, of which there are many cultivars, and the Seville or bitter orange, *C. aurantium*, the fruits of which can be made into marmalade. These are the hardiest of the citrus trees (can usually survive up to 5°C of frost) apart from the calamondin (see below) and could perhaps be grown outside in northern climes if carefully situated in a south-facing, sheltered position with very well-drained soil.

The calamondin (x *Citrofortunella microcarpa*) is said to survive up to 7°C below freezing and is generally the one most recommended for northern European weather. Like the orange tree, the calamondin flowers are fragrant and it produces a fruit that can be used for marmalade. Other, less hardy (perhaps only tolerating –3°C of frost) citrus species are: *Citrus aurantifolia* (lime), *C. limon* (lemon), *C. reticulata* (mandarin) and *C.* x *paradisi* (grapefruit), all of which would require protection in winter.

Alternatives to Citrus

If you have the right position then a frost-hardy alternative to the high-maintenance citrus is the wonderful, bushy, evergreen shrub *Pittosporum tobira*, its creamy star-like flowers giving off a lovely scent in the spring (Fig. 156).

A hardy substitute for the high-maintenance citrus is, of course, the old favourite, the wonderfully versatile, tough and easy-to-grow shrub, the Mexican orange blossom, *Choisya ternata* (Fig. 157). It is planted widely in cooler climates, as well as Mediterranean ones, since it is happy in both situations as well as being reasonably tolerant of drought; its glossy evergreen leaves and good round shape can also be clipped into an informal hedge. In spring it produces marvellous creamy-white, orange-blossom-like, scented flowers which often appear again later in the season.

Fig. 158. Philadelphus 'Belle Etoile' (strictly speaking the name 'Mock orange' is given only to P. coronarius*).*

Another old favourite, but nevertheless wonderful alternative to the orange tree, is the 'mock orange' (*Philadelphus* species and cultivars), the scent of which is one of the most exquisite in the garden and bears a strong resemblance to orange-blossom itself. There are many cultivars of this: 'Belle Etoile' with its single creamy-white flowers has one of the most delicious scents, which wafts around the garden at all times of day and evening. Although the glory of the *Philadelphus* is short-lived, usually the middle to end of June and first week of July only, the scent is certainly worth the space it takes up.

There is also the more unusual and fully hardy Japanese orange tree, *Poncirus trifoliata*. This is a spiny, deciduous shrub or small tree with scented white flowers in spring and sometimes again in autumn (like the *Choysia*) and bears small orange-like fruits. It can make a good protective hedge if pruned well after flowering in early summer.

The orange tree is almost always to be found in the domestic courtyards of Fez, Marrakech, Cordoba, Seville or Damascus, as well as in mosque courtyards such as in the recently restored Koutoubia Mosque in Marrakech and the famous 'orange-tree courtyard' next to the Great Mosque of Cordoba (Fig. 46). Here

*Fig. 157. Mexican orange blossom (*Choysia ternata*).*

it is said that the oldest orange tree in Spain still survives from the eleventh century. Even in the smallest courtyard today, in one of the above cities, the most likely tree to be found is an orange, lemon or lime tree. A charming sight observed in a Damascus courtyard recently was an elderly man sitting on a rickety wooden chair beneath the miniscule amount of shade cast by one small citrus tree.

Other Trees

Acacias, Tamarisks and Vines

In the Quran, *talh* in Arabic, translated as 'serried acacias', are mentioned,[309] as well as 'palms and vines, with rivers flowing beneath, and all manner of fruit there'.[310] *Talh* has also been translated as a banana tree[311] but generally it is thought to be the *Acacia seyal*[312] or *Acacia arabica*, a thorny evergreen tree that only camels are able to eat, since they have the unique ability to strip off the foliage without being spiked by the thorns. In England and northern climates this acacia could be substituted for the *Acacia dealbata*, better known as the mimosa. This is the tree under which it is believed that the Prophet Muhammad and his followers signed the pledge of Hudaybiyah; it is also the tree over which the Prophet threw his hair after shaving his head on the same occasion.[313] Another, easy-to-grow alternative is the adaptable deciduous false acacia (*Robinia pseudoacacia*) of which there are several cultivars, the most well-known being 'Frisia', a pretty tree with slightly translucent yellow leaves giving light, dappled shade.

The tamarisk tree, *athl* in Arabic, is also mentioned in the Quran. The tallest one, *Tamarix aphylla*, can reach 10m high and has very long roots enabling it to withstand drought, wind and sea-spray. According to the Quran it can also withstand flood, since, along with 'bitter produce… and a few lote-trees', tamarisks were the only trees to survive the 'Flood of Arim'.[314] Other tamarisks are small to medium-sized trees with graceful, slender branches and feather-like foliage bearing white or pale pink flowers in spring or autumn depending on the species and/or time of pruning. They are tough trees and, as well as being essential for screening and shelter-belts in hot, desert

Fig. 159. Orange tree (possibly Citrus sinensis*), Alhambra gardens.*

conditions, are hardy down to –9°C. Therefore they can happily be planted in most parts of the United Kingdom.

Species such as *Tamarix gallica* (also known as the manna plant, since it has been suggested that the sweet gum obtainable from tamarisks is the manna mentioned in the Quran)[315] is one of the hardiest and thus probably one of the best to grow in northern climates; but be aware that the long taproots searching for water may deprive neighbouring plants of water and essential nutrients. They should be planted in sandy soil in a sunny position.

Grapevines are mentioned several times in the Quran,[316] as well as in plant lists, and are depicted in many miniature paintings, sometimes entwining themselves around other trees such as the mulberry. Vines are easy to grow in the United Kingdom, even if the grapes themselves are usually too small to eat unless grown in a greenhouse. However, for ornamental purposes, growing up through trees, covering a pergola or climbing a trellis, then *Vitis coignetiae* is one of the best, its large shade-giving leaves turning spectacular crimson and scarlet in autumn. If you are feeling ambitious and would like to recreate the miniature painting depicting the fruiting vine twining itself around the mulberry tree (Fig. 146) then the well-known *Vitis vinifera* 'Brant' or *Vitis vinifera* 'Purpurea' – both of which have leaves that turn beautiful colours in the autumn – are the ones to try. The vine may be trained – with some trouble – to grow up the mulberry and in mid-summer it will, literally, look a picture![317]

More Trees, and Avenues

Other hardy trees associated with Islamic gardens, either cited in early treatises, depicted in paintings or mentioned in poetry, although not specifically mentioned in the Quran, are: the Judas tree[318] (*Cercis siliquastrum*), the ash (*Fraxinus excelsior*) the holm oak (*Quercus ilex*), the cork oak (*Quercus suber*), the elm (*Ulmus* species) the hawthorn (*Cratageus* species), the sumach (*Rhus coriaria*) and the sweet bay (*Laurus nobilis*). Various conifers, besides the cypress, are characteristic of Islamic gardens and may be grown with care in cooler climates; for example, the fast-growing umbrella pine (*Pinus pinea*) and the Aleppo pine (*Pinus halapensis*) are hardy to around –8°C. All of these are cited in one or more of the early Islamic horticultural treatises, as well as depicted in paintings or included in poetry; however, unlike the trees discussed previously, they are not mentioned by name in the Quran. Another tree (on Ibn Bassal's list) recommended for your northern Islamic garden is the so-called service tree (*Sorbus domestica*). Native to southern Europe, North Africa and western Asia, many species of the versatile *Sorbus* have been growing in the United Kingdom for centuries, the most well-known probably being the native rowan or mountain ash (*Sorbus aucuparia*). In the United Kingdom the rowan was often planted near a house as it was traditionally held to be a protection against evil and illness and to bring good luck.[319] It could be suggested, therefore, that the rowan is Britain's equivalent of the piece of turquoise or the 'Hand of Fatima', often seen hanging in the houses of Muslims in many parts of the Islamic world as a protection against the 'evil eye'. Another native *Sorbus* that is easy to grow, besides *S. aucuparia*, is the lovely whitebeam, *S. aria*, which has a beautiful downy white covering on the underside of its leaves.

'God's gift of plane trees, poplars, cypresses and weeping willows were so large that they reached the sky. The green grass provided ample seating and the pure flowing water made it a splendid place for picnics,' wrote Evliya Celebi about Buyukdere, a favourite hunting ground for the Ottoman sultans.[320] The poplar, usually the *Populus alba* (so-called because its bark is white), was a favourite in Islamic gardens from early on. It provides good wind protection, is tolerant of salty sea-breezes as well as drought, and when mature is both graceful and majestic, the wind rustling its leaves in an unmistakeable fashion. Its near relation, more common in France, is the Lombardy poplar (*Populus nigra* var. *Italica*). The poplar is known as the *alamos* in Spanish, *alameda* meaning a small avenue or mall. Avenues or allées of trees such as poplars became fashionable in the royal gardens of Spain and the rest of Europe from the sixteenth century onwards: although planted as late as the nineteenth century, the cypress walk in the Generalife gardens is a good example of an Islamic-inspired formal avenue (Fig. 160). Similarly, the rich and powerful emirs and sultans in India, Persia and Turkey planted avenues with water in the centre, either still or flowing. The Bagh-I-Fin at Kashan, a large formal Islamic garden dating from the sixteenth century, boasts marvellous majestic avenues of cypresses and plane trees growing either side of a central channel of flowing water.

Looking at late-nineteenth century photographs of Mughal gardens, such as the mausoleum garden of Jahangir (Fig. 18), we can see this idea repeated, although in this case the trees are formally shaped shrubs growing either side of a fast-flowing rill. The garden at the Taj Mahal consists primarily of an avenue of cypresses either side of a canal of water with a row of fountains running down the centre, a raised pool in the middle of the avenue creating the *chahar-bagh* design (Figs. 5 and 172). In the United Kingdom and northern Europe, the avenue was also – and still is – very popular for those with space: for drives up to large houses; for roads or even for wide footpaths; and for drawing the eye away from the house across fields towards a focal point – a statue or folly. This latter idea is very un-Islamic. In an Islamic

Fig. 160. Avenue of cypresses, Generalife gardens.

garden the focal point would be water in some form or a pavilion or, in exceptional expansive locations such as Kashmir, parts of Iran, Turkey and elsewhere, the eye would be drawn to the distant horizon with mountains. There is no doubt that what transforms an avenue of trees from something European to something quintessentially Islamic is the channel or canal of water in the centre. For a large Islamic garden in northern Europe, it would be wonderful to plant an avenue of Lombardy poplars either side of a fast-flowing channel of water, interspersed perhaps with pools or even *chadors*. Alternatively, on a slightly smaller scale, the columnar hornbeam (*C. b.* 'Columnaris') or the incense cedar (*Calocedrus decurrens*) could be planted either side of a water-rill.

By the late-eighteenth century, the fashion for formality in Europe was giving way to the new vogue for grand landscaping schemes, and trees were ruthlessly felled to make way for great vistas. The general idea was for the garden to lead seamlessly into the park and countryside beyond (often using a 'ha-ha' so there was apparently no division between the two), 'Capability' Brown and Humphrey Repton being the well-known exponents of this fashion in England. It is interesting that Jane Austen's character, Mr Rushworth, says, 'There have been two or three fine old trees cut down that grew too near the house, and it opens the prospect amazingly, which makes me think that Repton, or anybody of that sort, would certainly have the avenue at Southerton down.'[321] All this is somewhat alien to the Islamic ideal, which in general aimed to close off the lush oasis within – often with rows of trees acting as wind-breaks – from the usually unfriendly environment without. Although a beautiful view was a valuable asset in an Islamic garden, it was only for those few fortunate enough to live in spectacular locations and was not a priority: water, shade and seclusion came first.

The willow (*Salix* species) is frequently depicted in Persian paintings and mentioned in poetry, and this is usually the beautiful weeping willow (*S. babylonica* or more generally now *S. x sepulcralis* 'Chrysocoma'), its feathery light green leaves looking striking when planted next to the cypress's dark spire. The willow is traditionally regarded as a symbol of mourning, while the flexibility of its branches is a symbol of youth; this latter quality is celebrated in a poem by Saadi, the thirteenth-century Persian poet, who reminds us of an age-old truth:

> A willow-branch reminds one that a youth
> Can easily be bent towards the Truth;
> Old reprobates a sterner fate require
> For they will straighten only in the fire.[322]

More sun-loving trees, like the graceful *Jacaranda* (*J. acutifolia* or *J. mimosifolia*) mentioned at the beginning of the chapter, will only thrive in a northern climate in the most sun-soaked, sheltered position as it is only hardy to −3°C. However much you may long for its great froth of lavender-lilac flowers in the spring it will not be worth attempting to grow this tree unless you possess such a spot. The evergreen carob tree (*Ceratonia siliqua*), mentioned in the medieval lists and commonly grown all over the Middle East today (and as a street tree in Los Angeles, along with palms and *Ficus retusa*), is only hardy to –5°C. Like the jacaranda this is probably best left to enjoy when on your travels.

Tropical Trees

Trees such as the banana (*Musa* species), mango (*Mangifera indica*), frangipani (*Plumeria*), as well as the more exotic species of fig mentioned earlier in the chapter such as the peepul or bo-tree (*Ficus religiosa*) and the banyan tree (*Ficus benghalensis*), are obviously going to present a greater challenge to grow in your Islamic garden of the north. Not only will they not thrive in our cooler, damper climate but also, like the date palm, they do not really look at home under our grey skies. So, if you wish to go for the more exotic and tropical Islamic garden, more typical of the Indian sub-continent and further East, then you need to be very fortunate indeed and have a large heated conservatory where the plants may be brought in during the winter. Even so, with large trees this would be a tremendous amount of work, not to mention expense. Also, although an integral part of what may be termed the 'Asian Islamic world', this tropical-style planting speaks more to us of an Indian–Hindu–Buddhist garden than the traditional Islamic garden of the Near and Middle East and North Africa that we are primarily looking at for inspiration here.

Despite being off-putting about such exotic trees, it is certainly possible to grow them in the milder areas of the United Kingdom as many have done with a certain amount of success. The banana tree (*Musa* species), in particular *Musa basjoo*, has been grown for some years now in frost-free gardens in southern cities and in the south-west of England. It can be grown along with the two or three palms mentioned earlier – always remembering that they will give a rather different 'look', as observed above.

Babur, the first Mughal emperor of India (d. 1530), first saw the banana tree when he conquered India. When he returned to Kabul in 1508 to one of the many gardens that he had laid out, the Garden of Fidelity (*Bagh-I-Vafa*), he ordered a banana tree to be sent to him there, as well as sending sugar-cane (*Saccharum officinarum*) to Bukhara and Badakhshan. Although we do not have space here, it is interesting to compare Mughal miniatures with Persian and Ottoman ones,

Fig. 161. *Flower of the Frangipani (*Plumeria*) tree.*

since there are identifiably different trees in Mughal miniatures. They include the more exotic and tropical trees discussed here such as the banana, the mango and the peepul, as well as the coconut palm (*Cocos nucifera*), the screwpine (*Pandanus odoratissimus*) and the frangipani (*Plumeria*, which can reach up to 3–4m/10ft, called *Yasmine hindi* in Arabic). The frangipani tree or shrub, with its fantastic-smelling cream and yellow waxy flowers in beautiful five-petalled swirls, can really only be grown in a conservatory in a northern climate as it loves heat and humidity – happier in Saudi Arabia than further west (Fig. 161).

Shrubs and Small Trees

The more exotic heat-loving shrubs mentioned earlier, and which are included in the medieval plant lists quoted previously, are the oleander (*Nerium oleander*),[323] hibiscus (*Hibiscus rosa-sinensis* or *H. mutabilis*, *H. syriacuse*, more commonly known as the 'shrub mallow' in early Islamic plant lists), plumbago (*Plumbago auriculata*) and gardenia (*Gardenia jasminoides*). Oleander may be grown in Northern Europe but only in sheltered south-facing gardens and outside may require protection in the winter to be safe; certainly, jacaranda, gardenia and most hibiscus species need protection if they are not brought inside.

Any or all of these shrubs will contribute to the Mediterranean and Islamic atmosphere of your garden, but remember that they are very high maintenance in northern climates. The *Hibiscus* species which is hardy and grown fairly widely in southern Britain now (in fact since the sixteenth century) is the deciduous *H. syriacuse*, of which the two cultivars, 'Blue Bird' and 'Red Heart', are widely available. If you have a sunny, sheltered spot, then either or both of these are a must since they lend a wonderful eastern note to the garden. The non-hardy and evergreen *Hibiscus* are to be found in many other colours, one of the most popular in Egypt and other Near Eastern countries being the deep red *H. rosasinensis* 'Brilliant', which grows into tall informal hedges (up to 3m/10ft high).

Other genera of shrubs or small trees included in Ibn al-Awwam's list,[324] which can easily be grown in your Islamic garden of the north, are broom, buckthorn, hawthorn and Persian lilac. Butcher's broom (*Ruscus aculeatus* and other species) is mentioned by name; it is a marvellous shrub since it is evergreen and tolerant of dry, shady sites, as well as sun, and bears beautiful, large deep red berries in the summer after small green flowers. Various other brooms may also be chosen such as the lovely, if slightly tender, pineapple broom, *Cytisus battandieri*, from the Atlas Mountains; this often grows into a small tree and has pineapple-shaped and scented yellow flower spikes. There is also the fully hardy, spring-flowering *Cytisus x praecox*, and the frost-hardy summer flowering *Genista hispanica*, both of which would fit in well in your Islamic garden as they are native to Europe, North Africa and Asia Minor. There are many species of the hawthorn or 'may' tree (*Crateagus* spp.), some of which are native to North Africa and Western Asia such as *C. azarolus* ('Azarole'), and our own native hawthorn, *C. monogyna*, is native to Europe, North Africa and Western Asia. So, you may plant a hawthorn hedge in the full knowledge of its being typical of England, planted as they were in their thousands during the land enclosures (sixteenth to nineteenth centuries), as well as being included early on in the Islamic gardens of Spain, North Africa and the Near East. Hawthorns are amongst the hardiest and most adaptable of shrubs or small trees, being tolerant of both dry ground and moisture, sun and shade. With their sharp thorns they form a near-impenetrable barrier, as well as looking beautiful in the late spring when covered in blossom. Another shrub native to the United Kingdom and Europe, and included on Ibn al-Awwam's list, is the common buckthorn (*Rhamnus cathartica*) which, like the hawthorn, is often used for hedging. A more interesting buckthorn, *R. imeretina*, comes from the Caucasus and has dark green leaves, which turn purple-bronze in the autumn. Then there is the lovely Persian lilac or 'bead tree' or Chinaberry, *Melia azedarach*, a large shrub or small tree, which likes the sun and should only be grown in northern climates against a sunny, south-facing wall. It has beautiful, scented, star-shaped pale lilac flowers in the spring.

Other reasonably hardy shrubs that would blend well into your Islamic garden of the north, even though they are not specifically mentioned in the early plant lists, are the popular small evergreen (ever-grey) ones such as *Convolvulus cneorum* with its delicate yellow-centred white flowers, the cotton lavender, *Santolina chamaecyparissus*, *Teucrium fruticans*, with its fine small silver-grey leaves and sky-blue flowers appearing all through the summer, *Senecio* 'Sunshine' (syn. *Brachyglottis* 'Sunshine', the bright yellow flowers often snipped off to retain the beauty of the grey-leafed shrub) Jerusalem sage (*Phlomis fruticosa*) and *Feijoa sellowiana*. A pretty, silver-grey leafed shrub or small tree is *Elaeagnus* 'Quicksilver', which is reminiscent of a small olive tree from the distance but has the great advantage of being fully hardy. (The weeping silver pear tree, *Pyrus salicifolia* 'Pendula' has a similar look but with a pendulous habit.) There is also the wonderful genus of mainly evergreen shrubs or small trees, *Ceanothus*, which although they hail from California mainly, would suit an Islamic garden of the north well because of their dazzling array of blue flowers ranging from pale sky blue to deep indigo in spring and summer; blue, the colour of the heavens, being a favourite colour in Islamic art.

Some of the above shrubs are departing from any particular notion of an Islamic garden, simply favourites, which may contribute towards the atmosphere we are attempting to create of an eastern Mediterranean, Near-Eastern, Islamic garden. An exact replica of a traditional Islamic garden is not what we are aiming at, more its serene and contemplative atmosphere, centred primarily on water and shade: scent, colour and flowers come second to this, albeit a close second. As long as the fundamental design is

*Fig. 162. Box hedges (*Buxus sempervirens) *in formal geometric shapes, Alhambra Gardens.*

adhered to and the intention is kept uppermost – that of reflecting the heavenly gardens – then the planting can be relatively flexible. Depending very much on your own project, the size of the garden, the related buildings and so on, discernment needs to be exercised constantly in order to create a balance between the given unchangeable site and conditions and the aim of creating something that is both inspired by, as well as resembling, a traditional Islamic garden.

The Muslim rulers and horticulturalists themselves were always interested in growing new plants if they were beautiful and especially if they were scented. (This is expanded upon in the next chapter on plants and flowers.) There are many other half-hardy shrubs besides those included above which, if placed carefully,

Fig. 163. Philadelphus *growing profusely within formal box hedge, Alacazar, Cordoba.*

may be grown in more northern climates and still echo the traditional Islamic garden. For example, the aromatic leaves of the evergreen shrub myrtle conjures up a Mediterranean atmosphere, not to mention reminding one of the Court of Myrtles at the Alhambra (Figs. 42 and 125). Originally, as with the Court of Lions, there would have been far more planting in the Court of Myrtles to soften the architecture. In this court, myrtle shrubs are planted as thick, square-cut hedges either side of the pool with a narrow channel of water running around their edge. They make a good strong dark frame for the water and give one some welcome rest from the glare of the sun on the pale stone. These hedges are probably the common myrtle (*Myrtus communis*) or possibly the more compact version, *M. communis susp. Tarentina*, a densely leafed shrub bearing scented white flowers in July and August followed by white berries rather than black berries, as *M. communis* has. Myrtle can be rather tender so in northern climates it needs a sunny, well-drained position. A hardier alternative which can tolerate some shade is the Chilean myrtle (*M. cheken*) which has bright green leaves and can grow into a small tree.

A good alternative to myrtle for shady situations in your northern Islamic garden is the hardy evergreen, Christmas box, *Sarcococca confusa* or *S. hookeriana var. digyna*. Both bear scented white flowers at Christmas, which last about a month, the sweet scent wafting through the air on cold winter mornings is a real delight. Either of these species can be planted as a fairly informal hedge, not as dense as myrtle as their leaves are slightly larger with a more relaxed habit, but nevertheless providing some structure to the garden. Hedges, like paths and water-channels, may contribute towards the geometric structure of an Islamic garden. They are used to great effect in the modern planting of the gardens in and around the Alhambra palaces (Fig. 162 and Chapter 2); for example, the gardens beyond the Partal Palace and the Garden of the Lindaraja (Fig. 143). Other useful shrubs for emphasizing formality and geometry, and also mentioned in the medieval plant lists, are box (*Buxus sempervirens*), *euonymus* (one of the best choices today would be the evergreen *Euonymus japonicus* 'Macrophyllus') and sweet bay (*Laurus nobilis*). In the traditional Islamic garden – and easy to imitate in your northern Islamic garden since it is similar to English-style planting schemes – is to have profuse, lush and informal planting within a formal structure (Fig.

163, see Chapter 6): 'real-life' geometry and arabesque as it were. In the Alcazar in Cordoba this idea is used to great effect with marvellous large flowering shrubs (mostly *Philadelphus* species) spilling out over the formal hedges, laid out to a four-fold design of paths with a central fountain (Figs. 36 and 164).

In your northern Islamic garden you could vary the formal hedge with such alternatives as yew (*Taxus baccata*), hornbeam (*Carpinus betulus*, remembering that this is not evergreen), holly (*Ilex aquifolium* cultivars) *Lonicera nitida*, *Griselinia littoralis* or even privet (*Ligustrum*) which gets a bad press but in fact makes a good, no-fuss formal hedge. *Euonymus alatus* 'Compactus' makes a good, low (approximately 1m) hedge, its leaves turning a brilliant red in autumn; *Rosa rubiginosa*, *Viburnum tinus* or camellias would make a less dense and less Islamic-looking hedge (e.g. *C. x williamsii* cultivars and some *C. japonica* cultivars); and species of cistus, rosemary or lavender (see Chapter 6) could be planted for a lower, even more informal hedge, perhaps either side of a path. Camellias, although providing a glossy evergreen hedge and giving a certain amount of privacy, are definitely more Far-Eastern than Middle-Eastern so if you are going for a more typical Islamic look it would be better to stick to sweet bay for a high hedge. If your garden is warm and south-facing, *Pittosporum tobira* is a marvellous shrub, as mentioned above, which may also be grown as an informal hedge; other species of this genus are very well worth considering (e.g. *P. tenuifolium*) as they do survive in the milder areas of northern Europe and yet they also conjure up a more Mediterranean/Eastern atmosphere.

Just as there should be no statuary in an Islamic garden, the topiary should be limited to geometric patterns and shapes such as the large oval shapes of clipped yew at Jahangir's tomb garden (Fig. 18) and the more rounded yew shapes at the fort of Lahore, the hexagonal stars in clipped box in the Alhambra gardens, and pyramids or cubes in clipped box mentioned in accounts of Ottoman gardens;[325] the hedges should not be clipped to imitate animals, birds or people (see Chapter 6).

A possibility for a shady, north or north-east facing garden, if you have the space, is to concentrate on fruit trees – both ornamental and productive – combined with an under-planting of spring bulbs. This fits in with the Islamic ideal, as well as being appropriate for this kind of space. However, if you have very little sun, as

Fig. 164. Box hedges bordering straight paths and enclosing a variety of shrubs and trees, Alcazar, Cordoba. Formal layout and abundant planting, with water as the central factor, are keys to a successful Islamic garden. With careful planning this kind of design and planting can easily be achieved in a northern European type of climate.

well as a small space – a courtyard in the centre of high buildings, say – then, as mentioned earlier, to create an Islamic ambience you would need to focus on geometric patterns in hard landscaping with some large containers planted with shade tolerant, mainly evergreen, shrubs such as box, *Choysia ternata*, species of *viburnum* (e.g. *V. tinus* 'Eve Price' or 'French White') and *osmanthus* (e.g. *Osmanthus x burkwoodii*); and perhaps a few shade-tolerant climbers such as the evergreen honeysuckle, *Lonicera japonica* 'Halliana' or various clematis (e.g. *C. alpina* cultivars or *C. montana*) and pyracantha (e.g. *P. coccinea* 'Orange Glow').

Other plants mentioned at the beginning of this chapter, such as jasmine and bougainvillea, are described in the next chapter along with herbaceous plants, climbers and herbs. These include such shrub herbs as rosemary, lavender and sage, as well as a brief summary of vegetables – an important element in the traditional Islamic garden.

CHAPTER 6

Plants and Flowers

The tulip's graceful chalice,
Which God's own hand hath made,
Is filled with glowing wine; it stands
Upon a stem of jade.

Anwari (died c. 1190)[327]

The idea of a 'wild garden' is totally alien to the Islamic concept of a garden in which one of the primary motivating factors was to keep out the 'wild'. Most of Europe, generally speaking, enjoys a relatively temperate climate but the lands where the Islamic garden may be said to have been 'born' and nurtured – Arabia, Persia, Iraq, Syria and Egypt – experience extremes of climate where desert temperatures often reach 49°C in the shade. Therefore, the principal aim of the garden was to create a sanctuary, as different from the desert as possible, where these extremes could be forgotten about for a while amidst cool shade and running water. The wild – in this case, arid or semi-arid environments – had no place in this enclosed area. The plants and flowers that the inhabitants wished to nurture in their secluded domains were therefore not the ones that we associate with desert conditions: plants such as succulents and cacti (e.g. various species of *Opuntia, Agave* and *Yucca*) and those with thorns or spines (species of *Parkinsonia* and *Prosopis*). This concept of the importance of a protected area, isolated by walls or a shelter-belt of tall trees such as cypresses (*Cupressus sempervirens*) or poplars (usually *Populus alba*) referred to in the last chapter, really only comes alive to an observer when travelling through the desert or barren, rocky ground such as the road through the Jordan Valley or the road from Cairo to Fayoum or the road between Jeddah and Mecca. These roads are well-travelled, not out-of-the-way places; however, away from the road – in the Jordan Valley, in particular – there are small cultivated

Fig. 165. Ottoman ceramic tiles depicting stylised flowers including tulips, prunus *blossom, hyacinths and roses.*

Fig. 166. Jordan Valley showing small lone tree in the distance.

areas of fertile green which contrast sharply with their surroundings. They are separated from the seemingly unending desert landscape by walls and trees and make very powerful images; the dark green of the trees offers such a wonderful soothing rest and cool to the eyes (as the Arab saying goes) next to the glare of the sun on the monotonous sandy ground (Fig. 166 and 151).

The urban landscape of the frenetic modern world also needs to be separated from, and prevented, as far as possible, from encroaching on the private oasis of family life and garden within, however small. The principle is the same – it is the context that has changed. This new context of small gardens within built-up cities offers plenty of opportunity for planting a verdant retreat along the lines of the original Islamic enclosed courtyard garden.

In the making of an Islamic garden in the United Kingdom or elsewhere with a similar climate, one needs to be extra-aware of the 'ecological, geological and climactic factors, as well as other aesthetic exigencies of colour harmonies, forms and

Fig. 167. Flowers in art: stylised poppies and other flowers embroidered on this susani *from Uzbekistan.*

textures'.[328] This is because, in a certain sense, one is transplanting a 'foreign' concept. This has been discussed earlier in the book and needs no further elaboration here. I just wish to emphasize that one must ensure, as far as possible, that the plants and flowers, like the shrubs and trees, have 'an air of belonging',[329] at the same time as reminding one of the essential atmosphere of a traditional Islamic garden. After the design, layout, water and hard-landscaping have been decided upon, and the trees and shrubs have been selected, you can have a wonderful time choosing the smaller flowering plants – perennials and annuals, climbers, herbs and vegetables – that will put the final touches to this twin objective. The prime subject of this chapter, after a short historical introduction, is to recommend plants that fulfil these criteria.

Sources

The sources for recommendations for these plants are the same sources as those used for the trees and shrubs stated in the previous chapter; in summary: the Quran, the medieval plant lists, travellers' descriptions, other historical accounts, Islamic miniature paintings, and poetry. The planting in Islamic gardens today has, generally speaking, altered too much to be of great use to us as a source of inspiration (apart possibly from

some of the trees; for example, at the Generalife gardens in Granada, the cypress, the orange trees, the sweet bay and possibly the palms were probably 'the last of the original planting', which had lasted for over six hundred years).[330] However, the various manifestations of Islamic art are a good substitute: since flowers are such a popular subject, depicted in every art/craft medium possible (see below, 'Flowers in Islamic Art') representations of them shall be referred to more widely. Information gathered from these sources shows that very many of the flowers, herbs and vegetables mentioned are similar to our own, and the problem of less sunshine and heat does not appear to matter so much as it does with many of the trees and shrubs observed in the previous chapter. In Islam, a garden should be productive as well as beautiful, similar to gardens in Europe in the Middle Ages, and in fact – apart from 'stately homes' and the better-off – vegetables and flowers were grown in close proximity to each other until the second-half of the twentieth century;[331] the Victorian cottage garden is a classic example of this. Such gardens consisted of a mixture of vegetables and flowers, and vegetables were the most important as the inhabitants relied upon them for sustenance.

Flowering Season

Many, but by no means all, plants that are grown in Islamic gardens are accustomed to a more Mediterranean-type of climate of hot and dry summers and cool and moist winters, rather different from the northern European climate of short summers, cold winters and wet most of the year.[332] Therefore, a factor to remember when selecting plants for your Islamic garden of the north is their growing and flowering period. In northern Europe it is the late spring and summer that we look forward to most, since this is the period when the majority of plants come into flower, the only period when there are enough hours of sunshine to give them the nourishment to bloom. However, in countries further south and east, this is not usually the case. In Egypt, for example, (and other near Eastern or north African countries), the summers are so hot and the soil so baked, that the summer is in fact a fairly dormant period horticulturally speaking; whereas the autumn, spring and, to a certain extent, winter, all witness a great array of plants blooming to their hearts' content. The flowering period in these countries is also much longer, or occurs twice, in spring and in autumn – the pomegranate and hibiscus, to take just two examples, seem to be in bloom most of the year.

You may ask what this has to do with your Islamic garden of the north. Well, it is interesting since the existence of an extended flowering period explains to a certain extent why it is always the same favourite flowers that are referred to again and again in Islamic miniature paintings and poetry: roses, tulips, hyacinths, carnations, daffodils and violets – to name some of the principal flowers beloved by the early Muslims. These favourite flowers are described in more detail later in the chapter. 'The love that all Easterners have for flowers is almost worshipful,' wrote the English traveller, Julia Pardoe in the nineteenth century. In Istanbul she noted that:

> Every fine mansion along the Bosphorus has a flower garden… here are cultivated shrubs yielding beautiful roses in a thousand and one different varieties… there are also rows of pergolas covered with rosebuds along a beautiful road, flowers spilling out of red earthenware flowerpots, row upon row of carnations, and an abundance of acacias that all provide a feast for the eyes.[333]

In northern Europe we are used to a fleeting performance from most spring flowers with compensation in the form of some generous perennials and annuals lasting throughout the summer and into autumn, if frequently picked or dead-headed. Another advantage of the increased heat and sunshine of most Islamic countries is that the scent of many fragrant flowers, roses in particular, is far stronger than those grown further north.[334] There are some I have noticed, the scent of which is as strong in England as in Egypt, for instance, old-fashioned sweet peas (in particular, *Lathyrus odoratus* 'Cupani's Original' syn. *L. o.* 'Matucana'), jasmine (both *Jasminum officinale* and *Jasminum polyanthemum*), *Philadelphus* spp. and some *Viburnums* and *Daphnes*.

So, your northern Islamic garden may not be as colourful or as scented for the length of time as its prototype grown in warmer climes, but it will, hopefully, be just as beautiful with its freshness and lush foliage that only a good fall of rain can bring. This increased rainfall brings that most heavenly of qualities mentioned so often in the Quranic descriptions of the paradise gardens, the sacred colour green (Fig. 168).

Background

Over a period of time the interaction of the Islamic revelation with the different cultures of the Islamic world (*Dar al-Islam*) led to the development of a wide variety of art and architecture which nevertheless was unmistakeably Islamic. Alongside this cultural explosion, great advances were made in the art and science of water-engineering, agriculture, horticulture, husbandry and botany. This knowledge and creativity was manifested in such peaks of garden design already observed – for instance, the Shalimar Gardens in Lahore (seventeenth century) or the Generalife Gardens in Granada (thirteenth to fifteenth centuries). Arab botanists, horticulturalists, gardeners and medical botanists were aided tremendously in their endeavours by the Abbasid caliph, Harun al-Rashid (AD764–809), who advised the Baghdad Academy to translate various Greek and Latin sources, the most famous being the *Materia Medica* of the Roman physician Dioscorides (see Chapter 2).

Fig. 168. The sacred colour green, mentioned so often in the Quranic descriptions of the paradise gardens, we tend to take for granted in our naturally verdant lawns; although the hot and dry summer experienced by most of Europe in 2003 saw the grass turn from lush green to hard brown all too quickly (see p.167).

Besides the important works written by the Muslim Arabs themselves mentioned in Chapter 5, there is also a Persian treatise on husbandry, the *Irshad az-Zara'ah* by Qasim ibn Yusuf, which he composed at Herat (Afghanistan) in 1515. This is an interesting story, since he wrote it as a result of a vision of a Sufi saint, Khawajeh Abdullah Ansari, bidding him to compose such a work as a sign of gratitude to God. Ibn Yusuf took his vision seriously and consulted the Quran, scholars, theologians and fellow Sufis before embarking on his treatise. It has a fascinating amount of practical information, including distinguishing between good and bad soils, the laying-out of the *chahar-bagh* and its pavilion, astrologically auspicious times for planting, and other useful advice.[336]

Horticultural Experiment

It is true that the same flowers tended to be represented in art and poetry in the Islamic world but it should not be assumed that because of this, horticultural experiment did not take place. In fact, many of the rulers were passionately interested in expanding the plant repetoire of their gardens – such as Abdul-Rahman, the first Ummayyad ruler in Spain (AD756–88). He encouraged the introduction of as many new plants as their gardeners and ambassadors could discover. Abdul-Rahman sent messengers abroad specifically to bring plants back to his estate, al-Rusafa, which 'became famous for the excellence of its plant varieties'.[337]

Another ruler well-known for his horticultural addiction was Babur, the first Mughal emperor (1526–30). His tremendous passion for gardening led him, on conquering India, to constantly search for suitable places to create beautiful gardens. His love of plants of every description, from roses and narcissi, to fruit trees and vegetables, is well-known and vividly communicated in his memoirs. At Agra he wrote that he had 'in every border rose and narcissus in perfect arrangement' and he introduced new flowers: 'In these places the oleander flower is peach, those of Gualiar are beautiful deep red. I took some of them to Agra and had them planted in gardens there.'[338] His descendants include Shah Jahan who built the Taj Mahal (Fig. 172) and the Shalimar gardens in Lahore, and Jahangir who was also a keen gardener. His

memoirs tell of the flowers of Kashmir, of the narcissi, violets and tulips – the latter he does not recognize and calls 'strange flowers'. His ancestor, Babur, had known better and counted seventeen different kinds of wild tulips on the hills around Kabul.

The Ottoman sultan, Mehmet II, was also a passionate gardener and, similar to Babur, he liked to contribute himself to the planning, digging and planting of his gardens, in particular of his New Palace in Istanbul (Yeni Saray), completed in 1465. He is also noted for sending emissaries far and wide to bring rare plants back to his domain, a later visitor remarking that the garden was 'a most wonderful confusion of exquisite trees, fruit trees and others, and with all sorts of flowers and herbs'.[339]

However, horticultural experimentation was not the domain of the artists and poets. They preferred to stick to the beauty, romance and symbolism of the flowers they knew and loved. It is mainly these ones we shall focus on when selecting plants and flowers for a northern Islamic garden. Bearing this in mind when planting your own Islamic garden, actually makes things easier. You do not need to search out unusual or rare plants, since on the whole the flowers the early Muslims loved are the flowers that were loved in Europe – and still are, in both cases, although much of the horticultural world has become hooked on cultivating ever larger and brightly coloured hybrids. When planting your Islamic garden, modern cultivars that depart far from their species parents[340] should be avoided along with grasses, 'prairie-planting' or exotic succulents like agaves or prickly pears. These latter plants, although today sought after and grown with some success in the milder areas of Northern Europe and some modern gardens in the Islamic East, were part of the 'wild' and kept firmly out of the traditional Muslim sanctuary. The wide variety of grasses that are fashionable now, however beautiful they may be, are also not really appropriate in a traditional Islamic garden; but there is certainly scope for areas of informal spring planting under the fruit trees such as a mixture of narcissi, crocus, colchicum, cyclamen and tulips (see below under 'Spring Flowers'). It is human nature to want something different from what we are given – in temperate climates we crave the exotic in the shape of the date-palm, the banana or the bougainvillea, and in desert climates they long for the lush green and water that we have in abundance. So, for your Islamic garden, it will be more in keeping to grow the genera that are repeatedly included in the historical accounts and the plant treatises, as well as our other sources. This, as we shall see in more detail later on in the chapter, still gives plenty of opportunity for a wide range of planting.

Flowers in Poetry, Travellers' Tales and Sultans' Memoirs

An initial foray into our sources reveals Islam's great love for all the best-loved and most well-known flowers you can think of, mentioned above. Of all these it is the rose that stands head and shoulders above the rest. It is the most exalted and beloved of all the flowers in Islam, and something of its profound and many-layered symbolism is described a little later in the chapter. It is these flowers and many more, such as poppies, hyacinths, tulips, carnations and irises that are most often referred to in poetry and depicted in Islamic art. As Firdawsi wrote in his *Shahnama* (*History of Kings*) in about AD1000:

Fig. 170. Tulipa praestens *'Fusilier' (see pp. 154–5).*

> Tulips and hyacinths abound
> On every lawn; and all around
> Blooms like a garden in its prime,
> Fostered by that delicious clime.

And Hafiz (d. 1389) wrote:

> Oh! Bring thy couch where countless roses
> The garden's gay retreat discloses...[341]

Fig. 169. Rosa *'Tuscany Superba' (see pp. 157–9).*

When the Muslims conquered Spain in the eighth and ninth centuries, they started cultivating gardens almost immediately, so fertile did the land – around Granada in particular – seem to them after the inhospitable land of Arabia. By the eleventh century gardens were the most popular theme of all Arab–Andalusian poetry, and the garden-poem had its own special term, the *rawdiya*. The poems, however fanciful and romantic they may sometimes seem to the more prosaic northern European mind, were not entirely flights of the imagination but frequently corresponded to the actual surroundings, witnessed by observers' descriptions. Only a fraction of these gardens survive today but in the early centuries of Islam, as Andrew Watson makes clear,

*Fig. 171. Flag Irises (*Iris pseudacorus*) (see p.156).*

many a city boasted a wealth of gardens, not just the famous Isphahan:

> Basra is described by the early geographers as a veritable Venice, with mile after mile of canals criss-crossing the gardens and orchards; Nisibin, a city in Mesopotamia, was said to have 40,000 gardens of fruit trees, and Damascus, 11,000; al-Fustat [old Cairo], with its multiple-storey dwellings, had thousands of private gardens, some of great splendour; in north Africa one learns of a multitude of gardens, surrounding and even inside cities such as Tunis, Tlemcen, and Marrakesh.[342]

In the seventeenth century, Isphahan was in its hey-day and Sir Thomas Herbert, who was attached to the British Embassy in Persia at the time, was enchanted by it:

> Gardens here for grandeur and fragour are such as no City in Asia out-vies; which at a little

distance from the city you would judge a Forest, it is so large; but withal so sweet and verdant you may call it another Paradise... You pass by Cherbaugh [Avenue of the Chahar-Bagh], through an even street near two miles long, and as broad as Holborn in London, a great part of the way being Garden-walls on either side of the street; yet here and there bestrew'd with Mohols or Summer-houses; all along planted with broad-spreading Chenar trees, which besides shade serves for use and ornament.[343]

The sad decline of the Avenue Chahar-Bagh in Isphahan has already been noted; however, in the past few years, there has been some movement towards a restoration of a few gardens nearby, such as the garden surrounding the Palace-pavilion of Chehel Sutun.

The traveller, Sir John Chardin, wrote in the seventeenth century: 'There are all kinds of flowers in Persia that one finds in France and Europe' and his list includes roses 'found in five colours: white, yellow, red, Spanish rose and poppy red', jasmine, tulips, anemones, ranunculi, 'seven or eight different sorts of narcissus', lily-of-the-valley, lily, 'violets of all hues', pinks [carnations], hyacinths and stocks.[344] The rose is usually referred to with the Persian word *gul*, which also means 'flower', *gulistan* meaning rose-garden, and a whole genre of poetry flourished called *gul-u-bulbul* (rose and nightingale) poetry. Al-Himyari, an eleventh-century Spanish Muslim horticulturalist, includes similar flowers in his list, as well as myrtle, wallflower, iris, poppy, water-lily, *uqhuwan* translated as 'marguerite or camomile', carnation, and oleander. He also includes several herbs such as marjoram, thyme, mint and saffron, and many fruit trees, which have been named in the previous chapter. [345]

In the sixteenth century, the French traveller, du Fresne-Canaye, visited the imperial gardens at Sultaniye in Turkey, observing:

> It is difficult to describe how fond the Turks are of flowers: they hold them in their hands or twine them in the folds of their turbans as if they were sacred. And the sultans, whenever they find a tree finer than all the others, immediately plant in its shade flowers of every colour and scent. There

are so many varieties of flowers in their gardens that one only has to stretch out a hand to gather a mixed bouquet of every shade of colour one can imagine. The paths, which are narrow as the sultans walk alone, are lined with cypresses.[346]

On another occasion the same writer notes that the Turks love their roses so much that they even eat them! For breakfast they ate rose jelly which was, he notes, quite delicious.

Later on, in the nineteenth century, Edward Lear wrote an ecstatic description of the garden of the Taj Mahal:

> What a garden! What flowers!... the accompaniment and contrast of the dark green cypresses with the rich yellow green trees of all sorts! And then the effect of the innumerable flights of bright green parrots flitting across like live emeralds: and of the scarlet poincinannas and countless other flowers beaming off the dark green. Poinsettias are in huge crimson masses, and the purple-flowered bougainvillea runs up the cypress trees.[347]

Fig. 172. The Taj Mahal – view from one corner of the garden.

*Fig. 173. Sweet pea (*Lathyrus odoratus*) climbing up cypress, Carpet Garden, Chelsea, 2001.*

This last observation, as remarked earlier, is a strong image immediately transporting one to an Islamic garden. With a little care this could be imitated in your own garden but probably with sweet peas (*Lathyrus odoratus* cultivars, see below), rather than the tender bougainvillea which rarely survives outdoors in northern climates.

It is interesting how Lear remarks on the bright colours set against – or rather, 'beaming off' – the dark green; definitely something else that can easily be emulated in your own garden although the effect will be less dramatic in northern sunshine. However, in the north we have the great advantage of a longer twilight which gives us more time to take in the extraordinary beauty and density of colour as the darkness gradually descends. Also, at this time of day, grey foliage and white flowers – as many readers will have observed – stand out 'glowing' against a dark background.

Flowers in Islamic Art

As we have seen, Islamic gardens are principally centred on water and shade, in memory of their importance to a religion born in a desert region. Flowers, it could be

Fig. 174–5. Ottoman ceramic tiles depicting stylised flowers including tulips, prunus blossom, hyacinths and roses.

In the first few centuries of Islam, as the religion extended its realm into Persia, Byzantium, Anatolia and farther East to India, as well as west to North Africa and Spain, it absorbed much of the love of plants that already existed in those cultures. Besides poetry, the visual art of Islam celebrated flowers and plants: they came to be represented in every craft and medium, from book illumination, textiles and carpets to ceramic tiles, pottery, carved gypsum and wood, engraved metal and tooled leather. It is probably Ottoman and Persian tile-work and textiles that are most famous for their depictions of the rose, the tulip, the carnation and the hyacinth. Here, these flowers are identifiable but often – in Moorish art especially – they are depicted in the form of the 'arabesque' (*islimi*, or *rumi* in Turkish), the rhythmic biomorphic form which balances the crystalline, geometric patterns (Fig. 87). In Islamic art the 'arabesque' encapsulates Nature and represents her inward essence in abstracted form rather than Nature in her outward visible form. Certainly, when you look at an arabesque design it is not identifiable as an individual species of plant or flower – that is not the aim: the aim is to represent Nature as a whole, the organic natural rhythms of the universe.

It is true that European art also shows a love of flowers and gardens – but it is in a significantly different way. In art such as the Dutch still-life paintings of the seventeenth century, the great bowls of carefully depicted flowers are often the same flowers as those preferred by the Muslim artists. However, the emphasis of such painters as Jan Davidsz de Heem is on naturalism and detail, on how clever the artist has been in creating an illusion of a 'real' flower. In contrast to this is an Islamic miniature painting, which makes no attempt at perspective or creating a 'lifelike' image, but aims to capture its 'fragrant soul'[350] (Figs. 26, 102 and 146). One of the principal reasons behind this flat perspective is the recognition that the painting is a two-dimensional medium and to attempt 'reality' would be to create an illusion; this illusion is in danger of capturing the imagination and becoming the 'real thing' itself, an idol. One of the roles of Islamic traditional art is to capture the imagination and direct it upwards towards heaven, to the Creator Himself, rather than drawing it down into the world and emphasizing the illusion. Nature is understood as a reflection of the glory of

argued, are the least important element in these gardens – and to a certain extent this is true. Nevertheless, as already observed, it is also true to say that Islamic culture in general had a great passion for flowers, especially in Ottoman Turkey where the love of flowers was verging on an obsession and was not second-place to design, water and shade.[348] 'The Turks very much love flowers. A lady might spend all the money she has for a flower to put in her hair' and 'The Turks love flowers. They will always carry one about held in their hand or set in a turban'.[349]

God, not an end in herself. Thus in Islam, naturalism in art is to be avoided. According to a Saying of the Prophet Muhammad, artists who seek to imitate the world of the Creator will be told in the afterlife to breathe life into their creations, and when they are unable to do so, they will suffer terrible torments.

One of the greatest writers on Islamic art of the twentieth century, trained as a sculptor in the European tradition, once asked to become the apprentice of a North African master-decorator and the master asked him, 'What would you do if you had to decorate a plain wall like this one?' The author replied, 'I would make a design of vines and fill up their sinuosities with drawings of gazelles and hares.' The Arab master-craftsman said, 'Gazelles and hares and other animals exist everywhere in nature, why reproduce them? But to draw three geometrical rose patterns, one with eleven segments and two with eight, and to link them up in such a way that they fill this space perfectly, that is art.'[351]

So Islamic miniature paintings do not contain naturalistic depictions of space largely because of their profound belief that this world, although highly alluring, is fundamentally temporary and illusory. They do not depict the 'here and now' of the corporeal world that we inhabit but rather, with their other-worldly and magical atmosphere, offer the viewer a glimpse of an imaginal universe, closer to the higher realms of heaven.

Fig. 176. Contemporary painting in traditional miniature painting style of cypress entwined with flowering tree, by ex-VITA student Sabat Rifat (see endnote 135).

Special Atmosphere of the Islamic Garden

I would venture to say that this is the special ingredient of the traditional Islamic garden: wherever it may be situated – from Afghanistan to Algeria, from India to, hopefully, the United Kingdom – it possesses an other-worldly atmosphere, which gives the visitor an intimation of the peace and joy that is to come when we depart this world. Even if one is entertaining guests rather than contemplating, it still retains, to a greater or lesser extent, this sense of something beyond what is seen by the eye, something mysterious, hidden and ultimately holy. As mentioned earlier, *janna* besides meaning garden or paradise also means 'hidden' or 'secret'. The flowers within the Islamic garden are grown not just for the shape and colour of their petals and their sweet scent but because their outward form conceals, while at the same time reveals – 'to those who have eyes' – the beauty of the Creator's invisible hand, *al-Jamal*, the Beautiful, being one of the names of God.[352] Their beauty is a symbol: in the Islamic garden there always exists this element of symbolism, which is not usually present in the post-Renaissance European garden.

The earlier courtyard houses of England and northern Europe reflect the more spiritually-centred society that existed in the Middle Ages, and this was more akin to the traditional Islamic society. Just as medieval European art has many similarities to traditional Islamic art,[353] many parallels can be drawn between the enclosed monastic garden, the *hortus conclusus*, and the Islamic *chahar-bagh* garden; these have been touched on elsewhere in this book

Fig. 177. Alhambra gardens.

(see Chapters 1–3). Interestingly, monastic gardens are being restored or recreated today, and these demonstrate careful research and understanding of the meaning and use of herbs, vegetables and flowers in medieval times, as well as an understanding of the four-fold design being a universal symbol of the natural world. At Buckfast Abbey in south-west England, a series of herb gardens have been laid out on four-fold plans with an interpretation of the symbolism of the plants, herbs and flowers grown; at Winchester Castle Queen Eleanor's garden is an example of the recreation of a royal thirteenth-century 'Herber';[354] and in Morpeth (northern England), a sixteenth-century herb garden has been created in memory of William Turner, who wrote a three-part herbal dedicated to Queen Elizabeth I.

Flowers and Love and Flower Symbolism

There is an overwhelming sense of ease, relaxation and romance, as well as spiritual yearning, when reading Persian poems about gardens, and looking at Persian, Ottoman and Indian miniatures in which gardens, flowers and love are often intertwined. Only in Persia, with its long history of wonderful gardens, would you find a young soldier, military uniform and rifle notwithstanding, reciting poetry about flowers whilst guarding the entrance to a conference centre![355] Sitting in restaurants and cafes in Iran today, young boys go around the tables offering scraps of paper with poetry printed on them, the subject of which is very often gardens and love. There are also quiz shows in Iran, which are of a higher order altogether than those we are used to here; they are entirely about poetry, the subject of which is again very often gardens and love – it is woven into their souls as a living tradition, you might say.

When visiting Istanbul in the nineteenth century, the English artist Thomas Allom, noted that the Turks' love for flowers extended to a kind of symbolic language. Every flower carried a meaning; for example, orange blossom meant hope, the tulip symbolized betrayal, and the marigold represented despair. Bouquets of flowers were sent instead of love-letters and were a way of communicating how lovers felt about each other.[356]

The story of Laila and Majnun, the lovers who only saw each other twice on earth, was, as Constance Villiers Stuart wrote in the early twentieth century, often memorialized in the floral symbolism of a garden:

Two low-growing fruit trees, such as a lemon and orange tree, planted in the midst of a parterre of flowers, are the lovers happy in Paradise; the same idea is also illustrated by two cypresses, or the so-called male and female date-palms, which are generally planted in pairs... Majnun's sad earthly symbol is the weeping-willow, whose Laila, the water-lily, grows just beyond his reach. Two cypress trees are frequently grown as their emblems, and the prettiest and quaintest emblem of all is Laila on her camel litter, a rose-bush on a little mound. Dark purple violets mean the gloss and perfume of her blue-black hair, *saman* ['jasmine', which also means a foaming stream] is Laila's round white throat, 'cypress slender' is her waist, tulips and roses are her lips and cheeks, and the fringed, starred narcissus her eyes.[357]

The Rose

The rose, as a well-known saying in Islam goes, was created from a bead of perspiration that dropped from the Prophet's forehead on his miraculous night journey (*miraj*) and is seen as the perfect manifestation of beauty and majesty on earth. The saying develops later on to claim that the different kinds of roses were created from drops that fell from different parts of his body. Ruzbihan Baqli (d. 1209) of Shiraz wrote that 'everyone who wants to look into God's splendour should look at the red rose'.[358] It was Baqli who confirmed the tradition that it was the Prophet Muhammad's favourite flower. The thorns of the rose represent the trials on the spiritual path and the wrath of the Almighty, whereas the flower itself represents God's mercy and love. In the Diwan of Jalal ud-din Rumi, the thorn has become sanctified through performing so many circumambulations around the face of the rose. For Rumi the garden was one of the most powerful symbols of divine beauty, 'manifesting and yet veiling the eternal gardener and his everlasting beauty'.[359] Muhammad Iqbal (d. 1937), the Indian poet, described the Prophet as being like the rose, united as one with his community, he being the centre and the petals his followers. The rose is also representative of the soul at peace.

Fig. 178. Rosa rugosa *'Blanc Double de Coubert' (see p. 157ff).*

Fig. 179. Tulipa *'West Point', lily-flowered and 'goblet'-shaped (see pp. 154–5).*

The Tulip

The tulip is probably the flower most associated with the Islamic garden after the rose – no self-respecting Islamic-inspired garden could possibly be without one. The Ottoman Turks especially adored and revered the tulip, and under Suleyman the Magnificent it became the most beloved flower for them, taking on a mystical aura, even overtaking the rose in popularity. The tulip's mystical associations arose partly from its Turkish name *lale*, derived from the Persian *lal* meaning 'red', and known across the Middle Eastern world by this name or close variations. *Lale* consists of the same letters as *Allah* and also *hilal*, the Arabic word for 'crescent', the symbol of Islam. There is also a Persian legend in which the hero, Ferhad, loved the young maiden, Shirin, but she spurned his love so he went into the desert to weep and die – his tears turning into flowers, tulips, *lale*, wherever they dropped. However, more prosaically, the English word 'tulip' is said to derive from *tulbend*, the Turkish word for turban, since the shape of the flower was supposed to be similar to that of a turban.[360] Also, the flower's graceful shape meant that it sometimes represented a lamp or goblet. A visit to Istanbul's Topkapi Palace, Blue Mosque or the Mosque of Sokullu Mehmet Pasha (Figs. 174–5) with their wealth of spectacular and colourful tiles depicting tulips as well as other flora, is testimony to the Ottomans' passion. The dominant colour in both Persian and Ottoman tiles is the celestial colour – blue of every shade. However, sometime during the sixteenth century the highly skilled Turkish craftsmen of Iznik discovered their incomparable rich red glaze, and some say it was inspired by the scarlet of the wild tulip (possibly *Tulipa sprengii*, see below). The Austrian ambassador, de Busbecq, arrived in Istanbul in the mid-sixteenth century and was astonished at the number of flowers there, commenting, 'Turks have such a love of flowers that they have banned marching soldiers walking on them'. It was de Busbecq who first introduced the tulip into Europe, eventually instigating the great tulip craze of the late-seventeenth and early eighteenth centuries.[361] Since this time, tulips have thrived in northern Europe and now, ironically, Dutch hybrids and cultivars are more popular in Turkey than the beautiful species tulips, many of which originate in Turkey and the surrounding regions such as Kazakstan, Turkestan, Iran and Afghanistan.

Other Flowers

The violet is usually seen to represent humility because of its sweet nodding head bent down as if in prostration before the Lord; and the poppy is often seen as a symbol of everlasting life because of its ability to stay dormant underground for years and then spring to life when the earth is turned over (most obviously represented for us in the West by the Remembrance Day ceremony, of which the poppy is the symbol). The narcissus was seen to be languid, and the cypress, as well as representing eternity, was sometimes likened to the tall, elegant stature of the beloved; and clover, to some poets, symbolized mercy: 'The clover has come as a veil of mercy/To cover evenly the laws of the earth'.[362] The hibiscus, which blooms throughout the year in warmer climates, was sometimes compared favourably by poets to the rose, which was accused of being 'faithless', while the hibiscus symbolized constancy.

From this brief glance at the symbolism of flowers, it can be gathered that there is plenty of scope for the individual imagination of the poets, as well as the more generally acknowledged meaning. Other flowers in Islam have a particular symbolism which there is not space to expand upon here; the principal meaning to most poets and mystics was the idea that every flower is praising God and is a reflection of its perfect archetype in the eternal heavenly gardens:

> Every tree, and every shrub stand ready to bend before Him;
> Every herb and blade of grass are a tongue to utter His praise.

> Rahman Baba, eighteenth century Afghan poet[363]

How to Plant in Your Islamic Garden

Before embarking upon the recommendations for plants to grow in your northern Islamic garden, it is worth pointing out certain aspects relating to planting 'style'. When you mention 'Islamic garden' to most people, they first observe that water is the most important element and, second, that the gardens are formal – and, as we have seen, both observations are true. However, the formality is in the geometric plan and need not be extended to the actual planting. If this were the case, then your Islamic garden might end up looking over-ordered, regimented and reminiscent of municipal-style 'carpet-bedding'. This style looks marvellous and colourful in the right place, brightening up large, formal public gardens and squares, but this is not the style of the traditional Islamic garden. Constance Villiers Stuart makes this clear in her book on Mughal gardens:

> The Mughal parterres must not be confused with the English 'carpet bedding' of mid-Victorian days – tiny coloured leaves and flowers worked into a tedious pattern along some border or bank – but were boldly massed flowers of varying heights and beautifully chosen colours, like the lily beds of the Taj dados, the red rose garden of Jahangir's Memoirs, the narcissus, anemone and tulip plots that so delighted Babur.[364]

So, although the traditional Islamic garden was ordered in its layout, and to some extent its planting was compartmentalized, the flowering plants, as far as can be gathered from our sources, were not rigidly divided up. However, travellers' memoirs vary in their observations: an Austrian visitor to the palace gardens at Uskudar in Istanbul in the seventeenth century wrote: 'The garden was a paradise of orderly beds of sweet-smelling herbs and flowers and all kinds of trees',[365] while another seventeenth-century visitor to what appears to be the same garden, wrote: 'There was a splendid pavilion only used by the sultan during the summer. Water flowing from a fountain in the centre of this kept it cool on hot days… The garden was not divided into formal plots. There were no flower-beds and mainly vegetables were grown here. There were only cypress and pine trees and these can be seen all around the city where the courtyard of every house is shaded by these trees.'[366] According to the author who included these excerpts in her book, Ottoman gardens were different from gardens in the rest of the Islamic world: they did not adhere to any particular formal ground-plan and were far more 'natural' in their planting schemes, 'they sought to preserve the look of a setting that might have developed naturally'.[367] This author has done some fascinating research and it certainly seems from her book that Ottoman gardens developed along rather different lines from the classic *chahar-bagh* of Persia, the Indian sub-continent, the Near East, North Africa and Islamic Spain, that we have focused on here.

However, here we are keeping to the geometric order of the classic *chahar-bagh* and its variations, and within this you may plant an abundance of informal foliage and colour – a fine balance, as it were, between formality and Ottoman naturalism. This gives one far more of a free rein with the planting, as indicated by Villiers Stuart, than may have been imagined: the important point is to maintain this balance between the formal and informal, restraint and freedom. The plants should not be placed in gentle drifts in the style of Gertrude Jekyll and the typical English country-house raised herbaceous border, but more in the 'carpet-garden' or 'garden-carpet' style, with a scattered rhythm arising from careful 'dotted' placing of colour, size and texture – perennials, biennials and annuals mixed together, with evergreen shrubs or trees (e.g. myrtle, cypress, box or yew) marking the angle of the design. This has a certain similarity to the

Fig. 180. Border of the Carpet Garden, Chelsea 2001, showing 'dotted' effect of planting.

Fig. 181. Garden in the south-east of England showing balanced 'dotted' effect of the three primary colours in Crocosmia *'Lucifer' (red),* Delphinium *(blue) and* Hemerocallis *(yellow).*

cottage-garden style of planting that England is famous for. The cottage-garden style is a bit more unkempt perhaps and pays not too much regard to height, texture and colour, and is not generally contained in a disciplined overall design with borders strongly marked. However, the actual concept of mixed planting of many flowers together in the same area but not necessarily in the same bed, resulting in an overall colourful floral carpet effect, is not entirely dissimilar (Figs. 180–1). In the Victorian cottage garden the familiar and best loved flowers were grown, flowers which the Muslim artists would have known and approved of; 'all the sweet old-fashioned cottage garden flowers, pinks and sweet Williams and love-in-the-mist, wallflowers and forget-me-nots in spring and holly-hocks and Michaelmas daisies in autumn. Then there was lavender and southern-wood, sometimes called 'lad's love'… and every garden had its rose-bush'.[368] Herbs were also grown, the same as those grown in the Islamic garden (see below) – all the well-known ones such as rosemary, thyme, parsley, sage, peppermint, chamomile, lemon balm and rue. Generally, the women looked after the herbs and flowers, while the men tended the vegetables.

When planting or sowing seed yourself, it is good to mix brightly coloured flowers with green and grey foliage if you can (e.g. species of *Artemesia* and *Euphorbia* – see below), otherwise the colours will be too strong and vie with each other for your attention. Good background hedging or walls are a superb foil for bright or strong colours. This is a well-known, universal principle of good garden design, not particular to Islamic gardens.

In the smaller urban garden, pots and containers can be put to great use and moved around according to the position of the sun and according to the time of year the plants are flowering (see Pots and Containers in Chapter 3). Even in these smaller gardens, your borders between shrubs may be planted in 'carpet-garden' fashion (see Chapter 7). If you have a larger garden, then again avoid the usual English raised-bed herbaceous border and 'drift' planting and, if possible, lower the beds and plant with a wide mixture of perennials and annuals with carefully chosen colours to give the effect of a carpet.[369]

Selecting Plants for Your Islamic Garden

Generally speaking, it is safe to say that you should aim to grow the species plants of the genera included in the early plant lists, rather than the later hybrids.

However, as observed with suggestions for shrubs and trees in the previous chapter, this is by no means a strict rule but more of a guideline to avoid the more garish hybrids, which have no place in the subtle beauty of a contemplative Islamic garden. On this craze for developing ever more 'perfect' flowers, Lord Northbourne wrote as far back as 1970, 'the general tendency is all towards the substitution of ostentation for elegance, crudity for subtlety, blatancy for beauty, quantity for quality. People do not seem to want to look at a flower, they want to be hit in the eye by it'.[370] This tendency is very much the opposite of the traditional Islamic garden, which should not 'hit you in the eye' but rather come upon you gradually, quietly and calmly; the trees and shrubs, the flowers and fruit, and above all the water, all contributing to a serene atmosphere where nothing is too loud or too gaudy.

It is usually very clear in good plant dictionaries and catalogues, which are the species plants and where they come from. Below, in the many flowering plants that are mentioned, as well as herbs and climbers, I have mostly indicated which species originate in the Islamic world and are therefore most likely to have been the ones grown in the early gardens.[371] In some instances I have selected a few favourite cultivars, which fit the growing conditions and, for one reason or another, are not out of place in an Islamic garden. In fact, the species plants are sometimes difficult to source as the breeding of popular garden hybrids is more commercially rewarding (e.g. hyacinths, see below). In this case one needs to do a little more research and track down the species in *The Plant Finder*,[372] since it is most likely that your local nursery will not stock them. In the case of roses, lilies and tulips I have included a little more information as these are three of the genera that are so important in an Islamic garden and from which most people will probably wish to select several species.

This chapter and the previous one are primarily concerned with communicating to the reader a selection of plants that are both typical of the earlier eastern and Mediterranean Islamic gardens, as well as suitable ones to grow in more northern conditions. The selection is by no means exhaustive, since this would mean including a list of encyclopaedic length, as so many flowering plants focused on here (not to mention vegetables, shrubs and trees) are native to the Islamic world. Also, we are not overly

*Fig. 182. Herb garden,
Helmingham Hall, Suffolk.*

concerned with selecting historically accurate species that were grown in the Middle Ages in Syria or North Africa or Moorish Spain, since the aim is not to reconstruct an archaeologically precise medieval Islamic garden. However, it is hoped that your Islamic garden of the north will capture something of the atmosphere of the earlier Islamic gardens, and conjure up images of the archetypal heavenly gardens.

Herbs

Scented flowers and aromatic herbs are especially high on the list of essential plants to grow in your Islamic garden. Not only, as mentioned earlier, is *al-raihan* mentioned in the Quran in *Surat-ar-Rahman*,[373] variously translated as 'sweet-smelling plants', 'fragrant herbs' or 'scented herbs', but also there is a Saying of the Prophet in which he states that: 'Perfume and women have been made dear to me, and coolness hath been brought to my eyes in prayer.'[374] This really puts perfume on a very exalted level; as mentioned in Chapters 1 and 4, even the fountains in the paradise gardens are scented. Also, incense, as it is relatively easy to obtain, is commonly used in Islamic households, whereas in the western world it is generally still seen as a bit exotic and out of the ordinary.[375]

In the traditional Islamic garden, as in medieval herb gardens in northern Europe, herbs were grown not only for their sweet smells and their contribution to the overall beauty of the garden but also, and more importantly, for culinary and medicinal purposes. Many good books have been written on herbs and herb gardens, the medieval knot garden and the monastic physic garden,[376] describing the properties of the different herbs and how they were grown in separate areas in geometric 'knot' patterns, usually separated by low box hedges. From miniature

paintings, early plant treatises and garden-carpets (see Chapter 7), it seems likely that in Islamic gardens the herbs may also have been grown in separate plots, but more research into early Arabic, Persian and Turkish manuscripts needs to be carried out.[377] Indeed, in your own garden, which may not be large enough to have a separate herb area, it can be just as attractive, or more so, to grow herbs in the border amongst the other flowering plants and shrubs.

For our purposes here, the main observation to be made is that, on the whole, the herbs grown in Islamic gardens are mostly the same herbs as those that have been growing in the United Kingdom and elsewhere in northern Europe since Roman times. This means that you may grow with relative ease all our well-known and best-loved herbs (see below) in the safe knowledge that they would also have been present in an Islamic garden. Visiting Buckland Abbey recently in the south-west of England, with its majestic high stone walls and yew hedges, its herb garden was one of the most delightful I have ever seen. Clinging precipitously as it was to the walls of the great cathedral-like barn, each herb planted in compartments separated by box, it somehow appeared very natural and, unlike many herb gardens, happy in its place. In this area of the abbey grounds

*Fig. 183. Rosemary (*Rosmarinus officinalis *'Tuscan Blue').*

the atmosphere was exceptionally peaceful and, despite there being no water present, was strongly reminiscent of the contemplative atmosphere of an Islamic garden.

Sweet Basil

Al-Raihan, the 'sweet-smelling plant' in the Quran, is usually agreed to be sweet basil (*Ocimum basilicum*, from the Greek meaning 'aromatic' or 'royal'). Its powerful fresh-smelling leaves are used a great deal in cooking, as well as for keeping flies away from the kitchen. Sweet basil is grown wild in Arabia and India, and also Persia, where it is known as the 'king of herbs'. In northern climates basil is usually grown as an annual and kept in a pot on a south- or west-facing window-sill, but may be planted outside in your Islamic garden, providing you have a sunny, well-drained area. As well as being highly fragrant and good to eat, sweet basil serves a variety of medicinal purposes; the essential oil is considered to be stimulating and a diuretic.[378]

Lavender, Rosemary and Geranium

There is a legend that the Virgin Mary (known as *Sayyidatna* Maryam in Islam, to whom a whole chapter is devoted in the Quran) spread the baby Jesus' (known as *Sayyidna* Isa in Islam) clothes out to dry on an insignificant grey shrub. After she had picked them up the shrub was left with heads of tiny blue flowers, which had the most beautiful fragrance. The plant was lavender, *Lavandula*, from the Latin *lavare*, 'to wash'. There is a similar story relating to rosemary (*Rosmarinus officianalis*), the flowers of which turned blue after the Virgin Mary hung her clothes out to dry on it. For your own garden it is probably best to choose from the species' of lavender that grow wild in Italy and the Mediterranean region and which have been cultivated in England since the Middle Ages – such as *L. angustifolia* (syn. *L. spica* and *L. officinalis*) or the slightly later arrival, *L. dentata*. One of the most popular cultivars today is the darker flowered *Lavandula angustifolia* 'Hidcote', which has rather brittle stems, or *L. dentata* 'Munstead' or 'Blue Mountain', both of which have softer, lighter grey foliage, lavender-blue flowers and a strong scent.[379]

'Rosemary is for Remembrance,' Perdita says in Shakespeare's *A Winter's Tale*, and it was Sir Thomas More's favourite herb: 'As for rosemary', he wrote, 'I let it run all over my garden walls, not only because my bees love it but because it is the herb sacred to love and remembrance, and therefore to friendship'.[380] Although not specifically mentioned in the early Islamic plant lists we are mainly referring to, this surely is an essential herb in your Islamic garden; it is native to the Mediterranean region, bears blue flowers in varying shades and is sweet-smelling, so important a quality for plants in an Islamic garden. Although there are only three species of rosemary, the most well-known being *Rosmarinus officinalis*, there are many cultivars available today with more intensely blue flowers such as *R. officianalis* 'Severn Seas', and *R. officianalis* 'Tuscan Blue'. Rosemary has many culinary and medicinal uses and makes a delicious and invigorating 'pick-me-up' tea.

There is another legend in Islam concerning the Prophet Muhammad and the geranium. It is said that he was walking one very hot day, and to obtain relief he took off his robe and rinsed it in a nearby pool around which grew a quantity of marsh mallows (probably *Althaea* or *Alcea officinalis*, a relative of the hollyhock, *Alcea rosea*; *altheai* is a Greek derivative meaning a cure and the pigment found in the flowers and the essential oil both have healing properties). He placed his robe on the branches of a nearby tree to dry, and water from it dripped onto one of the mallows beneath. It immediately turned into a beautiful red geranium, while the other mallows remained the same.[381]

Other Herbs

The following herbs (genera) are all included in the medieval lists of Ibn Bassal and Ibn al-'Awwam[382] and all of them have been tried and tested in northern climes for centuries. So, providing you save the warmest and, essentially, well-drained, area of your garden for your herbs, you have a wide variety to choose from: Sage, *Salvia officinalis* and *S. o.* 'Purpurescens' are two of the most commonly grown in the United Kingdom and perform a range of good deeds including use as an antiseptic as well as helping to arrest ageing;[383] Coriander, *Coriandrum sativum*, is used for the digestive system; Sweet marjoram, *Origanum majorana*, may be used to relieve headaches; Mint, *Mentha* spp., such as the most common and easy to grow garden mint, *M. spicata*, peppermint, *M. x piperita*, and helps soothe the stomach, and Moroccan mint, *M. spicata* var. *crispa* 'Moroccan', probably makes the best tea; Lemon balm, *Melissa officinalis*, may relieve tension; Thyme, *Thymus vulgaris*, may be used as a cough remedy – a pretty silver-grey leafed cultivar is *T.* 'Silver Queen'; Fennel, *Foeniculum vulgare*, may be used as a remedy for indigestion; and Southernwood, *Artemesia abrotanum*, or wormwood, *Artemesia absinthum*, may be used to stimulate digestion, and it is said that a dried branch placed among your clothes will help deter moths.

Then there is garlic, *Allium sativum*, which may be used as an effective anti-bacterial and anti-viral agent. The orange filaments of saffron are from the saffron crocus, *Crocus sativus*, and is said to make people cheerful.[384] Chamomile, *Chamaemelum nobilis*, is well-known for its soothing qualities. Mandrake, *Mandragora officinarum*, folklore tells us that if pulled

*Fig. 184. Lavender (*Lavandula stoechas*).*

up by the root, the mandrake lets out such a terrible scream that the perpetrator is driven to suicide. Marsh mallow, *Althaea officinalis*, has effective soothing properties used for digestive and other problems. Mallow, *Malva sylvestris*, may be used in similar ways to marsh mallow but not to such effect. Dill, *Anethum graveolens*, is a remedy for flatulence. Parsley, *Petrolselinum crispum*, is a rich source of Vitamin C. Elecampane, *Inula helenium*, can soothe and protect internal tissue. Rue, *Ruta graveolens*, whose name *Ruta* comes from the Greek word '*reuo*' meaning to 'set free'; it acquired this name in ancient times because of its reputation of being able to set one free from disease. However, it should be handled with care as it can easily be an irritant to the skin. There is also the well-known pot marigold, *Calendula officinalis*, a favourite annual in English gardens since its introduction from southern Europe in the Middle Ages or earlier. 'Love-in-the-mist', the hardy annual *Nigella damascena*, thought, as may be guessed, to come from Damascus; or *N. hispanica*, with slightly larger, deeper blue flowers, not known so much as a herb in the United Kingdom but in the Near and Middle East the black seeds are precious and sometimes made into an oil. It is known in Arabic as *Mahabatalbarakah*, and is said to help cure everything, *barakah*, meaning 'blessing' or 'grace' from God.[385]

Notes on Climate and Aspect

In most of the countries of the Islamic world that we are looking at, plants, as noted earlier, almost all have a longer flowering period than in Northern Europe, some going to sleep in the heat of the summer and coming to life again in the autumn and flowering through until December. In some of these countries roses, jasmine and spring flowers, such as narcissi and violets, may well bloom at similar times – roses and narcissi are sometimes depicted as flowering together in Islamic miniature paintings, as well as being linked together in poetry. On the whole this is not possible in northern climates, unless the roses are forced or the narcissi held back, a well-known and trying occupation for flower-show exhibitors.[386]

The spring flowers mentioned as being essential in an Islamic garden may, on the whole, be grown in semi-shade. However, most of the summer flowers need as much sunshine as possible in our temperate climate. There is no doubt that a south-facing or south-west facing garden with good drainage is the optimum position for your Islamic garden of the northern hemisphere. Then it means that you can grow, without too much anxiety for their hardiness, the sun-loving plants associated with Islamic gardens

Fig. 185. Tulipa 'White Triumphator' (see pp. 154–5).

of the Mediterranean and further east: plants such as the grey-leaved *artemesias* (referred to usually in the plant lists with the old-fashioned name of 'wormwood' or 'southernwood'), lavenders, rosemary, sage and jasmine – to name a few of the most popular. Indeed, all of these are widely grown already in northern Europe and thrive providing they are carefully sited.

So, apart from the herbs above, what are the other flowers and plants that you should grow in your Islamic garden of the north? Keeping in mind the flowers already noted as being the most popular in Islamic art and poetry, it will be observed that it is an easier task to choose the flowers and herbs for your garden than the trees and shrubs, since so many of them are the same. Therefore, one does not need to be unduly concerned whether, first, they will survive the different climate and, second, whether they will look as though they have 'an air of belonging'. To both questions the answer, by and large, is 'yes'. Even if you are creating your garden in a cooler climate with a generous amount of rain, there is still plenty of potential for achieving the look and ambience that we are aiming for. Providing the geometric layout is correct, there is some form of water and dappled shade, then you have a reasonably free hand for the rest of the planting.

Spring Flowers

Tulips

There is no doubt that, apart from the rose, the quintessential flowers of an Islamic garden, cited over and over again in poetry and historical descriptions, are what we would call spring flowers, many of which are grown from bulbs, corms, tubers or rhizomes. First of all, there is the tulip, the Turks' favourite flower, of which there are about one hundred species and thousands of cultivars. As there is so much choice amongst the species, and so many originate in Islamic lands, then it is not difficult to choose several of these for your garden; for example, *Tulipa greigii* from Turkestan, *T. sprengeri* from Turkey and *T. praestens* from Central Asia, and possibly cultivars of these, which do not depart much from their wild parents.

For example, for lightness of touch and a splash of colour in your northern Islamic garden, I would go for the small and delicate *Tulipa praestens* 'Fusilier' (Fig. 170) whose flowers are a marvellous deep red with pointed petals and look quite lovely appearing through fresh green leaves in early spring, and what's more appear year after year with no fuss. They could be planted in grass under fruit trees enjoying the dappled shade. Then there are the taller, more 'sophisticated' cultivars such as the lovely white *T. p.* 'White Triumphator' (Fig. 185) or clear yellow *T. p.* 'West Point' (Fig. 179). These are not tulips for naturalising in grass, more for the formal container or flower-bed. Two other pretty species tulips which would look beautiful grown in the rough grass, are the rose-pink and white *T. clusiana* (from Iran, Iraq and Afghanistan) and *T. turkestanica* from Turkestan and NW China, which has a multi-branched stem and may flower as early as February.

Daffodils and Jonquils

Daffodils (*Narcissi*) were another favourite flower in traditional Islamic gardens. There are estimates ranging from fifty to seventy species of *Narcissi* (and thousands of cultivars), mainly native to southern Europe and north Africa, although the Lent lily (*Narcissus pseudonarcissus*) is the wild daffodil of western Europe and the United Kingdom. This is a lovely, small, pale yellow daffodil, far more beautiful in my view than all the larger or double-flowered cultivars, and should be grown if possible in your Islamic garden as it is similar to the wild daffodils of the Mediterranean region (e.g. *N. tazetta*). As with the tulips, as far as possible you should aim for the understated species rather than the overblown hybrids. Others to be recommended to grow either in your orchard area (if you are fortunate enough to have one),[387] under the fruit trees or in the flower borders, are: *N. tazetta*, from the Mediterranean region; *N. triandrus* (the species is not known in cultivation, so *N. triandrus* 'Angels' Tears' is a good substitute) native to Portugal, Spain, Lebanon and Iran; *N. humilis*, found growing wild in Spain, Algeria and Morocco; *N. poeticus* is a pretty, highly scented, white-petalled form native to the Mediterranean region; *N. atlanticus*, from the Atlas mountains in Morocco; and the jonquil, *N. jonquilla*, native to Spain

and Portugal. The easily available cultivars of *N. cyclamineus*, such as *N. cyclamineus* 'Tete-a-Tete' or 'Peeping Tom' or 'February Gold', could also be grown as they are small, delicate daffodils, scented, and similar to the wild species *narcissi* that grow all over the Iberian peninsular.[388]

Crocus and Colchicums

Other favourite spring bulbs are the crocus and colchicum. There are over eighty species of *Crocus*, mainly native to the Mediterranean region, north Africa and parts of Asia. They include the saffron crocus, *Crocus sativus*, as well as *C. speciosus*, both of which grow wild in Turkey and the Caucasus, as well as *C. tommasinianus* from eastern Europe and *C. aleppicus* from the Near East. Any of these could be grown in your Islamic garden to brighten up the autumn and spring. There seem to be estimates varying from sixty-five to eighty species of *Colchicum*, many of which come from Colchis, a mountainous area near the Black Sea in Georgia, as well as being native to Europe. *Colchicum speciosum* comes from Turkey and the Caucasus, *C. luteum* comes from Central Asia, northern India and Afghanistan and *C. autumnale* is native to Europe and the United Kingdom. *Colchicum speciosum* 'Album' is one of the best known, prettiest and easiest to grow colchicums and should be planted under deciduous trees rather than in borders. *Colchicum byzantinum* is also good for planting in dry soil under trees.

Hyacinths and Grape Hyacinths

Fortunately, there are only a few species of hyacinths in cultivation (although many cultivars, especially of *Hyacinthus orientalis*), so one does not have quite so much agonizing about which to choose. There is *Hyacinthus transcaspicus* from Turkmenistan and north-east Iran, *H. litwinowii*, from Turkey, northern Iran and parts of Asia, and the common hyacinth, *H. orientalis*, which is native to the Near East and Southern Turkey. Unfortunately, the species *H. orientalis* is hardly grown today and, although there are many cultivars available, they bear little resemblance to the original wild species. For your Islamic garden, if you have a small orchard area, it would be more in keeping to plant our native

*Fig. 186. Bluebell (*Hyacinthoides non-scripta*).*

hyacinth, the bluebell (*Hyacinthoides non-scripta*), rather than the *H. orientalis* cultivars, which would look too large and out of place in an area of more delicate bulbs. Alternatively, or in addition, you could plant the grape hyacinth, e.g. *Muscari armeniacum* ('Blue Spike' is a recommended cultivar) or *M. azureum*, both of which are native to the Caucasus and eastern Turkey. An assortment of spring bulbs would look beautiful and be very much in the spirit of the Islamic garden; however, with bluebells and grape hyacinths you have to be careful as they do multiply.

Irises

The iris (Fig. 171 and 187) is another favourite bulb, often represented in Islamic miniature paintings, and in Christianity is associated with the Trinity as well as the *fleur-de-lys*. There are over three hundred *Iris* species (and thousands of cultivars) to choose from, all native to the northern hemisphere. Out of this vast choice, those I would choose to grow in my Islamic garden of the north are: first of all, the lovely deep blue *I. reticulata*, native to the Caucasus, Turkey, northern Iraq and Iran; then *I. histrioides*, native to Turkey; *I. unguicularis*, the beautiful, sweetly-scented pale to rich lavender-blue Algerian iris; the common iris, *I. germanica* (said to be the *fleur-de-lys*), which comes from the Mediterranean region, although its wild origin is uncertain; *I. damascena*, from Syria, the flower of which is white spotted with purple; our

Fig. 187. Iris sibirica, *a beautiful substitute if the species listed below are not available.*

native flag iris, *I. pseudacorus*; and, finally, *I. kashmiriana*, from Kashmir and Afghanistan, which Constance Villiers Stuart thought the most beautiful. After walking in the hills of Kashmir and admiring the many flowers growing wild there, she wrote: 'Each flower as we passed it I thought the loveliest of all, but the craftsman who crowned the crescent of the Taj with an Iris knew best, for the memory of the other lilies fades before the blue Kashmir iris.'[389]

Cyclamen

The cyclamen is also known as the 'Persian violet', and estimates of the number of species of this exquisite flower vary from fifteen to thirty. These are mainly native to the Mediterranean lands and further east, and have been grown in Islamic gardens since the Middle

Ages or earlier. The most well-known, easily available and not hard to grow are, first, the delicate *Cyclamen coum* from the Near East, Turkey and the Caucasus; second, *C. hederifolium*, native to southern Europe; and third, the beautiful *C. persicum*, from the east Mediterranean regions. The large-flowered and less hardy hybrids, widely grown as pot plants, should be avoided. When seen next to their delicate wild ancestors they seem rather overblown and vulgar. Less well-known species and slightly less hardy are *C. africanum* from north Africa and *C. cilicilum* from Turkey.

Anemone

The name 'anemone', also known as 'lily-of-the-field' and 'wind-flower', comes from the Greek *anemos* meaning 'wind'. Estimates of the number of species range – amazingly – from twelve to one hundred and fifty and most are native to both northern and southern Europe, as well as further east to Turkey and Turkestan. The species to choose from are: the well-known *Anemone nemorosa*, the wood anemone, native to the United Kingdom and Europe; *A. blanda*, native to south-east Europe and further East towards Turkestan; or *A. coronaria* ('poppy anemone'), thought by some to be the 'lilies-of-the-field' of the sermon on the mount, since they grow wild in the east Mediterranean region.

Ranunculus and Violets

The *Ranunculus* is also mentioned in the early Muslim plant lists and this is a genus of a large number of species, estimates varying from two hundred and fifty to four hundred. You could perhaps grow *R. asiaticus*, from Turkey, Asia Minor and North Africa or *R. rupestris*, from Morocco. The violet (*Viola*) was another spring flower much planted in Islamic gardens and referred to many times in poetry. Once again, there are many species but my preference would be to grow *Viola odorata* (sweet violet), native to Europe including the United Kingdom as well as Asia and North Africa; *V. cornuta*, from the Pyrenees or the pretty heartsease, *V. tricolor*. There are also many hybrids of the cultivated species, the pansy, *Viola x wittrockiana*. Happily, the lovely wild *V. odorata* seems to be making a comeback in one of its native homes, Devon and Cornwall (south-west England).

Summer Flowers (Perennials, Biennials and Annuals)

The most important summer flowers in an Islamic garden are the rose and the lily, the same two flowers that were so important for Christians, both being associated with the Virgin Mary. According to the Persians, roses are the 'messengers of the garden of souls' – perhaps because their beauty is of such an ethereal quality that they seem to have dropped straight from the heavenly garden.

Roses

When deciding on a rose or roses for your own Islamic garden there is an *embarras de richesses*. To limit the vast choice and to pick those most suited to an Islamic garden in northern Europe – or elsewhere with a similar climate – it is best to go for the 'old roses' as far as possible. This still leaves one with a great choice, but a more manageable one. To narrow it down further, we can concentrate on the earlier cultivars of the two spieces *R. damascena* and *R. gallica*, both of which are believed to originate in the Near East, and have been cultivated in Europe since the Middle Ages. Not only were varieties of these

Fig. 188. Rosa Ispahan, Carpet Garden Highgrove.

roses grown in the earlier Islamic gardens, but also their flowers are, generally-speaking, more subtly beautiful and with a stronger scent than many rather artificial-looking hybrids bred today. However, this is not to say that there are not some wonderful modern roses (i.e. those bred in the last seventy years or so); for instance, those cultivated in old rose style, such as David Austen's 'English Roses'. For greater reliability, a longer-flowering period and resistance to disease, you could choose one or two from this group, in particular the lovely shrub rose with scented pink flowers, R. 'Sharifa Asma', its name indicating its appropriateness for an Islamic garden.[390] However, to be more true to the roses of the earlier Islamic gardens, then I would recommend almost any of the early Damask roses.

Damask roses are an ancient group originating, if not precisely in Damascus, then at least not far away in southern Turkey and Asia Minor. It seems that their origin cannot be clearly traced, but the frequent use of the term 'Damask roses' in Elizabethan times indicates that at this period they were thought to have come from Damascus, and were most probably introduced into Europe by the crusaders or early travellers. The gardens of Damascus have impressed travellers for centuries, from Al-Maqdisi's tenth-century paeons of praise to Alexander Kinglake's nineteenth-century observations on how damask roses grew in Damascus 'to a great profusion' and 'load the slow air with their damask breath. There are no other flowers'.[391] They are thought to be hybrids between *Rosa gallica*, grown by the Romans, and *Rosa phoenicia*, the white-flowered, wild musk rose of southern Turkey. Vita Sackville-West is rather disparaging of an article she read saying that it must be 'pure poetry', nevertheless quoting it: 'In the twelfth century the dark red Gallic rose was cultivated by the Arabs in Spain with the tradition that it was brought from Persia in the seventh century.'[392] In fact this 'pure poetry' is probably true.

Varieties of *R. damascena*, in particular *R. x damascena* 'Trigintipetala', are grown in Turkey, Morocco and elsewhere for their essential oil, which can be extracted and distilled to make attar of roses (now called 'Rose Otto' by some western cosmetic companies). This ancient damask rose has pink, loose double flowers and a wonderful scent. Not only are other cultivars of the damask rose very beautiful and

originate in the Islamic world, but also they have a long history of flourishing in the United Kingdom. So it would be very possible, should you wish, to plant only damask roses in your garden; although they do not repeat flower on the whole, their usually pale blossoms are highly fragrant and will conjure up images of peaceful, rose-filled Damascus courtyards, the only sounds being trickling water and the song of birds. The exception to the once-flowering rule among old roses is the ancient R. 'Quatre Saisons' (listed sometimes as *Rosa x damascena* var. *semperflorens*) also known as the 'Autumn Damask', since it flowers in both early summer and autumn.[393] Another ancient damask rose is R. 'St. John's Rose', also known as *Rosa sancta* or *R. x richardii*, 'The Holy Rose', which, although not strongly scented, would be worth growing for its association with St John. I understand this to be St John the Baptist (*Sayyidna Yah-Yah* in Arabic) revered in both Christianity and Islam, whose head is believed to be buried in the great Ummayyad Mosque in Damascus. His shrine in this mosque is a place of pilgrimage for both Christians and Muslims and is a very peaceful area of the mosque in which to sit.

Of the other, later, cultivars of the damask rose, which would make beautiful and evocative summer-flowering shrubs in your Islamic garden, a few favourites are: R. 'Ispahan' (spelt like this rather than 'Isphahan' like the Persian city), a shrub rose with double, scented, deep pink flowers, which has the added bonus of being shade tolerant; its name indicates its eminent suitability, although its association with the town of Isphahan seems to have been lost in the mists of time; R. 'Celsiana', another shrub rose with pink flowers fading to white; and R. 'Omar Khayyam', which has a good scent and is so-called as it was found growing on the poet's tomb in Nashaipur in north-east Iran.

Other 'old roses' to plant in your Islamic garden could include R. 'Rose de Resht', possibly an ancient cross between a damask and a china rose and suitable because of its source (after which it is named, Resht being a city in Persia). It was discovered by Nancy Lindsay who 'happened on it in an old Persian garden in ancient Resht, tribute of the tea caravans plodding Persia-wards from China over the Central Asian Steppes; it is a sturdy yard-high bush of glazed lizard-green, perpetually emblazoned with full camellia flowers of pigeon's blood ruby, irised with royal purple, haloed with dragon sepals like the painted blooms of Oriental faience'.[394] How could one omit a rose with such a description?

The Gallica roses are also marvellous old roses to grow in your garden and, despite their name, are thought to have originated in Syria, arriving in France in the thirteenth century. Three of my favourites for their marvellous deep ruby-red coloured flowers are *R*. 'Tuscany Superba' (Fig. 169), *R*. 'Cardinal de Richelieu' and the ancient 'Apothecary's Rose', *R. gallica* 'Officinalis'. This was used for healing purposes, as well as for rose-water, and is probably the rose being held by Mehmet the Conqueror in the famous miniature painting in the Topkapi Museum.

Lilies

Lilies, along with the rose, are essential in the summer Islamic garden – they always lend a certain aristocratic grace and elegance, rising majestically above most other perennials in the border, not to mention their intoxicating scent. Most of the approximately one hundred species originate in the Islamic lands of the eastern Mediterranean, Turkey and Asia Minor, so once again there is a wealth to choose from. The queen of them all, cultivated from ancient times, is the white Madonna lily (*Lilium candidum*), famous as the flower most associated with the purity of the Virgin Mary, and adopted as the principal flower of the Annunciation from the Middle Ages onwards. It was, and still is, also beloved by Muslims and is depicted in miniature paintings, as well as mentioned in the plant lists and poetry.

This is not the easiest lily to grow but should be tried, if possible, since no other lily quite equals its grace and purity. Other species that may well have been grown in the earlier Islamic gardens are the clear yellow Caucasion lily (*L. monadelphum*), which grows wild in the Caucasus and parts of Turkey. Like the scarlet Turk's cap lily (*L. chalcedonicum*) and the martagon lily (*L. martagon*), it has the so-called 'Turk's cap' flowers, meaning they have petals curling back on themselves ('recurving' as opposed to trumpet-shaped).[395] These two species are also found growing wild in the eastern Mediterranean region and grow well in northern and western Europe. Most of them are scented and providing they are planted in

Fig. 189. Lilium regale.

full sun or light shade in rich soil would be good specimens to plant in your Islamic garden.

However, although it may seem disloyal to the Islamic perspective, I have to put in a word for the superb and justifiably praised regale lily (*L. regale*) which hails from China rather than the Islamic world. Its beautiful white trumpet flowers with dark pink lines, growing atop long waving stems definitely add a bit of class to any garden and have a scent to die for; they make it an irresistible choice for pots around the central pool or fountain of your Islamic garden. Its sister, the pure white *L. regale* 'Album' with a golden centre is almost as wonderful. Although the Madonna lily is the first choice, it is sometimes a trial to grow and seems to fall prey to the vile lily-beetle sooner than the others. In contrast, the regale lily gives generously of itself year after year, and as Robin Lane Fox writes, 'its powerful scent lifts you beyond all worldly distractions on a cool, clear evening in July'. What more can one ask for?[396]

The wonderful day-lily (*Hemerocallis*) was probably also grown early on in Islamic gardens since its medicinal uses were described by the twelfth-century medical botanist, al-Ghafiqi. This would probably have been the Asian species, *H. fulva*, which has now naturalized in Europe, the other species mainly coming from China and Japan. Instead of attempting to navigate your way through the twenty thousand or more day-lily cultivars that are available today (from about fifteen species), I would recommend avoiding

*Fig. 190. Poppy (*Papaver rhoeas*).*

them all and aiming for the species only, *Hemerocallis fulva*, available in several specialist nurseries. Otherwise go for well-established cultivars of *H. fulva*, such as the deep yellow and long-flowering 'Golden Chimes' or the lemon yellow 'Nighthawk'.

Poppies

After the rose and the lily, one of the next favourite flowers in the Islamic garden was the poppy (*Papaver*) of which there are about one hundred species and many cultivars to choose from today. Although the brightly coloured Iceland poppies (*P. nudicaule*) and the lovely pastel-coloured Californian poppies (a different genus in fact, *Eschoscholzia californica*) are very tempting, the species that were most probably originally grown in the early Islamic gardens are: first of all, the opium poppy, *P. somniferum*, which is native to Greece, the Near East and parts of Asia, and is mentioned in the early Muslim treatises; second, there is the simple and beautiful corn poppy or field poppy, *P. rhoeas* (native to Europe and from which the 'Shirley' poppies were bred in England in the late-nineteenth century, and available from specialist nurseries); then there is *P. glaucum*, the tulip poppy from Syria (not listed in *The Plant Finder* and therefore not easily available); *P. pilosum* from Asia Minor; and the perennial oriental poppy, *P. orientale*, originally from Armenia, from which many cultivars have been bred such as the wonderful deep scarlet

'Beauty of Livermere' and the appropriately named *P. o.* 'Abu Hassan'. However, to my mind, there are few more beautiful sights than the swathes of field poppies that appear in many parts of England in early summer. With a little care these can be introduced into the garden and hopefully seed themselves everywhere (providing your soil is not too heavy), giving scarlet glory in May and early June as well as conjuring up visions of wild poppies in the East.

Carnations, Wallflowers, Delphiniums and Larkspur

Another beloved flower in the Islamic world – largely because of its marvellous scent no doubt – was the carnation or pink (*Dianthus*) of which there are approximately three hundred species and numerous cultivars. The species include: *Dianthus caryophyllus*, which grows wild in southern Europe; *D. barbatus* (Sweet William); *D. neglectus*, also from southern Europe; and *D. noeanus*, from east Europe and Turkey. If the species plants are hard to find, the so-called 'old-fashioned' cultivars such *D.* 'Mrs. Sinkins' could be a substitute. Indeed, Robin Lane-Fox says that he finds the 'wild forms far less interesting than the ones that gardeners have bred. In the wild, the pink of a pink's flower is sour or rosy, while there are some beastly deviations into lilac or mauve'.[397] Maybe so; selecting pinks for yourself it is probably best to go to a good nursery in the early summer when they are in bloom or perhaps aim for our native pink, *Dianthus caesius* (syn. *D. gratianopolitanus*, confusingly called 'Chedder Pink' and also found growing wild in Europe), heavily scented and good to grow under roses.

*Fig. 191. Carnation (*Dianthus*).*

*Fig. 192. Wallflower (*Erysimum cheiri, *syn.* Cheiranthus cheiri, *and tulip).*

The Islamic garden was usually home to wallflowers (*Cheiranthus*, *al-khairi* in Arabic) too, which is estimated to have approximately ten species, the most common being *C. cheiri*; and there is the dwarf form, *Erysimum cheiri*. Harvey comments that by the twelfth century in Spain, the wallflower and stock (*Matthiola incana*, see below) 'already had numerous cultivated varieties'.[398] Both wallflowers arrived in England with William the Conqueror in 1066, perhaps from Moorish Spain via France. They have been a popular garden plant in this country ever since, many cultivars now being available – for example, the marvellous deep crimson *Erysimum cheiri* 'Blood Red'.

Another popular flower in the Islamic garden was the stately, and equally popular today, delphinium, of which estimates range from two hundred and fifty to three hundred and fifty species, and numerous cultivars. The species include: *Delphinium elatum*, *D.*

cashmerianum (from Kashmir), *D. semibarbatum* (syn. *D. zatil*) from Afghanistan (all of these available from a few specialist nurseries only), and *D. grandiflorum*. *D. g.* 'Blue Butterfly' is a recommended cultivar as its single flowers are more delicate than many and are a good royal blue. Indeed, *D. elatum*, the species native to Europe and Asia, is not widely available and only the garden hybrids are easy to find, such as the so-called 'Galahad' group, the colours of which are not to be recommended, none being a 'true blue'. Other cultivars (of other species) such as *D.* 'Blue Jay', *D.* 'Bluebird' and the royal blue *D.* 'Molly Buchanon' are good blues for your garden. Aim for the truest blues you can find, rather than the mauvy-lilac or the purple ones. In fact, although delphiniums are found in other colours, such as red in the wild, I would always aim for a blue – there is something slightly shocking about a delphinium being any colour other than blue! The so-called 'Belladonna group' are highly recommended since, although they do not hail entirely from the East (they result from a cross between *D. elatum* and *D. grandiflorum*), they are more delicate than some of the outsize 'improved' hybrids. They do not flop over if left without support and carry on flowering all summer if dead-headed. Mary Keen recommends 'Volkerfrieden' and 'Atlantis' for good strong blues and the paler blue 'Clivedon Beauty'.[399] There is also the lovely larkspur, *Delphinium consolida*, the annual delphinium, which, like the Belladonna group, is probably more suitable

*Fig. 193. Delphinium (*Delphinium *'Blue Butterfly').*

*Fig. 194. Hollyhocks (*Alcea rosea *syn.* Althaea rosea*).*

for your Islamic garden than the more sumptuous delphinium hybrids.

Stocks, Hollyhocks and Lupins

Stocks (*Matthiola incana*) and the night-scented stock (*Matthiola bicornis*) were also favourite flowers in early Islamic gardens, both included on the medieval plant lists, native to Southern Europe. These are easy to grow annuals or biennials, and essential for their fragrance. The beloved flower of our cottage gardens, the biennial hollyhock or 'holy-hoc', also known as rose mallow (*Alcea rosea* or *Althaea rosea*), is another plant featured on the early lists and essential in your Islamic garden. The wild hollyhock grows in the Holy Land and was most probably introduced into Britain by returning crusaders. *Hoc* is the Anglo-Saxon word

for mallow and the original word 'holy-hoc' has become 'hollyhock', evidently suffering the same fate as the word 'holy-day', now 'holiday'. The species, *A. rosea*, is easily available (as well as many cultivars) in a range of colours including pink, cream and yellow.

The lupin (the species *Lupinus albus*) is also mentioned in the Hispano-Mauresque medieval plant lists and was probably introduced into Britain from the eastern Mediterranean in the fourteenth century. There are in fact about two hundred species of lupin, including a sweet-smelling one, 'Spanish violet' (*L. luteus*) from south-western Europe. However, once again many garden hybrids have now been bred and are more easily available than the species.

Cornflowers, Water-Lilies, Pond-Lilies and Sweet Rocket

Other summer flowers mentioned on the medieval lists are the wonderful deep blue cornflower, *Centaurea cyanus* – this species is native to the United Kingdom. Other species originating in Islamic lands are *C. dealbata*, from the Caucasus and Persia, *C. moschata* (also known as Sweet Sultan) from Turkey

*Fig. 195. Cornflower (*Centaurea cyanus*).*

and further east, and the tender *C. pulchra* from Kashmir. Water-lilies (*Nymphaea alba* is the best species to choose)[400] are also an important plant for an Islamic garden, which, besides needing several hours of sun every day to flourish, prefer still water to fountains and flowing channels. Also mentioned on the plant lists is *Nuphar lutea*, the yellow pond lily, the flowers of which are nowhere near as beautiful as the water-lily but the plant does have the advantage of growing in shade and not being so particular about moving water. Sweet Rocket, also called damask violet (*Hesperis matronalis*) comes from southern Europe and was also planted in Islamic gardens, for its pretty white or purple flowers which give off a delicious sweet scent in the evenings.

In northern Europe it is marvellous how colours, as well as white, really sing out and 'glow' against the green as dusk descends after a rainy day. It was a tradition in Mughal gardens to plant scented white flowers, which 'glowed in the dark', one of the most popular being jasmine (see Climbers). A welcome newcomer would be the heavenly-scented tobacco-plant, the annual or biennual white *Nicotiana alata*, which only starts to give its slightly spicy fragrance at sunset to attract the moths for pollination. The scent grows gradually more intense until it reaches its most powerful, the experts say, at three in the morning.

Fig. 196. *Water-lily* (Nymphaea alba).

Climbers

The two climbers that spring to mind first when thinking of Islamic gardens are probably jasmine (both *Jasminum polyanthemum* from China and *J. officinale*, the common hardy jasmine from Persia, India and China) and bougainvillea (*Bougainvillea spectabilis*). *Jasminum polyanthemum* is one of my most favourite plants as it produces such a generous abundance of very sweet-smelling star-shaped flowers

Fig. 197. *Tobacco plant* (Nicotiana alata).

Fig. 198. *Jasmine* (Jasminum officinale).

Fig. 199. Jasminum polyanthemum, *Alhambra gardens.*

against small dark green leaves, and continues all summer. However, in northern Europe this has to be on a south-facing (or perhaps west-facing) wall as it is frost-tender. The common jasmine is a poor producer of flowers by comparison but does have the great advantage of being hardy and tolerant of some shade, and its little white flowers still glow at night smelling delicious. Another climber that would suit an Islamic garden very well, although not on the medieval lists, is the wonderful jasmine-like evergreen from China with scented star-shaped white flowers in summer, *Trachelospermum jasminoides* or *T. asiaticum*, both of which are hardier than *J. polyanthum*, but still need a good sunny free-draining site.

Bougainvillea, *Bougainvillea spectabilis* (*Jahanamiyeh* in Arabic) or *B. glabra*, both of which originate in Brazil, although we usually associate them with Islamic, eastern and Mediterranean gardens, is not included on the medieval plant lists since it was not introduced until later. If you have a very sheltered, south-facing, well-drained site it might be worth trying this outside. Otherwise I am afraid only the lucky ones with conservatories may grow this spectacular climber in northern conditions. A conservatory, although marvellous for growing tender plants, is hardly a feature of an Islamic garden, since it increases heat in a cool country rather than the opposite – as was the role of the open-sided pavilions. However, there is no doubting the conservatory's practical use for over-wintering such sensitive souls as a bougainvillea. There are many cultivars of this lush and evocative plant and in an array of fantastic colours, mainly in scarlets, pinks and purples, such as 'San Diego Red', 'Pink Tiara', or the pure white 'Jamaica White'.

As mentioned previously, instead of the bougainvillea climbing up the evergreen cypress or yew, you could plant the marvellous-smelling old-fashioned sweet-peas, such as *Lathyrus odoratus* 'Cupani's Original' (cultivated by Father Cupani in a monastery in Palermo, Sicily, in 1699) *L. odoratus* 'Black Knight' or *L. odoratus* 'Painted Lady'.[401] Even if not growing up a columnar tree, sweet peas are a must in your Islamic garden, growing up trellis, entwined around a hazel 'teepee' or, even better, a whole tunnel of them. There are over one hundred

Fig. 200. Bougainvillea spectabilis.

*Fig. 201. Sweet peas (*Lathyrus odoratus *'Cupani's Original').*

ivy and bell-ivy (Harvey suggests it may be *Convolvulus* or *Calystegia sepium*) called 'Poor Man's Cord' by Ibn al-'Awwam: 'Both these may be moved to gardens, taking them up with their roots in February, and planted near the water-channels.'[402] So, although it may not immediately spring to mind as being a plant of an Islamic garden, you may grow ivy in your garden knowing that it flourished in medieval Hispano-Mauresque and North African gardens. However, rather than growing the common English ivy (*Hedera helix*), it would be preferable to choose one from the Islamic world, such as the half-hardy Algerian ivy (*Hedera algeriensis*, syn. *H. canariensis* var. *algeriensis*) or the fully hardy Persian ivy (*H. colchica*).

species, mainly native to southern Europe although *L. rotundifolius* is native to Asia Minor as well, its common name being 'Persian everlasting pea'.

Ivy (*Hedera* spp., *kissus* in Arabic) was introduced into cultivation, it seems, in twelfth-century Islamic Spain. Harvey quotes Ibn al-'Awwam's observations of

Fig. 202. One of many beautiful scalloped-edged fountain basins or 'lotus pools' to be found throughout the Alhambra and Generalife gardens.

The Sacred Lotus

The sacred lotus, *Nelumbo nucifera*, revered by Hindus and Buddhists in particular, possesses a many-layered symbolism. The most important and universal meaning of the lotus is that its unfolding on the surface of the waters represents burgeoning or nascent life. Although far more closely associated with the ancient Eastern religions, the lotus was, nevertheless, absorbed into the Islamic culture of the Indian sub-continent. Reflections of this merging of cultures are found as far away as the Alhambra and Generalife, where the beautiful scalloped-edge fountain basins found throughout the gardens are sometimes called 'lotus pools' or 'lotus fountains', reminiscent as they are of the unfolding lotus itself and of those on which the Buddha is often sculpted (Fig. 202). This is a good example of the blending of Islamic and Hindu cultures which thrived under Mughal rule for many centuries.

A tender perennial, the sacred lotus would not be possible to grow in northern Europe without some protection and, since it is more associated with Hinduism and Buddhism than Islam, it is probably best to direct your energies towards the water-lily rather than the lotus.

Euphorbia

Many species of *euphorbia* (Spurge) are grown in Mediterranean and hotter climates, as well as being very popular in northern Europe, since they provide good foliage to balance the bright colours of the flowers – species such as *E. characias*, *E. oblongata*, *E. sikkimensis*, *E. amygdaloides* subsp. *robbiae* and *E. mellifera*, to name a few of the more well-known ones. There are nearly two thousand species, which include annuals and perennials, shrubs and succulents. What is their relevance to the Islamic garden? Well, unfortunately it is not a poistive one. This arises from several grim references in the Quran to the 'Tree of Zaqqum', which has been identified as *euphorbia*.[403] In the Quran it is written, 'the Tree of Zaqqum. For we have truly made it [as] a trial for the wrong-doers. For it is a tree that springs out of the bottom of Hell-fire: the shoots of its fruit-stalks are like the heads of devils: Truly they will eat thereof and fill their bellies therewith. Then on top of that they will be given a mixture made of boiling water. Then shall their return be to the blazing fire'.[404]

The idea of the head of the plant being similar to the devil is emphasized by the species from South Africa called the 'Medusa's Head' (*E. caput-medusa*), perhaps the same as the one called the 'Gorgon's Head' (*E. gorgonis*). Either way they do not sound very attractive. It is well-known that the white latex that exudes from the *euphorbia* is poisonous and causes severe irritation to the skin and to the eye (even blindness), although, as with many toxic plants, if used very carefully it can also be an important medicine. Unfortunately, the more one looks into this genus in the light of Islam, the more off-putting it becomes. The only positive aspect, after reading Dr Iqtedar's thorough

Fig. 203. Euphorbia sikkimensis.

chapter on the Zaqqum tree, is that the particular species of *euphorbia* with which this tree of hell is associated, has not been positively identified. Let us hope that it is one of the more thorny or cactus-like species that are native to the hot, dry lands of the Arabian peninsular (e.g. *E. arabica* or *E. cactus*) rather than one of those mentioned above so valued by gardeners in the United Kingdom!

Lawns

Lawns (Fig. 228) have hardly been mentioned at all so far. This is not because of their lack of importance but mainly because the climate in the majority of the Islamic countries we are looking at does not allow for any simple solution to maintaining this sought-after element in the garden. A beautiful green lawn is something very much to be prized in the Islamic world – especially after colonial powers like the British, for example, imported their love of them into India; but in a predominantly dry climate, constant watering is required and this takes time and money. Indeed, in many of the hotter Muslim countries, such as those in the Gulf region, special drought-tolerant grass is required – Bermuda grass (*Cynadon dactylon*) or *Zoysia* grass being two of the most common choices. A northern European location with its higher rainfall and cooler temperatures definitely has tremendous advantages when it comes to lawns. There is nothing like the fresh green colour of a lawn – together with surrounding shrubs and trees – after rainfall, somehow both restful and invigorating at the same time, and a wonderful compensation for the lack of sunshine.[405] Maintaining and mowing a lawn is said to be the English obsession – and this obsession may be assimilated smoothly into your Islamic garden, and for some gardens could well be a substitute for water (see below).

As we have seen in previous chapters, the centre of a traditional Islamic garden is usually water in some form or other. Practically-speaking, in a northern location this may not always be possible: the garden may be too small or surrounded by high buildings or trees or facing predominantly north (or all of these factors), so a small lawn or area of grass could be an alternative. Overhanging trees often present a problem to growing a healthy lawn in an urban environment and many people with small courtyard-type gardens opt for hard-landscaping instead, especially if the area is used for sitting and eating in with a table and chairs. However, although you may have some beautiful geometric-patterned stone and *zellij* in your small urban garden, an empty space of green grass is worth considering in spite of its upkeep: it really is a 'rest for the eyes' after the endless roads and pavement the city-dweller looks upon much of the time, and is a less expensive and simpler alternative to a fountain.

Symbolically, there is a good case for lawns being claimed as the Western equivalent of the Islamic pool or fountain. It was mentioned earlier that the open fire or stove, being the focal point of a house in a cold climate, represented the equivalent of the fountain in a hot climate – and to a large extent this is true. But there is also something to be said for this parallel of a lawn to a pool or fountain. Although the lawn will never possess the many layers of symbolic meaning that the fountain possesses, nevertheless, aspects of the function and symbolism are similar: in particular, that of providing a centre, a tranquil and calm space around which the rest of the garden is focused. A lawn is not busy and crowded with colour and texture like a planted border: it is a void, a green and soothing space and, in the absence of a pool or fountain, offers a restful place to sit and contemplate, to 'refresh and nourish the eyes' (as quoted in Chapter 1) as well as the soul. As noted earlier, the most important colour in the Quranic descriptions of the paradise gardens is green, and this, together with the colour's revered status in lands where green vegetation is rare, are two of the main reasons why this colour holds special significance for Muslims.[406]

Vegetables

A fruit-tree or trees, as noted in the last chapter, is essential in an Islamic garden, and after this, vegetables are important. For your own garden, much will depend on space and aspect, and most people, where space is restricted, will probably prefer to include flowers and herbs rather than vegetables. However, if you are able to, and you love to eat your own home-grown produce, then certainly this is very much in keeping with the Islamic ideal of a garden, since in the paradise gardens 'produce is eternal'.[407] In the Quran there is a verse in which the people ask Moses to intercede for them and ask God for a greater variety of vegetables: 'Moses, we will not endure one sort of food; pray to thy Lord for us, that He may bring forth for us of that the earth produces – green herbs, cucumbers, corn, lentils, onions.'[408]

Most of the well-known vegetables we grow in northern Europe seem to have been grown in the early Islamic gardens, as well as more exotic ones. The following vegetables are on the medieval plant lists referred to above, so you may grow your favourite traditional vegetables knowing that they were also grown in the Islamic gardens of the past. The vegetables are: broad beans, cabbage, carrot, cauliflower, celery, cress, onion, garlic, leek, lettuce, parsnip, radish, sorrel (which grows wild in parts of the United Kingdom), spinach, turnip, lentils (which have been grown and eaten throughout the Middle East for thousands of years and arrived as early as the thirteenth century in the United Kingdom), globe artichoke and gourds. This last vegetable is more ornamental than edible. Other, more exotic and less hardy, vegetables and spices, which are grown in many countries in the Islamic world and which some people grow in northern Europe in greenhouses or in very sheltered, sunny positions, are: cucumber, aubergine, endive, ginger and a variety of red, green and black peppers.

It may be added that the cabbages, cauliflowers and other vegetables grown today in Egypt, for example, are quite vast compared to their European cousins – and they taste just as good, so one cannot claim superiority on that front! Seeing the donkeys struggling along beside the traffic overloaded with their great specimens is an amazing, if rather horrifying, sight. Due to the tastelessness of many supermarket vegetables, as well as concern about genetic engineering, it is once again becoming very popular today to 'grow your own'. An increasing number of people in urban,[409] suburban and rural regions have a small area set aside for growing vegetables and fruit.

Reading *Lark Rise to Candleford* recently, the similarity between the mixed planting of an Islamic garden with the Victorian cottage gardens of the poor rural labourers struck me. The author describes the garden of one of the larger cottages in the hamlet:

> Nearer the cottage were fruit trees, then the yew hedge, close and solid as a wall, which sheltered the bee-hives and enclosed the flower garden. Sally had such flowers and so many of them, and nearly all of them sweet-scented! Wallflowers and tulips, lavender and sweet William, and pinks and old world roses with enchanting names – Seven sisters, Maidens Blush, moss rose, monthly rose, cabbage rose...[410]

The author adds that it was unusual for the labourers' gardens to have so many flowers, since due to their poverty most of them needed all the space they could lay their hands on to plant their vegetables, an essential part of their families' diet, so 'most of the gardens had only one poor starveling [rose] bush or none'. The positive aspect of the lack of flowers was that the families ate plenty of choice, home-grown, freshly dug vegetables and their diet, although meagre, was very healthy.

Conclusion

Although the following passage may seem a little extreme to end this chapter with, it nevertheless seems appropriate considering the increasingly threatening times in which we live. It is written by Reginald Farrar, the famous English plant-hunter, gardener and writer, whose words, written towards the end of the First World War, ring all too true today:

> Mortal dooms and dynasties are brief things, but beauty is indestructible and eternal, if its tabernacle be only a petal that is shed tomorrow. Wars and agonies are shadows only cast across the path of man: each successive one seems the end of all things, but man perpetually emerges and goes forward, lured always and cheered and inspired by the immortal beauty-thought that finds form in all the hopes and enjoyments of his life. *Inter armes silent flores* ('In time of war

flowers are silent') is no truth; on the contrary, amid the crash of doom our sanity and survival more than ever depend on the strength with which we can listen to the still small voice that towers above cannons, and cling to the little quiet things of life, the things that come and go and yet are always there, the inextinguishable lamps of God amid the disaster that man has made of his life.[411]

*Fig. 204. Lilies (*Lilium regale*) under apple trees.*

CHAPTER 7

HRH the Prince of Wales' Carpet Garden, Highgrove: a Case Study

Introduction

The Carpet Garden at Highgrove, The Prince of Wales' house in Gloucestershire, is based on his own idea, originally conceived in 2000. It was initially designed and constructed for the Chelsea Flower Show of 2001 and, after the show was over, was dismantled and transported to Highgrove. This sounds deceptively simple – in fact it took two months of intensive work to prepare the site and re-lay the garden in its permanent (as permanent as any garden can be) home. This chapter tells the story of how the Prince was first inspired to carry out his idea of a Carpet Garden and the main stages involved in the process, as well as giving something of the historical background.

The Carpet Garden at Highgrove is, in effect, a garden based on principles of traditional Islamic garden design. It incorporates a central fountain from which flows, symbolically, the four rivers of paradise, and its formal four-fold plan includes many of the trees and plants that are essential to a *chahar-bagh*, the earthly symbol of a heavenly archetype. The Carpet Garden is one of the first interpretations of a traditional *chahar-bagh* in the United Kingdom. Designing and constructing such a garden in a very different environment from the large geographical area referred to as the *Dar al-Islam* (the Islamic world, see Introduction) makes an interesting study. The design itself, starting from the Prince's idea based on his two carpets (see below) went through many stages and developments: from Michael Miller's first designs for the garden at Chelsea to various modifications under consultation with Khaled Azzam

Fig. 205. Fountain, centre of the Carpet Garden, in preparation at the Chelsea Flower Show, May 2000.

(Director of the Visual Islamic and Traditional Arts Programme [VITA] at the Prince's Foundation in London, see Endnote 3 and 135) to the final adaptations required to place it in the new site at Highgrove. The biggest change at Highgrove was the inclusion of an entrance 'viewing platform'. This is important since it means that visitors are able to see the full glory of the garden's design and planting – and its likeness to a beautiful carpet – laid out before them, something that was not possible at Chelsea.

Originally, the Prince of Wales, inspired by the designs of two of his own carpets, thought how beautiful they could be if turned into a garden. The idea was to commission an enclosed formal garden based on the patterns and colours of these two Anatolian tribal carpets, one of which is a prayer-rug (Figs. 208 and 209). In fact the Prince was taking a traditional Islamic concept – that of the garden-carpet, a carpet woven with a bird's-eye view of a formal garden – full circle (Fig. 210). Indeed, it seemed appropriate that the Chelsea Flower Show should be graced with a 'Carpet Garden', which could then be 'rolled-up' and taken to Highgrove.

In the translation from a two-dimensional woven wool surface to a three-dimensional foliage and flower garden with footpaths and water, the patterns in the carpets needed to be amalgamated and modified. Nevertheless, it was possible to retain some of the patterns and colours that appeared in the carpets, even if not all of them could be employed. It will be seen from the plan (Fig. 207) that the overall design is the classic Islamic *chahar-bagh* with a fountain in the centre. The principal designer responsible for turning the carpets into a garden was Michael Miller of Clifton Nurseries who worked in collaboration with VITA (see above) which included myself, at the Prince's Foundation.[412]

Historical Background

In the past, it was not unusual for the wealthy and influential in the Islamic world to commission carpets that imitated gardens, some of the most famous now being in museums; for example, the Wagner Carpet in the Burrell Collection, Glasgow or the Aberconway Carpet in the Al-Sabah Collection (Fig. 210). Also, some of the greatest carpets, such as the famous Ardebil Carpet and the Chelsea Carpet (both in the Victoria and Albert Museum in London) although not strictly speaking 'Garden Carpets', in that they are not centred on a *chahar-bagh* plan, are nevertheless, in their dense and luxurious woven floral and arabesque designs, essentially depictions of the heavenly gardens. There is a famous garden carpet on which all subsequent ones are thought to be partly based, and this is the carpet known as the 'Spring of Chosroes'. Chosroes I (AD531–579) was a powerful Sassanian king who ruled from the winter capital Ctesiphon on the river Tigris, south of Baghdad. However, he was not powerful enough to withstand the Muslim Arab invaders who, on sacking the city of Ctesiphon in AD637, discovered this magnificent carpet portraying a richly bejewelled paradise garden – and promptly cut it up and distributed it. A barbaric act it seems but revealing because it demonstrates the deep suspicion the early Muslims felt for what they no doubt regarded as man's vanity in seeking to create something perfect on earth without acknowledging their dependence on God. According to a contemporary source, the carpet was used in the palace by the Sassanian kings for festivities in the winter when the weather was too cold to be out in the garden. It was therefore the 'Winter Carpet, although, because it depicted the beauty of springtime, was known by the Persians as 'the Spring of Chosroes'. A contemporary writer observed that 'Its material, which was marvellous and costly, consisted of silk, gold and silver, and precious stones. On it was represented a beautiful pleasure ground with brooks and interlacing paths, with trees and flowers of springtime'.[413]

Ironically, although the early Muslim invaders destroyed this carpet, a few centuries later the

Fig. 206. Planting the Carpet Garden at the Chelsea Flower Show, May 2001.

Persian Muslims became the supreme weavers of the Islamic empire, producing such fine examples of garden carpets as those mentioned above. It is a good example of how the Islamic civilization developed hand-in-hand with the indigenous civilization of the country it invaded. The Persian Muslims eventually saw that the representation of an 'eternal' spring on a carpet was not in opposition to the Word of God, providing it did not attempt to imitate nature in any naturalistic way but rather sought to represent symbolically the mysterious and invisible power that gives life to nature. Like Persian miniatures, the garden carpets are stylised portrayals of a garden, depicting more the essence and atmosphere of an eternal spring than a literal rendering. There is a beautiful and atmospheric Persian poem which begins, 'Here in this carpet lives an ever-lovely spring'.[413A]

The carpets that the Prince of Wales based his design upon, although not formal garden carpets, nevertheless embody aspects of a garden with their stylised floral motifs and harmony of colour and pattern. Like the garden, they are symbolic expressions of praise and love of God. In addition, a prayer-rug with its arch motif (*mihrab*) is representative of the entrance to paradise: it is only through prayer and submission to the Almighty (demonstrated most fully in the act of prostration, an integral part of the five-times-daily ritual prayer) that one may enter the gardens of paradise.

As mentioned above, one of the principal ideas behind these carpets was that in the winter months the beauty of nature could be brought inside through capturing its spirit in a carpet woven with flowers, trees and plants, sometimes with birds, deer and other animals or with ducks on a central pool as in the Wagner carpet. In a traditional Islamic home, one actually sits on the carpet, not on a chair removed from it, and this intensifies the illusion of sitting in a garden. There is little furniture in such a home and so the carpet is the main item of decoration, both functional – for warmth and prayer – and beautiful, with a few cushions for greater comfort, and perhaps a low table on which to place food. The floor of the house is sacred since one prays on it, and this is the underlying reason for shoes being taken off when entering the home.

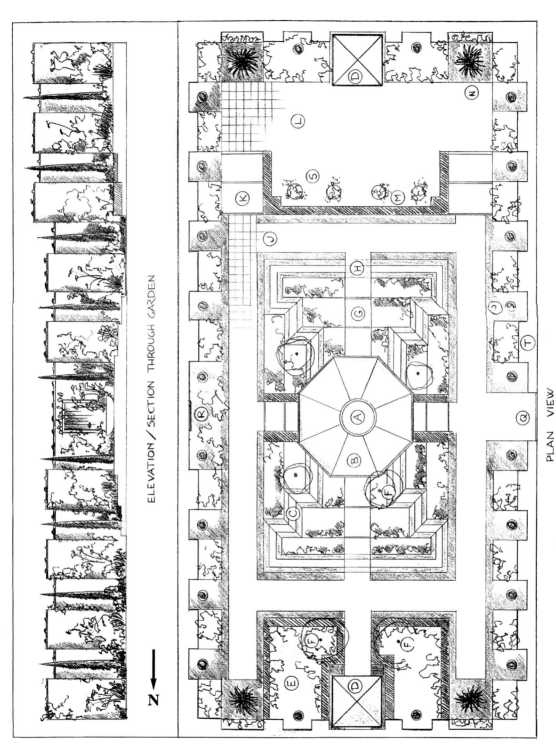

ELEVATION / SECTION THROUGH GARDEN

N

PLAN VIEW

THE "CARPET GARDEN" AT HIGHGROVE HOUSE
DESIGNED BY MICHAEL MILLER

SCALE 1:50

Fig. 207. Design of the Carpet Garden at Highgrove (this design modified from the original design for Chelsea to fit into the new, larger, dimensions) by Michael Miller.

The Carpet Garden

This was a challenging project to be involved in, as it meant the practical application of the existing patterns and colours of the two Anatolian carpets, as well as relating them to traditional Islamic *chahar-bagh* design principles and planting ideas. It was also a marvellous opportunity to bring to life, as far as possible, not only the carpets themselves but also passages from Persian poetry, scenes from miniature paintings and, importantly, the passages describing the gardens of paradise in the Quran. Although the carpets were the original inspiration for the garden, we wanted to capture something of the atmosphere of serene joy and contentment that is suggested by the Quranic gardens, where the blessed souls will have 'such fruits as they shall choose', and dwell 'mid thornless lote-trees and serried acacias, and spreading shade and outpoured waters, and fruits abounding'.[414]

We did not manage to plant the 'thornless lote-trees' (see Chapter 5) and 'serried acacias'[415] in the Carpet Garden but some shade is provided by the evergreen cork oak (*Quercus suber*) and tamarisks (*Tamarix tetandra*), and the two small pavilions at either end. 'Outpoured waters' are in the form of a marble fountain in the centre, and fruits are present in the form of citrus (calamondin – *Citrofortunella microcarpa*, and kumquat, Fig. 230), pomegranate, fig and olive trees – three of the four principal trees in the paradise gardens (see Chapter 5).

In the centre of the garden is a Moroccan-inspired scalloped marble fountain, the bowl set on an octagonal plinth, covered in coloured *zellij* (ceramic tile

Figs. 208 (top) and 209 (bottom). The Prince of Wales' Anatolian tribal carpets on which the design of the Carpet Garden is loosely based.

pieces). The octagon *zellij* pattern was designed by VITA alumnus, David Feuerstein, together with Dr. Khaled Azzam. The fountain and *zellij* were made in

	LEGEND FOR HIGHGROVE DRAWING (left)		
A	Marble fountain bowl	**J**	Terracotta tiles on pathways
B	Geometric tile patterns decorate octagonal plinth	**K**	Steps down from terrace
C	Rill in celadon green tiles bordered by purple berberis	**M**	Myrtle hedge at pathway level forms edging to terrace
D	Pavilions guard east and west entrances to garden	**N**	Square lead container planted with astelia on area of porphyry gravel
E	General planting	**P**	Cypress with surround and path edging of porphyry gravel
F	Pomegranate trees	**Q**	Main entrance to garden
G	Steps up to central plinth edged with celadon green tiles	**R**	False door
		S	Terracotta containers with standard form citrus
H	Access covers to fountain pumps in coloured tiles to match rill and berberis	**T**	Boundary wall capped with old terracotta tiles

Fig. 210. 'Aberconway' garden carpet, Persian, eighteenth century.

Spain and transported to Chelsea, where it was installed by water expert, Bamber Wallis. The base under the *zellij* is a heavy galvanized steel frame, strengthened with fibre-reinforced cement made in eight triangular sections bolted together. At the end of the Chelsea flower-show this all had to be dismantled and then re-assembled at Highgrove.

Design and Planting

Around the perimeter of the Carpet Garden, planted against the walls, are the Italian cypress, *Cupressus sempervirens* 'Stricta', and three of the four trees mentioned in the Quranic descriptions of the gardens of paradise are also planted: the fig (*Ficus carica*), the olive (*Olea europea*) and the pomegranate (*Punica granatum*). In esoteric Islam, the pomegranate is considered the highest fruit in paradise.[416] At High-grove, a few of the pomegranates are placed in large containers outside the entrance to the Carpet Garden on the west side, next to the Orchard Room, the Prince's room for public entertainment, and three are planted in the beds inside the garden. During the second winter of the garden's life (2002–03) the Head gardener at Highgrove, David Howard, experimented leaving them outside to see if they would survive. Two of them have survived and hopefully will survive many more in the future. The fourth tree mentioned in the descriptions of the paradise gardens is the date-palm (*Phoenix dactylifera*), which would most likely not survive outdoors in Gloucestershire and would also look very out of place. Also, this garden is principally a 'carpet garden', not a literal rendering of the Quranic paradise gardens – bearing in mind that on a more profound level every Islamic *chahar-bagh* is in a sense a recreation of the heavenly gardens.

Shrubs, Roses and Climbers

When constructed at Chelsea, the Carpet Garden was approximately 15m long by 10m wide and the design, as can be seen (Fig. 207), was based on the traditional *chahar-bagh* plan combined with certain geometric motifs and colours that are woven into the carpets. The central marble fountain set on the octagonal *zellij* platform is surrounded by plants largely corresponding to the patterns and colours of the prayer carpet. For instance, the four rills flowing from the centre, lined with sea-green tiles, are laid out in a zig-zag pattern in imitation of the zig-zag on the arch of the prayer-niche (*mihrab*) (Fig. 208). These rills are edged with a deep purple hedge of *Berberis thunbergii* 'Atropurpurea Nana' to match the border around the central prayer-area of the carpet (Fig. 211). The pale aquamarine of this area of the carpet was the basis of the choice of a variety of Mediterranean plants with foliage of a similar pale grey-green, such as *Santolina incana*, *Artemisia* 'Lambrooke Mist' and *Lavandula multifida* 'Blue Wonder' or *L. pinnata*. Roses are essential in an Islamic-inspired garden (see Chapter 6) and, to retain the idea of walking on a carpet, the roses were planted in sunken beds, a device used in many gardens in the Islamic world since it made irrigation easier (see Chapter 2). These beds were sunk to approximately 50 or 60cm (in the past they were often much deeper, see Chapter 3) and, unlike the sunken beds of old, which were made of brick or stone, were constructed of steel. They were then painted in a shade of fired earth in order to blend in with the Mediterranean colours of the wall and of the later paths, also so as not to detract from the colour of the roses. As far as possible, old roses that may well have been used in eastern gardens in the past, were chosen which were also of similar shades as the crimsons,

Fig. 211. Close-up of Berberis *zig-zag in garden.*

Fig. 212. Rosa 'Charles de Mills' a Gallica rose.

Fig. 213. Detail of flower-beds showing roses, Highgrove.

purples and deep pinks of the carpets. Roses such as the lovely pink scented damask rose, *Rosa* 'Ispahan',[417] the deep crimson-flowered Gallica roses, *R.* 'Charles de Mills' and *R.* 'Tuscany Superba',[418] and for obvious reasons we chose *R.* 'Prince Charles', which has wonderful dark maroon flowers.

In preparing the garden for both the Chelsea Flower Show and later at Highgrove for the Prince of Wales to show his visitors at the beginning of August 2001, an intense amount of planting took place in addition to the trees, shrubs and roses mentioned above. There was a constant weighing-up between plants and flowers that both recreated the colours of the carpets, those that were known to have been cultivated in the Islamic world in the past[419] and those that would be suitable and available for the Flower Show, as well as at Highgrove. There are myrtle hedges (*Myrtus communis* 'Tarentina' which flowered well in May, 2002 and were clipped not long after, in July). Climbers around the walls at Highgrove include: the evergreen and beautifully scented, *Trachelospermum jasminoides* on the south wall,

either side of the entrance pavilion; ivy (*Hedera helix*); roses, such as 'Sanders White' and 'Felicité et Perpetué'; as well as the evergreen climber, *Muehlenbeckia*. It is interesting to read what the twelfth-century Ibn al-Awwam writes in his *Book of Agriculture* about transplanting ivy from the wild into gardens:

> The ivy called *kissus* [*Hedera* spp.] is a wild plant which climbs trees and hangs down from them. Both these may be moved to gardens, taking them up with their roots in February, and planted near the water-channels they are watered from time to time until they become established. For these climbers one makes a trellis of stakes on which both kinds climb and are sustained.[420]

Of course today it is illegal to dig up any plants in the wild, so please do not follow his recommendation! Also, in damper climates ivy can become a real problem, not just clinging to walls and trees but eventually being the cause of their downfall. However, using a trellis as he advises would avoid this problem, if one is vigilant. The use of ivy is also interesting as, on the whole, it is associated more with wet, woodland environments than the warmer, drier areas of the south. It looks good at Highgrove as there is not too much of it climbing the walls and the green against the Mediterranean-style buff-terracotta wall colour (see below) makes a subtle and warm background to the more colourful planting in the rest of the garden.

Flowers

At the beginning, the same plants were planted at Highgrove as at Chelsea but over the past three years, since things have settled down, there have been some changes and replacements including annuals and biennuals, as well as a few other introductions to fill in the larger garden area (see below). In the flower-beds around the edge of the garden, a mixture of perennials, biennials and annuals were originally planted, chosen for the similarity of their colours to the colours in the carpets, the harmonious blending of height and texture,

Fig. 215. *Flower-beds either side of path, Chelsea.*

as well as considerations of Islamic horticultural history, symbolic meaning and, very important, availability – all to give an even, beautifully-patterned carpet effect. In order to pick up the indigo blues, deep reds, crimson, terracotta, white and greens of the two tribal carpets, we chose a variety of plants including: *Astrantia* (*major alba* and *A. major rubra*); *Achillea millifolium* 'Terracotta' and 'White Beauty'; various lilies, including *Lilium* 'Martagon'; *Angelica archangelica* and *Angelica gigas* to give some background height; *Knautia Macedonica* for its beautiful claret colour; *Scabiosa atropurpurea* 'Chile Black'; and *Heliotrope* 'Princess Marina' to match the dark-purple-blacks. For a deep velvety blue, *Anchusa* 'Lodden Royalist' was chosen and, for a range of blues, various delphinium and *Salvia* cultivars (including *S.* 'Indigo Spires') were planted as well as larkspur (*Consolida* cultivars), cornflowers (*Centaurea cyanus*) and love-in-the-mist

Fig. 214. *Flower-beds, Chelsea.*

(*Nigella hispanica*). There were also poppies (e.g. *Papaver* 'Pattie's Plum'), valerian (*Centranthus ruber*), *Cosmos astrosanguineus, Nicotiana alata* (to recreate more of the white highlights in the carpet as well as because of the wonderful evening fragrance) *Geranium* 'Kashmir White' and *G.* 'Kashmir Purple'.

No true Islamic-inspired garden could be without tulips and, again, the ones we chose reflected the colours in the carpet, such as *Tulipa* 'Queen of the Night' and *T.* 'Abu Hassan'. This latter tulip is a good strong red and also the name Hassan is a popular Muslim name; Hassan was one of the Prophet Muhammad's grandsons, and 'Abu' means 'father of'. As the garden has developed in its early years at Highgrove, other tulips have been tried out such as the lily-flowered *T.* 'White Triumphator' and *T.* 'Burgundy'. The Ottoman Turks, in particular, loved the tulip, and in the seventeenth century, under Suleyman the Magnificent, it became the most beloved flower for them. (see Chapter 6).

As scent is so important in an eastern garden, it was originally intended to place eight pots filled with lilies around the central octagonal plinth on which the fountain is placed, specifically, *Lilium candidum* or *L. regale*. Unfortunately, these lilies were not ready in time for Chelsea and were substituted with delicate white pelargoniums. In the summer of 2002 and 2003 these pots were planted with pelargoniums (the beautiful claret coloured 'Sidoides') and oxalis, and next year other species of pelargoniums may be tried as well as lilies. In general, David Howard, the head gardener, is aiming over the next few years (2004-06) to restore more of the original colours of the carpet, as were planted in the garden at Chelsea. Many of the plants that were selected for their temporary performance at Chelsea do not flourish and perform well in Gloucestershire, so there is, as with all new gardens, a constant experimenting to discover plants which both reflect the original colours as well as enjoying the conditions at Highgrove. For the summer of 2004 David is planting more deep blue viola and replacing both the *santolina* and the *artemesia* both of which have become too big and woody. The new *artemesia* is *A. schmidtiana* 'Nana', a dwarf variety, and instead of the *santolina* they are planting *Pericallis lanata* 'Kew Form'. The pots used at Chelsea were aluminium, some of which have been replaced at Highgrove by terracotta, since the natural material and earthy colour fit in better with the traditional Islamic garden theme, as well as weathering prettily.

Construction at Highgrove

When the time came to transport the garden from Chelsea to Highgrove a vast amount of preparation was required before the garden could be installed there. The completed garden had to be 'up and running' by the first week of August 2001, when the Prince of Wales was due to open it to visitors. The

*Fig. 216. View of garden showing citrus trees (*Calamondin*) in terracotta pots and Moroccan lamps for night-time lighting, from Lavender Garden entrance at Highgrove.*

Fig. 217. View of the Carpet Garden from main entrance platform on Lavender Garden side, Highgrove.

Water and Fountain Construction

When the fountain was moved to Highgrove, Bamber Wallis devised the plumbing and water system to make sure that the water was constantly at the correct pressure. In fact, underneath the garden there lies a sophisticated irrigation system put in place by the construction team, headed by Colin Withycombe, together with the local building firm, R. Williams, led by Nigel Selwyn. However, before any irrigation or fountain-plumbing could be carried out, the area of ground where the garden was to be placed required some heavy digging, particularly after it was discovered to be solid clay. The construction team had to dig down nearly 1m, remove as much clay as possible and replace it with eighty tons of top-soil. If the clay had remained, the sunken beds for the trees and roses would have been constantly water-logged and this would eventually have ruined the plants. So water was drained away from the surface and pipes were laid and connected

area where the garden was to be laid out was between the west side of the Orchard Room, the room for public functions, and a traditional Cotswold stone barn. There are fields to the north and the Mediterranean-style Lavender Garden, a partially enclosed area planted entirely with lavender hedges and lawn, is to the south. The main entrance to the Carpet Garden is in this south wall, leading directly off the Lavender Garden – highly appropriate it could be said, stepping from the Mediterranean to an exotic, more eastern scene.

Fortunately, the space allocated for the Carpet Garden at Highgrove was at least a third larger than its original size at Chelsea – that is, approximately 20m by 15m. Although this meant some adjustment of measurements all round, the extra space has made a huge improvement on the rather cramped Chelsea site. It has also allowed for a kind of raised 'viewing platform' as you enter, about 45cm above the rest of the garden so that, as visitors walk from the Lavender Garden they are given a good overall view of the formal lay-out slightly below them. This view (see Fig. 206 taken from above) was lost to visitors at Chelsea, since they could only observe it from the same level as the paths, or even slightly below; at Highgrove, happily, it is possible to see the whole garden-carpet effect before stepping down to walk around it.

Fig. 218. The Carpet Garden showing its high walls – a typical feature of the traditional Islamic garden, creating a haven of lush growth within; here, cypresses flank a tamarisk.

into the drainage system already existing for the Orchard Room (underneath the area between the north wall of the Carpet Garden and the field beyond). This system lies on a natural fall into the field beyond where pipes for draining into the lake farther away were already laid.

After constructing the drainage system, the walls were built using concrete blocks, rendered with a subtle Mediterranean/North African style buff-terracotta colour, already mixed into the render. Local Cotswold stone was used around the three entrances to the garden, on the south, north and west sides, as well as on the four corners (see Fig. 222). There is no doubt that, since the garden is now a good third larger than it was at Chelsea and there are walls all the way around instead of only on two sides, it achieves one of its main aims of being a garden secluded from its surroundings. The walls have a coping of Italian terracotta-red tiles, and roses and other climbers may be planted to grow up the outside walls as the garden develops.

Before the planting took place, the octagonal steel and concrete structure forming the base of the fountain was transported from London in its eight segments and rebuilt on site. The scalloped marble fountain bowl was set on a one-inch marble ring and placed on top of the *zellij* octagon. There are two underground water-tanks in the garden, the larger one providing water for the central fountain and two of the rills, the smaller one providing water for the other two rills. There is an automatic top-up system and an ultra-

Fig. 220. Detail of zellij *surrounding fountain.*

violet (UV) sterilizer to prevent algal growth. The water is pumped through the UV bulb and the light, which is inside a sealed unit, kills the algae and prevents the water from turning green. This is working well as the water was crystal clear when I last visited in August 2003, and the white-grey of the marble fountain does not have a trace of green algae. In winter, the fountain is wrapped up to prevent frost damage; the water is turned off, the tanks are drained and the marble bowl is covered in straw and plastic. The garden is put to sleep for the winter, hibernating until the spring arrives the following year and it can come alive again. The Carpet Garden is most definitely a late spring and summer garden. As remarked before, in a garden centred on water, as the Carpet Garden at Highgrove is, when there is no water there is no heart and no soul; in the spring when the water is flowing again, life is renewed. As W.H. Auden wrote so beautifully:

> In the deserts of the heart
> Let the healing fountains start.[421]

Fig. 219. Detail of marble fountain.

Fig. 221. View of garden showing original tall cypresses, with the roof of the barn in the background.

How are the Plants Faring?

It was one thing preparing for the Chelsea Flower Show, a temporary affair when it was relatively easy to pick and choose the flowers and trees we wanted, but quite another to build the Carpet Garden in the middle of Gloucestershire, a rather exposed part of England, which probably would not support the tender plants and shrubs chosen for Chelsea. The only major alteration that has been necessary is the substitution of smaller cypresses for the original tall ones. These were placed at regular intervals around the walls of the garden, and when moved from Chelsea to Highgrove proved to be too tall and slim to withstand the strong Gloucestershire winds. The smaller ones, approximately the same height as the wall now (summer 2003), in fact look more in proportion with the garden than the original ones.

The garden is in its early years yet (three and a half years old at the time of going to print) but at least the olive and fig trees are still alive as well as – more remarkably – two of the pomegranates, and look as happy as can be expected in spite of the exposed

Fig. 222. View of entrance to garden (Orchard-room side) showing new cyresses appearing over the top of the wall, and local Cotswold stone around door.

position. The open site means they receive as much sunshine in the summer months as an English summer will allow and the summer of 2003 has been one of the hottest and driest ever recorded. With the knowledgeable care of the Head Gardener, David Howard, and his team, these relatively tender trees, along with the other half-hardy plants will hopefully last a few more winters yet, depending on the frosts. The other trees – the new cypresses, the tamarisks and the cork oaks are also doing well. The citrus trees need to be brought in during the winter and this is usually carried out in mid-October before any serious frosts descend. These are growing in large pots so that they can be moved inside, with relatively little trouble, for nearly eight months of the year. The more informal habit of the cork oaks provides a balanced contrast to the fastigiate cypresses, offering shade as they grow taller. The cork oaks were chosen partly as an alternative to the oriental plane tree

(*Platanus orientalis*), a tree present in many traditional Islamic gardens (and represented, along with the cypress, in many Persian miniatures; see Chapter 5) because of its shade-giving properties. In Persian poetry, the plane trees' leaves are often compared to human hands outstretched in supplication and it is they who lead the way when, as Rumi writes, 'The trees are engaged in ritual prayer'.[422] However, the oriental plane would have grown too large too quickly at Highgrove and the cork oak, being slower-growing (and not so tall eventually), is a fine alternative. Cultivated widely in Spain it is very much a part of the Hispano-Mauresque and North African Islamic world.

With more wall space to cover in its larger home, the garden now has extra climbers such as the hardy jasmine (*Jasminum officinale*) added to it on either side of the entrance pavilion on the north side. At Chelsea, inspired by miniature paintings in which

Fig. 223. View of garden showing new, smaller, cypresses, the pencil-thin Cupressus sempervirens *'Stricta' group; unfortunately, no sweet peas trained up them now as this task is too high maintenance to keep up every year.*

fruit trees are often depicted with their flowering branches embracing the tall dark form of the conifer, highly scented sweet peas were planted to climb up and entwine the cypresses. Cultivars such as the old-fashioned *Lathyrus odoratus* 'Cupani's Original', 'Lord Nelson' and 'Indigo King' were planted to grow up and cling lovingly to the dark evergreens (Fig. 173). Sadly, this idea has not always been continued at Highgrove due to its high maintenance. So far the *Trachelospermum jasminoides*, *Muhlenbeckia* and tender perennials, such as the salvias, have survived three winters and hopefully will survive the next. The gardeners have taken cuttings in case they suffer losses. Last year (2003) they grew the exotic trumpet vine (*Campsis radicans*), which climbs over walls and perhaps up the cypresses. Next year they are experimenting with *Albizia lophantha*, *Sophora tetraptera* 'Golden King' as well as possibly the crab-apple, *Malus hupehensis*, with the aim of making some crab-apple jelly.

Design Notes

The paths are wider at Highgrove than at Chelsea and also more terracotta tiles have been laid down the centre of them to make walking easier, with gravel borders either side. Hopefully, night-scented stock and love-in-the-mist will be sown amongst the gravel to enhance both the fragrance in the garden and the illusion of walking on a carpet. Two of the walls, on the west and east sides, have large wooden doors set into them painted with bold Saudi Arabian designs. There are also various favourite pieces of artwork belonging to The Prince of Wales set into the walls, such as a ceramic plate with Arabic calligraphy, and Spanish tiles, both of which fit well into the overall theme of the garden. When the construction team was preparing for the Prince of Wales' opening in August 2001, the last week was dedicated to an intense amount of planting, as well as irrigation, including installing taps in the corners and an automatic system for watering the perimeter borders. Lighting was a very important consideration for the first evening and subsequent evening gatherings, and subtle, low-level, electric lights were installed behind the cypresses and amongst the foliage in the central beds. More exotic lighting was

Fig. 224. Paths showing gravel border and tiles: the colour of the gravel and of the tiles could be paler in order to set off the plants more effectively; in fact, when dry the tiles are a much paler and prettier colour.

Fig. 225. One of two doors with Saudi Arabian-carved and painted traditional designs.

Fig. 226. Carpet Garden in the evening with subtle low-level lighting.

added in the form of Turkish geometric-patterned brass paraffin lamps around the fountain, as well as candles to light the pathways. A romantic Arabian Nights atmosphere was created in the Cotswolds! Perhaps another year the Prince of Wales may be more ambitious in his lighting effects and follow the Persians' example: gathering together hundreds of tortoises and fixing candles to their shells (somehow) to create an even more magical scene with the flickering flames moving about amongst the flowers and shrubs.[423] (See pages 84–5 on Lighting.)

Fig. 227. One of two painted wood pavilions in the Carpet Garden – one at each end; design by the Prince of Wales based on a motif in one of the two carpets.

Pavilions

The geometric shape of the top of the prayer-niche (*mihrab*) shown in the prayer-carpet was the basis of the Prince of Wales' sketch for the small pavilions at each end of the garden. These were made by VITA alumnus, Farid Aliturki, a specialist woodworker. Pavilions, as mentioned in Chapter 3, are an important feature in an Islamic garden, often placed in the premium position for the best view, as well as to receive cool breezes – such as at the intersection of water-channels. Sometimes they are placed at one end of a garden for the best view as is the case here. The European equivalent is the summer-house, often used to hide from the rain as much as from the sun. These pavilions provide the only shade in the Carpet Garden until the cork oaks and olive trees grow taller.

A Summer Garden

The Carpet Garden is a summer garden as mentioned above and requires fairly high maintenance if the array of carpet colours are to bloom every year. Hopefully, this will be possible – only time will tell which ones will thrive in their Gloucestershire home – since maintaining the colour is one of the main objectives. The garden's glory may not be long-lasting each season but it is a spectacular sight at its height in late May and June, and much of the flowering lasts into September; and in a way the garden is all the more special because of its fleeting character. This is not just in the nature of gardens but very much in keeping with the Islamic view that nothing lasts long in this world – we should be grateful for every moment and then move on. In the winter the garden is 'a fine and private place' but seems rather forlorn since there are no flowers, some foliage from the evergreens, in particular the cypresses and oak, but above all, the water is not running, and an Islamic garden without water is a desolate place rather than the healing oasis it should be. However, its melancholy may be to some people's taste, and on those few bright winter days that cast a gentle light in the pale English skies, it could offer, for a short time, a different kind of contemplative atmosphere than when the flowers are out and the water is running. This garden in winter may remind

Fig. 228. Summer house raised on stone platform, Devon.

the visitor that its beauty is more than the sum total of the visible parts: it is the secret invisible power which only reveals itself to 'those who have eyes' or 'people who reflect'.[424]

Is the Garden Successful?

It must be admitted that it was with some trepidation that I first visited the Carpet Garden at Highgrove (July 2002) almost exactly a year after it had been packed up and moved from the Chelsea Flower Show and re-constructed and re-planted. I doubted that such a garden could be 'installed' in the Cotswolds and not look very out of place. In fact, since it is laid out within its own Mediterranean/North African style walls with local Cotswold stone around the doors and at the corners, it works surprisingly well. A formal garden such as the Carpet Garden needs a formal separation from its surroundings – this is the key to its happy 'placement' in the Gloucestershire countryside. The garden itself does not attempt to blend in with the surroundings: it is hidden within its walls and the walls fit in well in the space between the Cotswold stone barn and the Orchard Room.

I have been fortunate in visiting the garden on hot, sunny days when the walls, fountain, water, planting, colours and textures all looked as they should. The water was flowing from the fountain at the right speed, low and gentle – 'murmuring', not shooting up into the air;[425] it was running clear in the rills slightly below one's feet with planting either side. The rose bushes planted in the sunken beds, with the rest of the planting around the central fountain at one level, meant the flowers were just above ankle-height, so the visitor really does have

the impression of walking on a luxurious, scented carpet. There is no doubt that spending time in this garden is to give one the sensation of being spirited into a kind of Arabian Night dream, entirely cut off from the outside world, the sound of the water lulling one into a dreamlike peace.

So the answer to the questions, is it successful? can a carpet garden, an Islamic-style garden, work in different surroundings and climate to those in which it was born?… is yes! Of course, since I was closely involved with the planting it could be suggested that there is some bias here (of course not!). Well, it must be admitted there is some truth in this. However, I also had many reservations, since what may work at Chelsea for one week will not necessarily – to say the least – work as a permanent (or for several years hopefully) garden in the very English surroundings of Gloucestershire. But this potential problem was solved before it arose, since no attempt was made to make it blend in with its surroundings: it is indeed a separate 'room'. This garden shows that it is possible to create an Islamic-style garden in an environment very different from what we perceive as the Islamic world, and for this garden to succeed. The planting still needs some experimenting with since, as mentioned before, making a garden 'for life' rather than for a week at Chelsea requires quite a different approach.

Fig. 229. View of the Carpet Garden from one corner.

Considerations of changing weather, temperature, maturity of plants and so on have to be taken into account. But even a sceptic, I dare say, would be won over by the Carpet Garden. In detail it does not bear a great deal of resemblance to the original carpets but the essence of the carpets is there and Islamic art is all about capturing the essence: it is not, as has been noted earlier, so much about the individual ingredients, as about the underlying unity of the whole, the harmonious balance between the architecture, the geometry of structure, the arabesque of nature – all tied together by the all-important element of water, the life-giving force, the *rahma* (mercy) of God.

So, at the risk of sounding rather fanciful, to enter the Carpet Garden at Highgrove is to enter a secluded place, a magical world, a world that (in spite of there being no lawns) conjures up a Persian poem:

Within this scented garden close
Whoso desires may win repose;
An earthly Paradise it seems –
Of cypresses, green lawns and streams –
And if your host you wish to please
Converse of nothing else but these.[426]

Conclusion

The Quran is 'the great theophany of Islam'[427] and thus its importance cannot be overestimated when considering any aspect of Islamic civilization. It is the primary inspiration for all true Islamic art and architecture, including the art of the garden. All art, to be truly worthy of the name, should to a greater or lesser extent, reflect the principles of a more profound order of reality. This means that its outward beauty should stir the soul into contemplation of its inward essence. This process should be subtle and reveal itself gradually after time and meditation by the beholder. The human scale of the Islamic garden, embracing rather than overwhelming the visitor, can be seen as an example of this. 'The object of art is beauty of form, whereas the object of contemplation is beauty beyond form.'[428]

In Islam, no barrier separates God from His supplicant – the worshipper can lift up his or her hands at any time, anywhere, and even perform the *salat* (ritual prayer) almost anywhere.[429] No priest or intermediary is required and no mosque is necessary, since the whole world is a mosque, strictly speaking: 'And if thou speakest aloud, then lo! He knoweth the secret [thought] and that which is yet more hidden.... He knoweth what is in the land and the sea; not a leaf falleth but He knoweth it; not a grain amid the darkness of the earth, naught of wet or dry, but [it is noted] in a clear record.'[430] The Islamic garden is the outdoor sanctuary wherein may be found the beauty of God and the peace 'which passeth understanding'.

The Quranic descriptions of the *jannat al-firdaws*, the gardens of paradise, are the divine archetype on which all traditional Islamic gardens are based; centred on a spiritual vision of the cosmos, these gardens on earth – mirrors of their heavenly counterparts – aim, like all sacred art, to draw the visitor closer to God. Hopefully this book has imparted some understanding of the source of their inspiration and that this will be of value in creating gardens today in the western world. The four-fold form of the *chahar-bagh* is a kind of summing-up of an ancient, timeless and universal cosmology, as well as a more particular reminder of the paradise gardens

Fig 230. Citrus tree in the Carpet Garden, Highgrove.

portrayed in the Quran. This form, like traditional Islamic art and architecture in general, is therefore not subject to changing fashion. Providing it is adhered to, there is tremendous scope for creativity in planning the water, the hard landscaping and the planting. Like tradition itself, each generation can re-interpret and breathe new life into inherited principles, while simultaneously remaining true to the source. Tortuous topiary, fantastic grottoes, figurative sculpture and water contorted into extraordinary feats, have no place here. This garden is about simplicity, purity, and a harmony between geometry and nature, reflecting more than anything else a peaceful resignation to the natural order. It is not about being original and different but is focused on capturing a fragment of the eternal in our ephemeral world. 'Paradise is an eternal springtime, a garden perpetually in bloom, refreshed by living waters; it is also a final and incorruptible state like precious minerals, crystal and gold.'[431]

When Washington Irving, the famous American diplomat and traveller, lived at the Alhambra for a few months in 1829, he used to walk about the neighbouring hills in the evenings, and vividly described the difference between the fruitful orchards of Granada and the nearby adverse wilderness:

> We… soon found ourselves amidst wild and melancholy mountains, destitute of trees, and here and there tinted with scanty verdure. Everything within sight was severe and sterile, and it was scarcely possible to realise the idea that but a short distance behind us was the Generalife with its blooming orchards and terraced gardens and that we were in the vicinity of delicious Granada, that city of groves and fountains. But such is the nature of Spain – wild and stern the moment it escapes from cultivation. The desert and the garden are ever side by side.[432]

In today's world, the wilderness or the desert is, for most people, replaced by the city which, unlike the

Fig. 231. Moroccan courtyard, drawing by Khalid Seydo after Titus Burckhardt.

desert, has no redeeming aspect of purity. The physical pollution of the city in the form of noise, dirt, crowded streets and transport is a strain on the physical energy and mental well-being of those who live and work there. Like the early Muslims who longed for a secluded retreat from a hard desert existence, many a city-inhabitant desires to create an inner sanctum of order, beauty and peace in the form of a garden.

For many people living in the city, gardening has become a kind of therapy, since it encourages one to submit to nature's pace and let go of the desire to impose one's own. Certainly, spending time either being involved in gardening itself, or just sitting in a garden, can have a profoundly beneficial effect, especially an Islamic one with its emphasis on an underlying cosmology. This has been said many times before, but remember that the Islamic gardening tradition excels in the contemplative aspect, prompting the visitor to wonder and meditate upon the source of the beauty observed. The marvellous descriptions of the paradise gardens in the Quran, symbolic as they are, are also intended to open the eyes of those with little faith so 'that the hearts of those who believe not in the world to come may incline to it'.[433] It was fascinating to learn recently that very many people who have undergone near-death experiences, not necessarily religious, have described gardens of extraordinary beauty and serenity.[434]

As everybody is aware, especially in the United Kingdom – a tiny country compared to many of our European neighbours – the countryside is increasingly disappearing under tarmac and towns. This is an inevitable fact of modern life, with growing populations and increasing expectations of material comforts. Never before in the history of humankind have there been such enormous and densely populated urban areas as there are today; and never before has there been such an intense desire to escape these areas – usually through travel to remote places 'untouched' by humans – but also, on a smaller scale, through creating gardens. These gardens are not only beautiful to behold and places of quiet but are also (often unconsciously) a recreation of the heavenly garden, itself reflected within all of us – our inner garden: 'Look for the garden within yourself, in your indestructible divine Substance, which will then give you a new and imperishable garden.'[435]

Endnotes

Preface

1. Burckhardt, T., *Sacred Art in East and West* (Perennial Books, 1967), p.9.
2. Quran XVI: 69 and other verses. A.J. Arberry's Interpretation of the Holy Quran is used throughout unless otherwise stated (The World's Classics edition, Oxford University Press, 1989).
3. In the Visual Islamic and Traditional Arts Department (VITA) 1988–90. VITA transferred from the Royal College of Art to the Prince's Foundation (London) in 1993 and was recently (2003) re-named The Prince's School of Traditional Arts. (See endnote 135.)
4. The term 'art' is used very widely here to include the art, architecture and landscape design of the world's great traditions, not just the Islamic civilization.
5. Quran XVI: 12.
6. See Vicenzo Olivetti, *Terror's Source* (Amadeus Books, 2002), Chapter 1.
7. Greenfield, M., *Newsweek*, 26 March 1979, p.116.
8. Please see Select Bibliography for a selection of the best.

Introduction

8A. These are the areas concentrated upon for the purposes of this book. There are a great many Muslims in China and south-east Asia where the gardening traditions could be said to be a mixture between Islam and other local cultures and the climatic and landscaping conditions.
9. This was particularly true in Ottoman Turkey. See Nurhan Atasoy, *A Garden for the Sultan, Gardens and Flowers in Ottoman Culture* (Koc Culture, Arts and Communications Inc. for Aygaz, 2002), Chapter 3.
10. The most well-known being de Busbecq, the sixteenth-century ambassador of the Austrian empire to Istanbul, who first sent the tulip bulb back to Europe.
11. It is a tragedy that so many gardens in the Islamic world no longer exist except in travellers' tales or old prints.
12. In Arabic *Jannat tajri min tahtiha al-anhar*. This is the phrase most often used in the Quran to describe the gardens of paradise, e.g. XXII: 18. See Chapter 1.
13. There are many exceptions to this but if you are born and bred in a very hot climate it makes perfect sense not to physically exert yourself unless absolutely necessary.
14. Sir John Chardin, quoted by Jonas Lehrman in *Earthly Paradise: the Garden and Courtyard in Islam* (Thames and Hudson, 1980), p.112.
15. In Islam the Sayings or Traditions (*Ahadith*) of the Prophet Muhammad are second only in importance to the Quran.
16. See Hadith 16 in *Forty Hadith Qudsi*, Selected and Translated by Ezzeddin Ibrahim and Denys Johnson-Davies (The Holy Koran Publishing House, 1981), p.80.

17. David Slawson, *Secret Teachings in the Art of Japanese Gardens* (Kodansha International, 1991), p.13.
18. Huston Smith, *The World's Religions* (Harper Collins, 1991), Chapter 3.
18A Reproduced in Brigid Keenan's marvellous book, *Damascus, Hidden Treasures of the Old City* (Thames & Hudson, 2000).
19. George William Curtis, quoted by Brigid Keenan, *ibid*, p.91.
20. The roots of Judaism, Christianity and Islam all start with the great prophet Abraham, father of Ishmael and Isaac. It was Abraham and Ishmael who built the Kaaba at Mecca, the place towards which Muslims turn in their five daily prayers. The Kaaba is symbolically the centre of the world for Muslims; its shape is almost exactly a cube and the word Kaaba means 'cube'. One of the principal rites of both the major pilgrimage (*haj*) and minor pilgrimage ('*umrah*) is the circumambulation (*tawaf*) of the Kaaba. The circle represents Heaven and the Kaaba represents earth and thus symbolically man is linking Heaven and earth.
21. By which I mean all of humanity, male and female – the use of 'man' or 'mankind' is to indicate 'human beings as such' not any individual person or gender.
21A. Plato, *The Republic, Part Ten*, Penguin Classics, 1975.
22. From the ancient Latin aphorism *Pulchritudo splendor veritatis*, a phrase attributed to Plato who clearly said the same thing in different places although in different formulations. (I am grateful to Roger Gaetani of World Wisdom Books for clarifying this.)
23. If something is worshipped for itself alone, and not as a reflection of its divine archetype, then it becomes an idol.
24. This is an understatement! The most obvious example being the Central Mosque in Regent's Park, London, built in the 1960s. Interestingly, mosques built in the late-nineteenth or first half of the twentieth century in Europe, adhered to traditional Islamic design and are attractive buildings. Two examples are, firstly, the main mosque in Paris (dating from the 1920s and built in traditional North African style, and which also has a beautiful garden, see Fig. 23), and secondly, the earlier mosque in southern England, the Shah Jahan Mosque in Woking. This latter mosque, the earliest known purpose-built mosque in Europe, dates from the 1880s and is in what might be called 'neo-Mughal' style. The surroundings are currently (summer 2003) being landscaped with Islamic garden design principles in mind. Fitting a car park around these principles requires imagination!
25. Russell Page, *The Education of a Gardener* (Penguin edition, 1983), pp.360–1.
26. Hassan Fathy, *Architecture for the Poor* (The American University in Cairo Press, 1989).

Chapter 1

27. A little later (c.1500BC), a garden was also the symbol of the Afterlife for the ancient Egyptians, who often had models of gardens placed in their tombs.
28. Quran LVI: 27, and II: 268
29. Quran XXX: 18.
30. Vita Sackville-West, *Passenger to Tehran*, quoted by John Brookes in *Gardens of Paradise: A History and Design of the Great Islamic Gardens* (Weidenfeld and Nicholson, 1987), p.13.
31. Titus Burckhardt, *Moorish Culture in Spain* (George D.W. Callwey, Munich, 1970). English translation by Alisa Jaffa, George Allen & Unwin, London, 1972), pp.209–210.
32. Huston Smith, *The World's Religions* (Harper Collins, 1991), p.236.
33. Quran XXXII: 18.
34. For example, Quran XXV: 15.
35. For example, Quran LVI: 12.
36. For example, Quran XXXII: 19.
37. For example, Quran XVIII: 30.
38. For example, Quran LXI: 12.
39. Quran XV: 45.
40. A term from the *Fatiha*, the opening sura (chapter) of the Quran, which Muslims recite several times in each of the five daily prayers.
41. Religion comes from the Latin *religio* meaning to 'tie' or to 'bind', that is, to the heavenly world.
42. Martin Lings, *The Quranic Doctrine of the Afterlife*, Lecture, The Temenos Academy, London, March 1993; available on cassette from The Temenos Academy, The Prince's Foundation, London EC2. (See List of Useful Addresses.)
43. Quran II: 38.
44. Quran LXXVI: 18–20.
45. Quran LXXVIII: 35, LXXXVIII: 11, LVI: 25.
46. Quran XV: 46–47.
47. Quran LXXVI: 13.
48. It is traditional for Muslim men not to wear silk or gold; along with wine, these are saved for paradise.
49. Quran LXXVI: 21.
50. Quran XV: 48.
51. Quran LVI: 20–21.
52. Quran LXXVI: 15.
53. Quran LVI: 19.
54. For example, Quran LVII: 12.
55. Quran LXXVI: 22.
56. Sufism is the inward or mystical dimension of Islam. See Martin Lings *What is Sufism?* (Mandala., Unwin paperbacks, 1981).
57. See Chapter 2 and Martin Lings, *Symbol and Archetype, A Study of the Meaning of Existence* (Quinta Essentia, 1991), p.67. Al-Ghazali, the great eleventh-century Persian theologian, defined symbolism as 'the science of the relation between multiple levels of reality'.
58. See endnote 15.
59. See endnote 20.
60. Quran XLVII: 15 (translation by M.M. Pickthall).
61. Genesis II:10. See Chapter 3 for further explanation of the number four.

62. Titus Burckhardt, *Moorish Culture in Spain, op.cit.*, p.209.
63. Quran XXX: 18.
64. Please refer to the author's book *'Underneath which Rivers Flow', The Symbolism of the Islamic Garden* (The Prince's Foundation, 1996). For a fuller explanation of Surat-ar-Rahman see *The Book of Certainty* by Abu Bakr Siraj ad-Din (The Islamic Texts Society, 1992) and Frithjof Schuon, *Islam and The Perennial Philosophy* (World of Islam Festival Publishing Company, 1976), Chapter 12.
65. See Chapter 4 and Russell Page's description of the Avenue Chahar-Bagh in Isphahan, from *The Education of a Gardener, op.cit.*, p.222–3.
66. Quran LVI: 25–6.
67. Huston Smith, *op.cit.*, p.222.
68. Quran XVIII: 32–42.
69. Quran XVIII: 38.
70. Washington Irving, *Tales of the Alhambra* (Ediciones Miguel Sanchez, Granada, 1994), p.130.
71. Ottoman gardens were also often referred to as *irem baghi*, gardens of Heaven.
72. It is only relatively recently, in the twentieth century, that the mass export of Western culture has meant a growing confusion in the more traditional civilizations of the world such as the Islamic, Hindu and Buddhist civilizations, as well as the tribal cultures in parts of Africa.
73. Titus Burckhardt, *Art of Islam, Language and Meaning* (World of Islam Festival Publishing Company, 1976), p.91.
73A. D. Fairchild Ruggles, *Gardens, Landscape and Vision in the Palaces of Islamic Spain* (Pennsylvania State University, 2000).
74. William Morris, the principal figure of the Arts and Crafts Movement, understood this very well; his dictum that 'everything in the home should be both useful and beautiful' is a faint echo of the traditional perspective.
75. *La ilaha illa-'Lllah*, usually translated as 'There is no god but God', comprises the first part of the *Shahada*, the Muslim declaration of faith and the first of the five pillars of Islam. The second part of the *Shahada* is *Muhammadan rasulu-Llah*, 'Muhammad is the Messenger of God'.
76. Titus Burckhardt, *Art of Islam, Language and Meaning, op.cit.*, p.46.
77. *Hamlet*, Act 1, Scene 2.
78. Quoted in *Gertrude Jekyll On Gardening, An Anthology*, edited by Penelope Hobhouse (Macmillan 1985), p.23.

Chapter 2

79. Confusingly, modern travel books have begun referring to the urban courtyard house in Morocco as a *riyadh* but traditionally it is this specific house-type.
80. Constance Villiers Stuart, *Gardens of the Great Mughals* (A. & C. Black, 1913), p.42.
81. The garden on the Hill of the Sun, opposite the Alhambra in Granada, southern Spain.
82. Titus Burckhardt, *Art of Islam, Language and Meaning, op.cit.*, p.75.
83. David Slawson's book, *Secret Teachings in the Art of Japanese Gardens* (Kodansha International Ltd., paperback edition,

1991) really brings home the importance of apprenticeship and contemplation in learning the art of Japanese garden design. 'A traditional apprenticeship, the aspirant is apt to be told more than once, was supposed to last for fifteen years – long enough to make even the most patient Westerner give up in despair', p.45.

84. Quoted by Kenneth Clarke in *Piero della Francesca* (Phaidon, 1951) p.1.

85. *The Concise Oxford Dictionary*, (Oxford University Press, fifth edition, 1964) p.981.

86. Ibn 'Arabi's *Book of the Description of the Encompassing Circles (insha'ad-dawa'ir)*, quoted by Keith Critchlow in Research Projects 1993 (The Prince of Wales' Institute of Architecture, 1993), p.7.

87. John Harvey, *Medieval Gardens* (Batsford, 1981), p.41.

88. *Ibid.*

89. In gardening, *plus ça change…* This was recently brought home on reading an unpublished translation (and forthcoming article in *Studies in the History of Gardens and Designed Landscapes*, formerly the *Journal of Garden History*) by the scholar and diplomat, Philip Watson, of *A Record of Famous Gardens of Luoyang* (China) written by LI Gefei in AD1095, in which he writes that the 'rise and fall of these gardens is an indication of the prosperity or decline of Luoyang'. The author continues by saying, 'Alas! No sooner have senior ministers and high officials been appointed to court than they abandon themselves to selfish interests, working for themselves and forgetting the good governance of the world. When they themselves wish to retire to enjoy these delights will they be able to?'.

90. Ibn Luyun, *Tratado* (Arabic) p.171–5. Translated by James Dickie, 'The Islamic Garden in Spain', in *The Islamic Garden*, edited by E.B. Macdougall and R. Ettinghausen (Dumbarton Oaks Trustees for Harvard University, Washington DC, 1976), p.94.

91. *Taifa* comes from the Arabic *muluk al-tawa'if*, meaning rulers of the 'parties' or 'factions'; see Richard Fletcher, *Moorish Spain* (University of California Press, 1992), p.81.

92. Cited by al-Maqqari, *Analectes*, 1: 411–2, quoted in D. Fairchild Ruggles, *op.cit.*, p.137.

93. Babur-Namah, *Memoirs of Babur*, (Luzac, London, 1922).

94. Quoted in *Mughal Gardens, Sources, Places, Representations and Prospects*, edited by James L. Wescoat, Jr. and Joachim Wolschke-Bulmahn (Dumbarton Oaks, Trustees for Harvard University, Washington DC, 1996) p.176.

95. Peter Levi, *The Light Garden of the Angel King, Travels in Afghanistan* (Penguin, 1984), p.39.

96. *Ibid.*, p.40.

96A. Constance Villiers Stuart, *Gardens of the Great Mughals* (A & C Black, 1913), p.68.

96B. See Nurhan Atasoy, *op.cit.*, Chapter 8

96C. Unpublished translation by Philip Watson, *op.cit.*

97. This is also true of Hindu and Buddhist civilizations.

98. Such as Balliol, Merton and University Colleges, all founded in the thirteenth century, their course of studies being the Seven Liberal Arts (see Chapter 3) taught in Latin.

99. Quoted by Sylvia Landsberg, *Medieval Gardens* (British Museum Press), p.36.

100. St Luke's Gospel, XXIII: 42–3.

101. See Sylvia Landsberg, *op.cit.*, pp.36–7.

102. Thomas Baskerville, c.1675, quoted in *The Oxford Book of Oxford*, Edited by Jan Morris, 1978, p.74.

103. Maggie Campbell-Culver, *The Origin of Plants* (Headline, 2001), p.34.

104. D. Fairchild Ruggles, *op.cit.*, Chapter 4.

105. Quoted in *Plants, Gardens and the Quran* by A.K. Khan (Jasmina, Karachi, 2001).

106. John Harvey, *Medieval Gardens*, *op.cit.*, p.40.

107. Doubtless there are some courtyards with fountains but in all of the many courtyards that we looked at no fountains or pools were to be seen.

108. Quoted by Martin Lings in *What is Sufism?*, (Mandala, Unwin paperbacks, 1981) p.49.

109. Titus Burckhardt, *Moorish Culture in Spain*, *op.cit.*, p.184. A friend confessed to me not long ago that on visiting the Alhambra he became so entranced by the Court of Myrtles that he never actually made it to the Court of Lions!

110. One cannot help thinking of the famous children's book, *The Secret Garden*, by Frances Hodgson Burnett (first published 1911, now a Puffin Classic, 1994).

111. See James Dickie, 'The Islamic Garden in Spain' in *The Islamic Garden*, edited by E.B. Macdougall and R. Ettinghausen (Dumbarton Oaks Trustees for Harvard University, Washington DC, 1976), pp.99–100.

112. Constance Villiers-Stuart, *Gardens of the Great Mughals*, *op.cit.*

113. Rodrigo Claro, quoted by James Dickie in 'The Islamic Garden in Spain', *op.cit.*, pp.97–8.

114. See, for example, John Brookes' *Garden Design Book* (Dorling Kindersley, 1991).

115. As the contemporary designer, Jill Billington, has written, 'Good designers are problem solvers as well as creative interpreters', (*The Garden*, Vol. 128, Part 2, Feb. 2003).

116. Constance Villiers-Stuart, *Gardens of the Great Mughals*, *op.cit.*, p.79.

117. Two famous gardens in England, the first laid out by Lawrence Johnstone at the beginning of the twentieth century and the second laid out by Vita and Harold Sackville-West in the 1930s.

118. Interestingly, the description of the original plan sounds quasi-Islamic with a rill that channelled water from the house into two pools before descending into a larger pool in the centre of a circular lawn – entirely enclosed within yew hedges.

119. George Dillistone, *The Planning and Planting of Little Gardens*, 1920; quoted in *The Castle Drogo Guidebook* (The National Trust, 2002), p.29.

120. This is an extremely simplified summary of something very profound. Please see Select Bibliography for further reading on the spiritual content of Islamic art.

120A. A visitor to the Court of Lions in the 1970s observed: 'In the middle of the pool is a fountain of twelve lions, generally resolute, but one at least looking rather glum at the appalling "municipal" planting displayed before him'. Jules Margottin writing in 'Tour of Gardens in Southern Spain' 7th-17th June 1974, *Journal of Garden History*, Vol. III, No.1, Autumn, 1974, p.23.

121. In *The Garden of General MIAO*, 'there are over ten thousand bamboos of two or three hand-spans in circumference, like jasper pillars dappled green'. From *A Record of Famous Gardens of Luoyang*. Unpublished translation by Philip Watson, *op.cit.*

Chapter 3

122. For example, the Nehru gallery at the Victoria and Albert Museum in London has particularly beautiful carved stone *mashrabbiyya* screens.

123. There are exceptions to this, but on the whole it appears that most contemporary art is subjective.

124. For further research see: Robert Lawlor, *Sacred Geometry, Philosophy and Practice* (Thames and Hudson, 1982); Keith Critchlow, *Islamic Patterns, an Analytical and Cosmological Approach* (Thames and Hudson, 1976); as well as various unpublished theses at the Visual Islamic and Traditional Art Department (VITA), The Prince's Foundation (see Useful Addresses).

125. The other six being Arithmetic, Music or Harmony, Astronomy – which together with Geometry make up the Quadrivium – and Grammar, Logic and Rhetoric, which make up the Trivium.

126. The Brotherhood of Purity. See S.H. Nasr, *An Introduction to Islamic Cosmological Doctrines* (Cambridge, Harvard University Press, 1964).

127. Robin Waterfield, translator, *The Theology of Arithmetic* (Kairos, 1988), p 56.

128. Titus Burckhardt, *Sacred Art in East and West* (Perennial Books, 1986), p.7.

129. The Holy Trinity as well as, on a more mundane note, 'three cheers'.

130. See endnote 20.

131. Titus Burckhardt, *Sacred Art in East and West* (Perennial Books, 1986), p.18.

132. Muhyideen Ibn 'Arabi (1165–1240), known as the 'Sheikh al-Akbar', the greatest Sheikh, was a great mystic, teacher and writer who was born in Murcia, Spain and later settled and died in Damascus.

133. See William L. Hanaway Jr., 'Paradise on Earth: The Terrestrial Garden in Persian Literature', in *The Islamic Garden*, edited by E.B. Macdougall and R. Ettinghausen (Dumbarton Oaks Colloquium, Trustees for Harvard University, 1976).

134. John Brookes, *Gardens of Paradise: A History and Design of the Great Islamic Gardens* (Weidenfeld and Nicholson, 1987).

135. One of the main reasons for the founding of The Visual Islamic & Traditional Arts Programme (VITA) at The Prince's Foundation was to revive the practice of geometry. Similar programmes are now being established in Islamic countries using VITA as their model.

136. Keith Critchlow, *Islamic Patterns, An Analytical and Cosmological Approach* (Thames and Hudson, 1976); Issam el-Said, edited by Tarek El-Bouri and Keith Critchlow, *Islamic Art and Architecture, The System of Geometric Design* (Garnet Publishing Ltd., 1993); and Robert Lawlor, *Sacred Geometry,*

Philosophy and Practice (Thames and Hudson, 1982). There are also one or two workbooks available from VITA at The Prince's Foundation. See List of Useful Addresses.

137. This is elaborated on in two marvellous books, one by David Slawson, *op.cit.*, and *Infinite Spaces, the Art and Wisdom of the Japanese Garden*, Introduction by Joe Earle, (Galileo Multimedia, 2000).

138. Nurhan Atasoy's book *A Garden for the Sultan*, *op.cit.*, refers to and translates many fascinating Ottoman Turkish documents relating to gardens, gardening, trees, plants and flowers but as far as I can see, not much on the actual training of the gardener. There is scope for interesting research here.

139. See endnote 135.

140. Always make sure that tiles and pots are frost-proof. See section on 'Pots and Containers'.

141. Traditionally, it is said there are ninety-nine names of God in Islam, each indicating one of His divine attributes such as *ar-Rahman* the Merciful, or *as-Salam* the Peaceful, or *al-Quddus*, the Holy.

142. See endnote 75. The *Basmalah* is the prayer of consecration, *Bismi-Llahi-r-Rahmani-r-Rahim*, 'In the Name of God, the Merciful, the Compassionate'.

143. Muhammad ibn Ahmar, a prince of the Nasrid tribe, made this the battle-cry of the Nasrid dynasty from the mid-thirteenth century.

144. A *mashrabbiyya* is a turned wood or slatted wood screen; see section later on in this chapter.

145. Ian Hamilton-Finlay's 'literary garden' near Dunsyre, Lanarkshire, Scotland, is well-known for its many pieces of letter-carving in stone, wood and other materials depicting a wide variety of sayings. Many of them are on the ground, which should not be the case in an Islamic garden.

146. Quran LV: 46.

147. Quran LVI: 24.

148. Quran XVII: 80 (Yusuf Ali's translation).

149. Both from *The Sayings of Muhammad*, translated and compiled by Allama Sir Abdullah al-Mamun al-Suhrawardy (John Murray, 1992).

150. Dorothy Frances Gurney (1858–1932), *God's Garden*. Indeed, the title of one of the gardens at the Chelsea Flower Show in 2003 was a couplet from a poem: 'What is this life if, full of care/We have no time to stand and stare?' (from *Leisure* by W.H. Davies, 1870-1940).

151. Annemarie Schimmel refers to this being an inscription in the audience hall in Delhi in her essay 'The Celestial Garden', in *The Islamic Garden*, edited by E.B. Macdougall and R. Ettinghausen (Dumbarton Oaks, Trustees for Harvard University, Washington DC, 1976).

152. Jalal-ud-Din Rumi wrote similarly in his *Mathnawi* IV: 1357, quoted by Anne Marie Schimmel, *op.cit.*, p.23, see endnote 153.

153. Rumi is a famous Muslim scholar, poet and mystic, originally from Persia but who settled in Konya in Turkey. He founded the Mevlevi Sufi order, known as the 'Whirling Dervishes' because of their beautiful circular dancing (*sama*) and music, both of which are supports on their spiritual path.

154. Today, if money is no object, materials can be transported all over the world and Italian marble floors can be seen from Abu Dhabi to Los Angeles.

155. Titus Burckhardt, *Art of Islam, Language and Meaning* (World of Islam Festival Publishing Company, 1976), p.61.

156. Dating from the nineteenth century, Minton is probably the most famous tile manufacturer in England. These tiles are found in churches and houses all over the United Kingdom.

157. The wide variety of materials available now has been used to great effect in many cities in the United Kingdom and the rest of Europe. They have improved public spaces tremendously.

158. See endnote 136.

159. Quran VI: 2.

160. Genesis, II: 7.

161. The science of alchemy is itself ancient and serves as a base for a spiritual tradition linked to Hermes Trismegistus and the Egyptian god, Thoth. Alchemy was centred upon the transmutation of base metal into gold, which symbolized the transmutation of the soul into the spirit.

162. Frithjof Schuon. This and the following quotations in the paragraph are from his essay, *The Principles and Criteria of Art*, in *Castes and Races* (Perennial Books, 1982) Chapter III, pp.61–88.

163. Both Chinese and Japanese gardens revere rocks and stones, aware of their ineffable quality.

164. See endnote 122.

165. Stephen Gerlach of the Austrian Embassy, quoted by Nurhan Atasoy in *A Garden for the Sultan, op.cit.*, p.311.

166. Field-Marshall von Moltke visiting Istanbul in 1837, quoted by Nurhan Atasoy, in *A Garden for the Sultan, op.cit.*, p.297.

167. See miniature painting in Nurhan Atasoy's *A Garden for the Sultan, op.cit.*, p.263.

168. *Ibid.*, pp.304–5.

169. See List of Useful Addresses.

170. Stephen Gerlach of the Austrian Embassy, quoted by Nurhan Atasoy in *A Garden for the Sultan, op.cit.*, p.311.

171. An exception to this general rule is shown in an Ottoman miniature depicted in Nurhan Atasoy's *A Garden for the Sultan, op.cit.*, p.53. The miniature is from the Hamse-I Atayi and is entitled 'A Meal in a Garden' in which gentlemen, mainly in European dress, are sitting and eating under a raised wooden pergola, the roof entwined with foliage. This dates from the eighteenth century and demonstrates the European influence that was gradually increasing at this time.

172. Sylvia Landsberg, *Medieval Gardens* (British Museum Press), Chapter 2.

173. Quoted by Constance Villiers Stuart, *Gardens of the Great Mughals, op.cit.*, p.67.

174. *Ibid.*, p.79.

175. In spite of Vita Sackville-West's view that they are a hideous colour!

176. Fire, emanating from the sun, is a symbol of the Spirit.

177. Both quotations are from: Sajjad Kausar, Michael Brand, James, L. Wescoat Jr., *Shalimar Garden, Lahore, Landscape, Form and Meaning* (Dept. of Archaeology and Museums, Ministry of Culture, Pakistan, 1990).

178. Flora Thompson, *Lark Rise to Candleford* (Penguin, 1973), the well-known trilogy about life in rural England in the 1880s, p.422.

179. The prettiest, simple to use, and inexpensive lights I have seen recently are Moroccan garden lanterns (using night-lights) attached to a wooden pole, which can be pushed into the ground wherever you wish, approximately 70cm high. These are available via mail order at Sarah Raven's Cutting Garden. See List of Useful Addresses.

180. It is enough to observe a Christmas-tree with fairy-lights and then one with lighted candles to see how profoundly beautiful the latter one is compared to the more superficial prettiness of the former. The magic of flickering candles captivates children in a way that electric light never does.

181. See Sally Storey, *Lighting by Design* (Pavilion, 2002). She reminds us never to leave candles burning unattended.

182. See Nurhan Atasoy, *A Garden for the Sultan, op.cit.*, Chapter 8.

183. Quoted by Sajjad Kausar in *Shalamar Garden Lahore, Landscape, Form and Meaning, op.cit.*, Chapter 4, p.74.

Chapter 4

183A. C. Villiers-Stuart, *Gardens of the Great Mughals, op.cit.*

184. Huston Smith, *The World's Religions* (Harper Collins, 1991), p.246.

185. For example, Philip Swindells, 'Water Gardening', *The RHS Encyclopedia of Practical Gardening* (Mitchell Beazley, 2001); and Anthony Archer-Wills, *The Water Gardener* (Frances Lincoln, 2000).

186. See Chapter 2 and Andreas Wohlhasen, *Living Architecture, Islamic Indian* (Macdonald, 1970), p.90.

187. Apparently Saddam Hussein liked to show off his 'muscle' by having swimming pools in all of his twenty palaces.

187A. Staying in Jeddah (Saudi Arabia) recently the weather became cloudy and overcast; my friend who lives there explained that locally this was considered the very best weather they could have – everyone wanted the day off to go to the beach!

188. This normally requires a simple turning-off of the pump switch; but if you suspect your material not to be frost-proof (always check when buying), such as some marbles, then the fountain needs to be packed up with anything warm you can find such as old blankets, straw or fleece and covered in a strong plastic sheet tied up firmly. This does not look beautiful but it will save much distress if a hard frost comes.

189. Genesis I: 2.

190. Quran XXI: 30 (M. M. Pickthall's Test and Explanatory Translation of the Glorious Quran, Taj Company, Lahore).

191. Quran XXV: 25.

192. Quran XXXI: 10.

193. Quran XLI: 39.

194. Quran XIX: 22–5 (A.J. Arberry).

195. When the Prophet Muhammad was asked by one of his disciples, 'My mother is dead; what is the best alms I can give away for the good of her soul?' the Prophet, thinking of the heat of the desert, answered, 'Water! Dig a well for her, and give water to the thirsty'.

196. It is interesting to note that the ritual ablutions (*wudu*) of a Muslim must be carried out with running water, not still water in a basin, since running water is constantly purifying itself. How many times have I heard Muslim friends complaining

about the separate hot and cold taps in England, which render it almost impossible to make the ablutions without freezing or burning!

197. John Wesley (1703–91), from his sermon no. xciii, *On Dress*. Ironically, when the Catholics gradually re-conquered Spain from the Muslims, they actively discouraged their Christian flock from washing too much, since in their eyes water and washing had become associated with the Muslims who were linked with lust and lasciviousness!

198. 'The soul resembles water, just as the Spirit resembles wind or air,' writes Titus Burckhardt in *Mirror of the Intellect* (Cambridge, Quinta Essentia, 1987), p.128.

199. See Endnote 56.

200. Titus Burckhardt, *Moorish Culture in Spain* (George D.W. Calley, Munich, 1970). English translation Alisa Jaffa (George Allen and Unwin, 1972), p.208.

201. Recently I was told that there is a saying in Hinduism that whoever looks upon the Himalayas is cleansed of his or her sins: such is the purifying power of virgin nature at her most majestic.

202. Titus Burckhardt, *Mirror of the Intellect*, Translated and edited by William Stoddart (Quinta Essentia, 1987) p.128

203. One cannot help thinking of Macbeth, whose sin was so great that 'all great Neptune's ocean' could not 'wash this blood clean from my hand'. (Act II: II).

204. St. Paul's Letter to the Corinthians, IV: 18.

205. Noble Ross Reat, *The Tree Symbol in Islam* (Studies in Comparative Religion, summer 1975), p.178.

206. Quoted in *Ibid.*, p.179.

207. Green is the colour of Islam and this is largely because of the many times it is mentioned in the descriptions of the paradise gardens in the Quran.

208. Quran LXXXIII: 26.

209. Quran LXXVI: 27.

210. See Abu Bakr Siraj ad-Din, *The Book of Certainty, the Sufi Doctrine of Faith, Vision and Gnosis* (Islamic Texts Society, 1992); and the author's book, *'Underneath which Rivers Flow', The Symbolism of the Islamic Garden* (The Prince of Wales' Institute of Architecture, 1996).

211. It is possible to see more examples in the Islamic museum in Cairo.

212. See Yasser Tabbaa, 'Towards an Interpretation of the Use of Water in Islamic Courtyards and Courtyard Gardens', *Journal of Garden History*, Vol.7, No. 3, p.205.

213. Quoted by Y. Tabbaa, *Ibid*, p.205.

214. Macbeth, Act V: I.

215. Russell Page, *op. cit.*, p.224.

216. *Ibid.*

217. Other large Mughal gardens in Kashmir may be mentioned here such as the Achabal gardens with its many fountains and the Nishat Bagh (Garden of Gladness) centred on water linking different levels.

218. Sajjad Kausar, Michael Brand, James L. Wescoat Jr., *Shalamar Garden, Lahore, op. cit.*, p.vi.

219. For example, Quran LXI: 12. See Chapter 1 for explanation of this phrase.

220. Russell Page, *op. cit.*

221. Chris Stewart, *Driving Over Lemons* (Sort Of Books, 1999), pp.112–3.

222. See Francisco Prieto Moreno, *Los Jardines de Granada* (Arte de Espana, 1983).

223. Burckhardt, *Moorish Culture in Spain, op. cit.*, Chapter XII.

224. There are two extremely comfortable leather armchairs at both ends of this courtyard and I highly recommend the visitor sit on one of these at the first opportunity and stay there for an hour or so – only then does the magic start to work and the visitors fade into the background.

225. The American author of *Tales from the Alhambra* (first published in 1832, Ediciones Miguel Sanchez, Granada, 1994)

226. *Ibid.*

227. *Ibid.*

228. *Ibid.*

229. See Richard Fletcher, *Moorish Spain* (University of California Press, 1992), p.66, who continues 'Well, it's what our sources tell us. Perhaps the loaves were extremely small'.

230. See John Harvey, 'Spanish Gardens in their Historical Background' *Journal of Garden History*, Vol. III, No.1, Autumn 1974, p.7–14.

231. Quoted by D. Fairchild Ruggles, *Gardens, Landscape and Vision in the Palaces of Islamic Spain* (Pennsylvania State University Press, 2000), p.31.

232. Quoted in *The Rough Guide to Morocco*, 1994.

233. Brigid Keenan, Damascus, *Hidden Treasures of the Old City* (Thames and Hudson, 2000).

234. Quoted in *ibid.*

235. Quoted in *ibid.*

236. Quoted in *ibid.*

237. Russell Page, *op. cit.*, p.222.

238. Quoted by Arthur Upham Pope in *A Survey of Persian Art from Prehistoric Times to the Present* (Oxford University Press, first published 1938) Vol. VI. It is interesting how many travellers talk about 'tanks', which today we tend to associate with something very functional with no pretensions to beauty; for instance, a fish-tank or an oil-tank, or indeed a water-tank. By 'water-tank' we usually mean a large metal or plastic container which may feed the boiler and which you probably would not view with much idea of aesthetic pleasure. Also, Herbert describes the 'pile' (some kind of pavilion) as being 'antickly garnished'. This presumably means that they made the pavilion look as though it had been there for years already, much as some antique dealers 'antick' their wares today before adding a few noughts onto the price.

239. See endnote 185.

240. However, there is no doubt that gravity-led fountains can still produce extraordinarily powerful jets of water. Paxton designed the Emperor fountain for the Duke of Devonshire at Chatsworth in the 1840s, which shot 260ft up into the air. See Kate Colquhoun, *A Thing in Disguise: the Visionary Life of Joseph Paxton* (Fourth Estate, 2003), p. 130 (see endnote 425).

241. This idea of a thin veil of water running over stone has been employed in fountains recently installed in the courtyard of the Royal Academy of Arts in London. It works quite well but the weather is cold and damp for much of the year and the water intensifies this.

242. One of our alumni at VITA, The Prince's Foundation, carved a marble *chador* for his degree show and set it up in the exhibition

with water falling over it. It looked very good but would look far better in the place for which it was intended – a garden.

243. Although the profound symbolism of these far-Eastern gardens is similar to the symbolism of Islamic gardens, that of a constant awareness of the invisible reality underlying all phenomena, the manifestation is quite different. This is due to complex and profound differences in perspective, which we do not have the space to consider here. Please see Selected Bibliography for recommended reading.

244. Another inspiring Lutyens and Jekyll garden with Islamic-style rills is Sonning in Berkshire.

245. BBC 2 Horizon programme, *The Quest for El Dorado*, 19 December 2002.

246. No endnote 246.

247. Muhammad Asad, *The Road to Makkah* (Islamic Book Service, New Delhi, 1994) quoted in Saudi Aramco World, Jan/Feb 2002, p.27.

Chapter 5

248. *Poems from the Persian*, translated by J.C.E. Bowen (Blackwell, Oxford, 1958), p.53.

249. Full names and more details about these trees and shrubs are included later in the chapter.

250. In Islam there is a well-known saying that 'Marriage is half the religion', the other half traditionally said to be patience or fortitude.

251. Richard Bisgrove and Paul Hadley, *Gardening in the Global Greenhouse: Climate Change and Gardens*, 2002.

252. John H. Harvey, 'Gardening Books and Plant Lists of Moorish Spain', *Journal of Garden History*, Vol. III, No. 2, 1975, pp.10–21.

253. See Nurhan Atasoy, *A Garden for the Sultan, Gardens and Flowers in Ottoman Culture*, *op.cit.*

254. Kritovoulos, quoted in Andrew Wheatcroft, *The Ottomans* (Penguin, 1993), p.27.

255. Quoted by Annemarie Schimmel in 'The Celestial Garden', *op.cit.*

256. No endnote 256.

257. The roses at the Alhambra and Generalife gardens, for example, seem mostly to be modern hybrids. If these were replaced by species roses, many of which originate in the Near East (such as the damask roses), the gardens would be closer to how they looked in the thirteenth to fifteenth centuries, as well as being, I feel, more beautiful. The 'old roses' are of a subtle and delicate beauty with stronger fragrance than the artificial-looking colours and vast flower-heads of many modern hybrids. See Chapter 6.

258. Quran, LV: 12.

259. See endnote 15.

260. John Harvey, *Medieval Gardens*, *op.cit*: 'Unlike the Greeks who ravaged the fields of their fellow Greeks with whom they were at war, cutting down their olive groves, the Muslims were at pains to avoid destruction and, as soon as possible, restored peaceful government and prosperity to the countries they overran', p.37

261. See Chapter 2, endnote 105.

262. Noble Ross Reat, 'The Tree Symbol in Islam', (*Studies in Comparative Religion*, Summer 1975) pp.164–82.

263. This is an evergreen tree up to 15m high, with whitish branches and thorns. It is commonly cultivated in Egypt for its timber and edible fruits. The crown of thorns of Christ is said to have been made of its spiky branches, hence its name *spina-christi*, literally spines of Christ.

264. Please see Abu Bakr Siraj ad-Din, *The Book of Certainty*, (Islamic Texts Society, Cambridge, 1992), Chapter 2; also see M. Iqtedar H. Farooqi, *Plants of the Quran* (Sidrah Publishers, Lucknow, 1997).

265. The Book of Psalms, CIV:16.

266. Ibn Hanbal, quoted by Noble Ross Reat, *The Tree Symbol in Islam, op.cit.*

267. *Ibid.*

268. Quran XIV: 24–5.

269. Martin Lings, *The Book of Certainty, op.cit.*, Chapter 7.

270. Quran XIV: 26.

271. See M. Iqtedar and H. Farooqi, *Plants of the Quran, op.cit.*, for a more detailed analysis.

272. Quran XIX: 22–5.

273. Maggie Campbell-Culver, *The Origin of Plants*, (Headline 2001), pp.24–5.

274. See M. Iqtedar and H. Farooqi, *Plants of the Quran op.cit.*, in which the author adds that in ancient Greece there were people called 'fig-informers' who gave information on the whereabouts of figs, *sukophantai*, which became the English 'sycophant'.

275. There is a particularly magnificent specimen of the banyan tree in the gardens of the Manial Palace in Cairo.

276. Genesis III: 7.

277. Quoted by Ibn Qayyim al-Jawziyya, *Medicine of the Prophet*, translated by Penelope Johnstone (Islamic Texts society, 1998) p.227.

278. Quran, XXIV: 35.

279. See M. Iqtedar and H. Farooqi, *Plants of the Quran, op.cit.*, pp.49-54.

280. Noble Ross Reat, *op.cit.*

281. Genesis VIII:11 and Quran VII: 59–60. There is no dove mentioned in the Quranic version of the flood.

282. F. Nigel Hepper, *Illustrated Encyclopedia of Bible Plants* (Three's Company, 1992), p.108.

283. Quoted by Ibn Qayyim al-Jawziyya, *Medicine of the Prophet*, *op.cit.*, p.227.

284. See Clive Simms, 'Olives al Fresco', *The Garden*, Vol. 127, Part 6, June, 2002, pp.444–5.

285. *Ibid.*

286. I noticed recently (March 2003) that at Kew Gardens they had experimented leaving this cultivar outside over winter in a south-facing border against a brick wall but unfortunately it had not survived.

287. The two other times are in Chapters VI: 99 and 141.

288. See Abu Bakr Siraj Ad-Din, *The Book of Certainty, op.cit.*

289. See M. Iqtedar and H. Farooqi, *Plants of the Quran op.cit.*, p.65.

290. Ibn Said, in al-Maqqari, Anelectes, 1: 305, quoted in D. Fairchild Ruggles, *Gardens, Landscape, and Vision in the Palaces*

of Islamic Spain (The Pennsylvania State University, 2000), p.17.

291. Russell Page, *The Education of a Gardener, op.cit.*

292. The Islamic world (the *Dar al-Islam*) is changing all the time and this is one of the reasons for writing this book, i.e. the problems experienced by traditional Islamic cultures settling into the predominantly non-traditional Western world.

293. An amazing example of an oriental plane tree is to be seen at Ham House in Richmond, outside London, where the oldest living specimen in the UK is growing. It dates from the 1770s and is quite magnificent.

294. Quran LVI: 30 and LV: 48.

295. See p.116 and Annemarie Schimmel, *The Celestial Garden, op.cit.*

296. Hilliers' *Manual of Trees and Shrubs* (David & Charles, 1974).

297. The only drawback is that the *Eucryphia*'s habit is not quite as dense as one may wish for an Islamic garden.

298. See Chapter 6 for the symbolism of trees and flowers in the story of Layla and Majnun. The cypress, as well as being symbolic of eternal life, is also sometimes said to represent a slim and graceful lady. Norah M. Titley, *Plants and Gardens in Persian, Mughal and Turkish Art* (The British Library, 1979), p.6.

299. C.M. Villiers Stuart, *Gardens of the Great Mughals, op.cit.*, pp.87–8.

300. According to ornamental fruit-tree specialists, the almond is highly vulnerable to the disease 'peach-leaf curl' and for this reason has become far less popular than in the past.

301. Quran LVI: 20.

302. Quran LV: 54.

303. See John Harvey, 'Gardening books and plant lists of Moorish Spain', *op.cit.*

304. So-called, as it was thought to come from Persia, though in fact in the nineteenth century it was found to grow wild in China.

305. A nursery in the west of England, Thornhayes, specializes in native varieties of fruit-tree. See List of Useful Addresses.

306. Maggie Campbell-Culver, *op.cit.*, p.55.

307. Quoted by Nurhan Atasoy, *op.cit.*

308. Before investing in a couple of beautiful large terracotta pots planted with orange or lemon trees, remember that they will need moving twice a year from their winter home to their summer location and back again. The best method I have found, requiring least labour, is on a sack-truck.

309. Quran LVI: 29.

310. Quran II: 267.

311. By M.M. Pickthall in his explanatory translation of the Quran, *op.cit.*

312. See M. Iqtedar and H. Farooqi, *Plants of the Quran, op.cit.*

313. See Martin Lings' *Muhammad, his Life Based on the Earliest Sources* (Unwin Paperbacks, 1988), p.255.

314. Quran XXXIV: 16.

315. Quran II: 57.

316. E.g. Quran LXXVIII: 31.

317. At Hampton Court Palace, just outside London, there grows what is said to be the oldest-known vine in the world. Planted by 'Capability' Brown in 1768 it is a *Vitis vinifera* 'Schiava Grossa' and has now grown to 120ft long with a 5ft girth.

318. So-called because of the tradition that Judas hanged himself from this tree and the deep pink flowers that appear before the leaves in spring represent his blood, or some say the blood of the betrayed Christ. Other say that it is simply the tree of Judaea.

319. For those interested in geometry, the red berries of the rowan tree each have a five-pointed star at the base. The number five is usually – and universally – associated with the human body, the torso having four limbs and a head.

320. Quoted by Nurhan Atasoy, *op.cit.*, p.305.

321. Jane Austen, *Mansfield Park* (Penguin edition, 1996), pp.47–8.

322. *Poems from the Persian*, translated by J.C E. Bowen (Blackwell, Oxford, 1958), p.55.

323. Remember that all parts of the oleander are poisonous, so it is better to avoid this if children are around.

324. Please refer to John Harvey's invaluable work, 'Gardening Books and Plant Lists of Moorish Spain', *op.cit.*

325. See Nurhan Atasoy, *op.cit.*, Chapter 8.

326. No Endnote 326.

Chapter 6

327. *Poems from the Persian, op.cit.*, p.47. Anwari was a Persian poet known for his skill in writing *qasidas*, poems or songs in praise of a living person or more mystical ones in praise of God.

328. Russell Page, *The Education of a Gardener* (Penguin, 1983), p.90.

329. *Ibid.*

330. Jules Margottin, 'Tour of Gardens in Southern Spain', *Journal of Garden History*, Vol. III, No.1, Autumn 1974, p.15ff.

331. Indeed, the recent vogue in 'Western' gardening for mixing vegetables with ornamental plants in a fairly geometric layout is quite Islamic. The large walled garden at Highgrove is a good example of this. It is laid out on an axial plan with a central fountain, the four quarters with geometric plantings of symmetrically coloured vegetables mixed with tunnels of sweet-peas and arbours of roses. Another example is the 'potager' or vegetable garden at Rosemore, the RHS garden in North Devon – in this case there is a central rose-covered arbour rather than a fountain.

332. Evidence shows that this is changing gradually as our winters, although still wet, are not as cold as they were and hard frosts are less frequent. See 'Changing Climate' in Chapter 5.

333. Quoted in Nurhan Atasoy, *A Garden for the Sultan, op.cit.*, p.338.

334. Friends told me recently how, on expecting a visit from a Persian lady, they had specially picked a selection of the most strongly scented roses and other flowers from their garden. When she arrived, she remarked on their beauty, inhaled deeply, looked up and said, 'What a pity they don't have scent; in our country the flowers all have a wonderful fragrance.'!

335. See John Harvey, 'Gardening Books and Plant Lists of Moorish Spain', *op.cit.*, pp.10–12. In this important and highly recommended article Harvey makes clear that there are difficulties in identifying a few of the genera listed.

336. See Ralph Pinder-Wilson, 'The Persian Garden' in *The Islamic Garden, op.cit.*, p.82.

337. Ibn Said, in al-Maqqari, Anelectes, 1: 304, quoted in D. Fairchild Ruggles, *Gardens, Landscape, and Vision in the Palaces of Islamic Spain* (The Pennsylvania State University, 2000), p.17.

338. Quoted by Elizabeth Moynihan, 'But what a Happiness to have known Babur!', in *Mughal Gardens*, edited by James L. Wescoat, Jr. and Joachim Wolschke-Bulmahn (Dumbarton Oaks Trustees for Harvard University Washington DC, 1996), p.123.

339. Quoted by Andrew Wheatcroft, *The Ottomans, Dissolving Images* (Penguin, 1995). Wheatcroft adds a grim note about Sultan Mehmet, whose love of gardens did not prevent him from performing savage acts such as, on 'finding one of his prize cucumbers missing, ripped open the stomachs of his gardeners to discover which one of them had eaten it', p.27.

340. This is elaborated on later in the chapter.

341. Both quoted by Donald Newton Wilber in 'Persian Gardens and Garden Pavilions' in *The Islamic Garden, op.cit.*, pp.16–17.

342. See Andrew Watson, *Agricultural Innovation in the Early Islamic World* (Cambridge University Press, 1983), Chapter 22.

343. Sir Thomas Herbert, quoted by Arthur Upham Pope in *A Survey of Persian Art from Prehistoric Times to the Present* (Oxford University Press, 1938), see Vol. VI. See Penelope Hobhouse's new book (Cassell 2003) *Gardens of Persia*, for up-to-date descriptions of Persian gardens.

344. Quoted by Donald N. Wilber in 'Persian Gardens and Garden Pavilions', *op.cit.*, p.6

345. See James Dickie, 'The Islamic Garden in Spain', in *The Islamic Garden*, edited by E.B. Macdougall and R. Ettinghausen (Dumbarton Oaks, Trustees for Harvard University, Washington DC, 1976).

346. Quoted by Nurhan Atasoy, *The Garden of the Sultan, op.cit.*, p.328.

347. Quoted by Jane Brown in *The Pursuit of Paradise* (Harper Collins, 1999), p.37.

348. See Nurhan Atasoy, *A Garden for the Sultan, op.cit.*, for fascinating and revealing research about Ottoman gardens.

349. *Ibid.*, p.46. Two sixteenth-century European observers of life in Istanbul.

350. 'O Rose, this painted rose/Is not the whole/Who paints the flower/Paints not its fragrant soul'. Carmina Burana, thirteenth century, quoted by Sylvia Landsberg, *The Medieval Garden, op.cit.*

351. Titus Burckhardt referring to himself, the author of *Sacred Art in East and West* (Perennial Books, 1986), pp.103–4.

352. Traditionally, it is said there are ninety-nine names of God in Islam, each indicating one of His divine attributes such as *ar-Rahman* the Merciful, or *as-Salam* the Peace, or *al-Quddus*, the Holy.

353. For example, icons, although depicting a human image, which was discouraged in Islam, are not naturalistic but are formalized and symbolic. It was not until the Renaissance that the Virgin Mary was painted as a human being and thus brought down to our level. The Muslim prohibition on images – at least in a liturgical setting – was in part to prevent the humanizing and therefore limiting effect that would inevitably take place.

354. See Sylvia Landsberg, *The Medieval Garden, op.cit.*

355. Overheard by a colleague at a conference on Religious Art in Tehran in 1995.

356. Nurhan Atasoy, *A Garden for the Sultan, op.cit.*, p.63.

357. C. M. Villiers Stuart, *Gardens of the Great Mughals* (A. & C. Black, 1913) pp.149–50.

358. See Annemarie Schimmel, 'The Celestial Garden' in *The Islamic Garden, op.cit.*, for a fuller and beautiful explanation of the symbolism of the rose in Islam.

359. *Ibid.*

360. It is true that the Ottomans specialized in exotic turban tying!

361. As has been well documented by Anna Pavord in her book, *The Tulip* (Bloomsbury, 1999) this flower took off into unprecedented realms of popularity, fashion and monetary value right across Europe.

362. Abu Talib Kalim, Persian poet in the court of Shah Jahan, quoted by Annemarie Schimmel in 'The Celestial Garden', *op.cit.*

363. Quoted by Annemarie Schimmel, *ibid.*

364. C. M. Villiers Stuart, *Gardens of the Great Mughals* (A. & C. Black, 1913), p.88.

365. Quoted by Nurhan Atasoy in *A Garden for the Sultan, op.cit.*, p.311.

366. *Ibid.*, p.312.

367. *Ibid.*, p.27.

368. Flora Thompson, *Lark Rise to Candleford, op.cit.*, p.115.

369. This has become quite popular in the last few years, a well-known example being the borders of the garden that won the 'Best in Show' prize at the Chelsea Flower Show 2000, the *Gardens Illustrated* garden, designed by Arne Maynard and Piet Oudolf.

370. Lord Northbourne, 'Flowers', essay included in *Seeing God Everywhere, Essays on Nature and the Sacred*, edited by Barry Macdonald (World Wisdom, 2002), pp.279–95.

371. More research needs to be carried out in this field to continue John Harvey's important work.

372. The *RHS Plant Finder*, devised by Chris Philip, principal editor Tony Lord, (Dorling Kindersley, 2002–2003).

373. *Sura LV*, referred to earlier as the longest description of the paradise gardens in the Quran.

374. Translation by Martin Lings in his book *What is Sufism?* (Unwin Paperbacks, 1981), p.56. The author adds a footnote that 'coolness of the eyes' is 'a proverbial Arabic expression signifying intense pleasure'.

375. Although it has become far more widely available since the 1960s, albeit in a very diluted form in incense sticks, which bear little resemblance to the real thing. A Saudi Arabian friend specialises in making her own incense from the finest ingredients including sandalwood soaked in jasmine oil. Burning it in the house or the garden seems to transport one to a heavenly realm.

376. For example, Sylvia Landsberg's *The Medieval Garden, op.cit.*, and Jekka McVicar's *New Book of Herbs* (Dorling Kindersley, 2002).

377. Nurhan Atasoy's book *A Garden for the Sultan, op.cit.*,

reveals fascinating information from Turkish sources but there is still plenty of scope for the Arabic and Persian scholar.

378. See M. Iqtedar and H. Farooqi, *Plants of the Quran op.cit.*, and Ibn Qayyim al-Jawziyya, *Medicine of the Prophet*, translated by Penelope Johnstone (The Islamic Texts Society, 1998).

379. A good place to observe many different species of lavender altogether, as well as other herbs, is at Buckfast Abbey in Devon, south-west England.

380. Roy Genders, *Flowers and Herbs of Love* (Darton, Longman and Todd, 1978).

381. H.G. Witham Fogg, *Geranium Growing* (W. & G. Foyle, 1955).

382. See John Harvey, 'Gardening Books and Plant Lists of Moorish Spain', *Journal of Garden History, op.cit.*

383. The word *salvia* comes from the Latin *salvere* meaning 'to heal' and the expression 'wise old sage' comes from the fact that sage may calm mental anxiety, and, interestingly, is now being tested for the treatment of Alzheimer's Disease.

384. One herbal reported that 'a lady of Trent was... almost shaken to pieces with laughing immoderately for a space of three hours, which was occasioned by her taking too much saffron'. Quoted by Alice Coats in *Flowers and their Histories* (Ebury Press, 1999). It is said that it takes 4,300 flowers to yield 1oz of saffron. The word 'saffron' comes from the Arabic *zafaran* and in south-eastern Turkey there is an orthodox Syrian monastery called Deir el-Zaferan. See Maggie Campbell-Culver, *The Origin of Plants, op.cit.*, p.82).

385. For detailed analysis of the medicinal properties of the herbs included here see David Hoffman's excellent *The Complete Illustrated Holistic Herbal* (Element Books, Shaftsbury, 1996) as well as Jekka McVicar's *New Book of Herbs* (Dorling Kindersley, 2002).

386. Further East in the Gulf countries, the climate is more extreme and most of the flowers mentioned would be too sensitive for the hot, arid conditions and would not last long, even if watered regularly. In these conditions, the real heat-loving, exotic plants, such as frangipani, gardenia and of course the date-palm, thrive providing they receive enough water.

387. This is even possible in crowded London. Two friends of mine were very fortunate in buying houses, one in south London and one in west London, each of which have a small area (approximately 15m x 10m) at the bottom of their narrow back gardens planted with a mixture of apple, pear and cherry trees.

388. Remember that the word *narcissi* contains 'narc', part of the word 'narcotic' so you may be forgiven for feeling rather sleepy after inhaling its scent!

389. C. M. Villiers Stuart, *op.cit.*, p.74.

390. The origin of this name seems to be lost. However, '*Sharif(a)*' is a title given to one who is a descendant of the Prophet Muhammad through one of his grandsons, and '*Asma*' is an ancient Arab name, difficult to translate, but very approximately means 'higher' or the 'highest'.

391. Quoted by Brigid Keenan in *Damascus, Hidden Treasures of the Old City, op.cit.*

392. Vita Sackville-West's *Garden Book* (Michael Joseph, 1987).

393. See Roger Phillips and Martyn Rix, *Traditional Old Roses* (Pan, 1998), p.20.

394. *Ibid.*, p.39. Nancy Lindsay was the friend of Lawrence Johnstone of Hidcote fame.

395. As noted above, the tulip was supposed to be similar to a Turk's turban and the 'Turk's cap' lily similar to a Turk's cap – well, the Turks certainly were besotted with their flowers!

396. Robin Lane Fox, *op.cit.*, p.137.

397. *Ibid.*, p.163.

398. John Harvey, 'Gardening Books and Plant lists of Moorish Spain', *op.cit.* He also says that the two lists he is analysing 'show that in one century (between c.1080 and c.1180) the number of species had doubled', p.12.

399. From *The Telegraph*, 14 June 2003.

400. See Anthony Archer-Wills, *The Water Gardener, op.cit.*

401. See Sarah Raven's *Cutting Garden Catalogue* in List of Useful Addresses.

402. John Harvey, 'Gardening Books and Plant Lists of Moorish Spain', *op.cit.*, p.13.

403. Dr M. Iqtedar H. Farooqi, *Plants of the Quran* (Sidrah Publishers, Lucknow, 1997), Chapter XX.

404. Quran XXXVII: 62–8.

405. In order to appreciate the special and mysterious beauty of the colour green, it is interesting to try and imagine how the natural world would look if it were another colour – red or blue, for example. Quite an uncomfortable thought! Green, as is well known, is the happy result of mixing the celestial colour, blue – a contemplative and cool colour – with yellow, the colour of the sun, warm and uplifting. When yellow is 'mixed with blue, it gives to the contemplativity associated with this colour a quality of "hope", of saving joy, and a liberation out of the enveloping quietude of contemplation'. Frithjof Schuon, *Spiritual Perspectives and Human Facts* (Perennial books, 1987), p.43.

406. The dome of the Prophet Muhammad's mosque at Medina has been painted green for several centuries. It is also said that the Prophet often wore a green turban.

407. Quran LVI: 20–1.

408. Quran II: 59.

409. The fortunate few have allotments, which provide great pleasure and reward for those who tend them. A 90-year-old allotment-keeper I heard remarking recently, 'It gives me a new lease of life... when I get here I forget myself entirely'.

410. Flora Thompson, *Lark Rise to Candleford*, p.78.

411. R. Farrar, *The Rainbow Bridge* (1922), quoted by Lord Northbourne in his essay 'Flowers', *op.cit.*, p.294–5.

Chapter 7

412. The garden at the Chelsea Flower show, as well as its installation at Highgrove, was sponsored by the Spanish specialist tile manufacturers, Porcelanosa, who provided the tiles for the pathways, rills and *zellij* (ceramic tiles in geometric patterns around the fountain), as well as the marble fountain itself – all of which were made in Spain.

413. Quoted by W.H. Hawley, *Oriental Rugs* (1913).

413A. Poem included in full in N. Ardalan and L. Bakhtiar, *A Sense of Unity*, University of Chicago Press, 1973.

414. Quran LV1: 20ff.

415. In fact 'serried acacias' is an idea that could easily be brought to life in an Islamic garden in northern Europe, since *Acacia dealbata* (mimosa), as mentioned in Chapter 5, grows well here in a sunny position, as well as looking spectacular when covered with its yellow flowers in spring.

416. See Chapter 1 and the author's book, *'Underneath Which Rivers Flow', The Symbolism of the Islamic Garden, op. cit.*

417. The damask roses, as is well known, are believed to have been brought back from Damascus by the Crusaders – like damask silk – so this seemed an obvious choice (see Chapter 6). The name 'Ispahan' was perhaps originally 'Isphahan' as it may have originated there but nothing is known for certain. Also, *Rosa* 'Sharifa Asma' was considered for the garden since, by virtue of its name, it is connected with the Islamic world (see endnote 390). However, it was eventually rejected for the Carpet Garden as its colour is too pale a pink and did not correspond to a colour in one of the carpets.

418. Gallica roses are particularly suitable for this garden because of their marvellous rich colours and their strong fragrance; also because of their short bushy habit and their compact flowers with tightly-packed petals. They are probably the oldest roses in cultivation, and although only flowering once in a season, are tough and able to withstand cold winds, something one needs to be aware of in the Cotswolds.

419. Mostly referring to the lists of the eleventh- and twelfth-century horticulturists/agriculturists Ibn Bassal and Ibn al-'Awwam included in John H. Harvey, 'Gardening Books and Plant Lists of Moorish Spain', *Journal of Garden History, op. cit.*

420. Quoted by John Harvey in *ibid.*, p.13.

421. W.H. Auden, from *In Memory of W.B. Yeats*, Pt. 2.

422. Jalal ud-Din Rumi, *Diwan-i kabir*, quoted by Annemarie Schimmel, *op. cit.*, p.25, see Chapter 5.

423. Beware of Health and Safety regulations and the Society for the Protection of Tortoises!

424. Quran III: 13 and 10: 24 – M.M. Pickthall's translation.

425. The fashion in fountains – public ones mainly – has for some time been 'the bigger the better'. In Manchester's new Piccadilly Gardens they have recently installed several fountains, which shoot at least twenty feet into the air. They require such a vast amount of water that a tank has been constructed beneath, so large that an underwater diver was recently called in to do some fixing!

426. By the Persian poet, Amir Khosro (1253–1325), included in *Poems from the Persian, op. cit.*, p.75

Conclusion

427. Frithjof Schuon, *Understanding Islam* (Allen and Unwin, 1963), p.43.

428. Titus Burckhardt, *Art of Islam, Language and Meaning, op. cit.*, p.197.

429. I recently saw a couple performing their evening prayer (*maghrib*) next to the Serpentine in Hyde Park, London.

430. Quran 20: 7 and VI: 59 (M.M. Pickthall).

431. Titus Burckhardt, *Art of Islam, Language and Meaning, op. cit.*, p.36.

432. Washington Irving, *Tales of the Alhambra* (Ediciones Miguel Sanchez, Granada, 1994), pp.104–5.

433. Quran VI:113.

434. I am indebted to Dr. Toby Mayor for pointing this out to me.

435. Frithjof Schuon, *The Transfiguration of Man* (World Wisdom Books, 1995), p.103.

Select Bibliography

The Quran and Hadith (The Sayings of the Prophet Muhammad)

Arberry, A.J., *The Koran Interpreted* (The World's Classics, Oxford University Press, 1989)

Muhammad Marmaduke Pickthall (translated by) *The Meaning of the Glorious Quran*

Abdullah Yusuf Ali (translation and commentary) *The Holy Quran: Text*

Ezzeddin Ibrahim and Denys Johnson-Davies (selected and translated by) *Forty Hadith Qudsi*, (The Holy Koran Publishing House, 1981)

Allama Sir Abdullah al-Mamun al-Suhrawardy (translated and compiled by) *The Sayings of Muhammad* (John Murray, 1992)

The Holy Bible, The Authorized version of King James I

Background Reading on Islam, Sufism, Islamic Art and Architecture

Ardalan, N. and L. Bakhtiar, *A Sense of Unity* (University of Chicago Press, 1973)

Asad, M., *The Road to Makkah* (Abdul Moin for Islamic Book Service, New Delhi, 1994)

Bowen, J.C.E. (translated by) *Poems from the Persian* (Blackwell, Oxford, 1958)

Burckhardt, Titus, *Sacred Art in East and West* (Perennial Books, 1967)

Burckhardt, Titus, *Art of Islam, Language and Meaning* (World of Islam Festival Publishing Company, 1976)

Burckhardt, Titus, *Moorish Culture in Spain* (George D.W. Callwey, Munich, 1970). English translation by Alisa Jaffa (George Allen & Unwin, London, 1972). New paperback edition by Fons Vitae (Louisville, Kentucky, 1999)

Burckhardt, Titus, *Mirror of the Intellect* (Cambridge, Quinta Essentia, 1987)

Coomaraswamy, A.K., *Christian and Oriental Philosophy of Art* (Dover Publications, first published, 1956)

Eaton, Gai, *Remembering God, Reflections on Islam* (The Islamic Texts Society, 2000)

Fathy, H., *Architecture for the Poor* (The American University in Cairo Press, 1989)

Fletcher, Richard, *Moorish Spain* (University of California Press, 1992)

Fletcher, Richard, *The Cross and the Crescent, Christianity and Islam from Muhammad to the Reformation* (Allen Lane, the Penguin Press, 2003)

Irving, W., *Tales of the Alhambra* (Ediciones Miguel Sanchez, Granada, 1994)

Lings, Martin, *Muhammad, his Life Based on the Earliest Sources* (Unwin Paperbacks, 1988)

Lings, Martin, *The Quranic Doctrine of the Afterlife*, Lecture, Temenos Academy, London, March 1993; available on cassette from Temenos, The Prince's Foundation, London EC2 3SG (see List of Useful Addresses)

Lings, Martin, *Symbol and Archetype, A Study of the Meaning of Existence* (Quinta Essentia, 1991)

Lings, Martin, *What is Sufism?* (Unwin paperbacks, Mandala, 1988)

Nasr, Seyyed Hossein, *The Heart of Islam* (Harper Collins, 2002)

Nasr, Seyyed Hossein, *Islamic Art and Spirituality* (Golgonooza Press, 1987)

Olivetti, V., *Terror's Source, The Ideology of Wahhabi-Salafism and its Consequences* (Amadeus Books, 2002)

Smith, Huston, *The World's Religions* (Harper Collins, 1991)

Schuon, Frithjof, *Islam and The Perennial Philosophy* (World of Islam Festival Publishing Company, 1976)

Schuon, Frithjof, *Spiritual Perspectives and Human Facts* (Perennial Books, 1987)

Schuon, Frithjof, *Understanding Islam* (Allen and Unwin, 1963)

Schuon, Frithjof, essay on *The Principles and Criteria of Art in Castes and Races*, (Perennial Books, 1982)

Siraj ad-Din, Abu Bakr, *The Book of Certainty, the Sufi Doctrine of Faith, Vision and Gnosis* (Islamic Texts Society, 1992)

Upham Pope, A., *A Survey of Persian Art from Prehistoric Times to the Present* (Oxford University Press, 1938)

Gardens and Gardening

Archer-Wills, A., *The Water Gardener* (Frances Lincoln, 2000)

Atasoy, Nurhan, *A Garden for the Sultan, Gardens and Flowers in Ottoman Culture* (Koc Culture, Arts and Communications Inc. for Aygaz, 2002)

Babur's Memoirs, National Art Library Edition, Victoria & Albert Museum

Brookes, John, *Gardens of Paradise: A History and Design of the Great Islamic Gardens* (Weidenfeld and Nicholson, 1987)

Campbell-Culver, Maggie, *The Origin of Plants* (Headline, 2002)

Clark, Emma, 'Underneath which Rivers Flow', *The Symbolism of the Islamic Garden* (The Prince of Wales' Institute of Architecture, 1996)

Dickie, James, 'The Islamic Garden in Spain', in *The Islamic Garden*, eds. E.B. MacDougall and R. Ettinghausen (Dumbarton Oaks Trustees for Harvard University, Washington D.C., 1976)

Earle, J., *Introduction to Infinite Spaces, the Art and Wisdom of the Japanese Garden* (Galileo Multimedia, 2000)

Gildemeister, H., *Mediterranean Gardening: A Waterwise Approach* (Editorial Moll, 1995)

Hanaway, W.L. Jr., 'Paradise on Earth: The Terrestrial Garden in Persian Literature', in *The Islamic Garden*, eds. E.B. MacDougall and R. Ettinghausen (Dumbarton Oaks Colloquium, Trustees for Harvard University, 1976)

von Hantelmann, C., (editor) and Zoern, D. (photographer), *Gardens of Delight, the Great Islamic Gardens*, (DuMont monte, 2001)

Harvey, John, *Medieval Gardens* (Batsford, 1981)

Harvey, John, 'Gardening Books and Plant Lists of Moorish Spain', *Journal of Garden History*, Vol. III, No. 2, 1975, pp. 10–21

Hepper, F.N., *Illustrated Encyclopedia of Bible Plants* (Three's Company, 1992)

Hobhouse, Penelope, *Plants in Garden History* (Pavilion Books, 1992)

Hobhouse, Penelope, *Gardens of Persia*, (Cassell 2003)

Hoffman, D., *The Complete Illustrated Holistic Herbal* (Element Books, Shaftsbury, 1996)

Iqtedar, M. and Farooqi, H., *Plants of the Quran* (Sidrah Publishers, Lucknow, 1997) al-Jawziyya, I.Q., *Medicine of the Prophet* (translated by Penelope Johnstone), (The Islamic Texts Society, 1998)

Kausar, S., Brand, M., and Wescoat, J.L. Jr., *Shalimar Garden, Lahore, Landscape, Form and Meaning* (Dept. of Archaeology and Museums, Ministry of Culture, Pakistan, 1990)

Keenan, B., Damascus, *Hidden Treasures of the Old City* (Thames & Hudson, 2000)

Landsberg, Sylvia, *Medieval Gardens* (British Museum Press, paperback edition (no date)

Lane Fox, Robin, *Better Gardening* (Penguin Books, 1985)

Lehrman, Jonas, *Earthly Paradise: garden and courtyard in Islam* (Thames and Hudson, 1980)

Margottin, J., 'Tour of Gardens in Southern Spain', *Journal of Garden History*, Vol. III, No.1, Autumn 1974, pp. 7–14

Maurieres, A. and Ossart, E., *Paradise Gardens* (Editions du Chene, Hachette Livre, 2000)

Moynihan, Elizabeth, *Paradise as a Garden in Persian and Mughal India* (George Braziller, 1979)

McVicar, J., *New Book of Herbs* (Dorling Kindersley, 2002)

Moore, E., *Gardening in the Middle East* (Stacey International, 1986)

Lord Northbourne, 'Flowers', essay included in *Seeing God Everywhere, Essays on Nature and the Sacred* (edited by Barry Macdonald), (World Wisdom, 2002)

Page, Russell, *The Education of a Gardener* (Penguin, 1983)

Phillips, R. and Rix, M., *Traditional Old Roses* (Pan, 1998)

Pinder-Wilson, Ralph, 'The Persian Garden' in *The Islamic Garden* (Dumbarton Oaks, Trustees for Harvard University, Washington DC, 1976), p.82

Prieto Moreno, F., *Los Jardines de Granada* (Arte de Espana, 1983)

Ruggles, D.F., *Gardens, Landscape and Vision in the Palaces of Islamic Spain* (Pennsylvania State University Press, 2000)

Sackville-West, Vita, *Garden Book* (Michael Joseph, 1987)

Schimmel, A., 'The Celestial Garden' in *The Islamic Garden*, eds. E.B. MacDougall and R. Ettinghausen (Dumbarton Oaks, Trustees for Harvard University, Washington DC, 1976)

Slawson, David, *Secret Teachings in the Art of Japanese Gardens* (Kodansha International Ltd., paperback edition, 1991)

Storey, Sally, *Lighting by Design* (Pavilion, 2002)

Swindells, P., *Water Gardening* (The RHS Encyclopedia of Practical Gardening, Mitchell Beazley, 2001)

Tabbaa, Y., 'Towards an interpretation of the use of water in Islamic courtyards and courtyard gardens', *Journal of Garden History*, Vol.7, No. 3, pp. 197–220

Titley, N.M., *Plants and Gardens in Persian, Mughal and Turkish Art* (The British Library, 1979)

Villiers Stuart, Constance, *Gardens of the Great Mughals* (A. & C. Black, 1913)

Watson, A.M., *Agricultural Innovation in the Early Islamic World* (Cambridge University Press, 1983)

Wescoat, J.L. Jr. and Wolschke-Bulmahn, J. (eds), *Mughal Gardens, Sources, Places, Representations and Prospects* (Dumbarton Oaks, Trustees for Harvard University, Washington DC, 1996)

Wilber, D.N., *Persian Gardens and Garden Pavilions* (Dumbarton Oaks, Trustees for Harvard University, Washington DC, 1979)

Wohlhasen, A., *Living Architecture, Islamic Indian* (Macdonald, London, 1970)

Geometric Patterns

Bourgoin, J., *Arabic Geometrical Pattern Design* (Dover Publications Inc., New York, 1973)

Critchlow, Keith, *Islamic Patterns, An Analytical and Cosmological Approach* (Thames and Hudson, 1976)

el-Said, Issam, (edited by Tarek El-Bouri and Keith Critchlow) *Islamic Art and Architecture, The System of Geometric Design* (Garnet Publishing Ltd, 1993)

Lawlor, Robert, *Sacred Geometry, Philosophy and Practice* (Thames and Hudson, 1982)

Waterfield, Robin, (translated by) *The Theology of Arithmetic* (Kairos, 1988)

Useful Addresses

The Prince's School of Traditional Arts (PSTA) (incorporating the Visual Islamic and Traditional Arts Programme [VITA]) The Prince's Foundation, 19-22 Charlotte Road, Shoreditch, London EC2A 3SG
Tel. 020 7613 8500
Fax. 020 7613 8599
www.princes-foundation.org
Through the Prince's School of Traditional Arts, artists and craftsmen specialising in Islamic and other traditional crafts may be contacted. These arts/crafts include: geometry, arabesque, calligraphy, stone-carving including lettering, ceramics – especially tiles with Islamic and geometric patterns, *zellij* (North African, mainly Moroccan, cut-tile work, see p.74), stained-glass, wood-carving (including *mashrabbiyya* – turned or slatted wood screens, see p.78), fountain design and construction; other architectural or building crafts such as Islamic-inspired pavilions, arbours and pergolas for the garden; and Islamic garden and landscape design.

Moroccan Interiors/Exteriors:
Habibi Ltd., Moroccan tiles and Interiors,
1C Greyhound Road, London NW10 5QH
Tel. +44 (0)20 8960 9203.
Fax. +44 (0)20 8960 9223
E-mail: nour@habibi-interiors.com
www.habibi-interiors.com

Dar Interiors, Arch 11, Miles St, London SW8 1RZ.
Tel. +44 (0)20 7720 9678.
Fax. +44 (0)20 7627 5129
E-mail: enquiries@darinteriors.com
www.darinteriors.com

Mainly Asian/Indian
Artique, Talboys House, 17, Church Street,
Tetbury, Gloucestershire, GL8 8JG
Tel/Fax. +44 (0)1666 503597
E-mail: george@artique.demon.co.uk

Michael Spink Design Ltd., 3, Georgian House,
10 Bury Street, London SW1Y 6AA
Tel. +44 (0) 20 7930 2288.
Fax. +44 (0) 20 7930 2988
www.michaelspinkdesign.com

Water: design and construction
Avalon Aquatic Nurseries, Broadford Bridge Road,
West Chiltington, West Sussex, RH20 2LF
Tel. +44 (0)1798 813204/344963

Bamber Wallis, 3, Hope Lane, Farnham, Surrey, GU9 OHY.
Tel. +44 (0)1252 715139
www.bamberwallisdesigns.co.uk

Ustigate Water Display Specialists, Unit 4,
Norfolk Road Industrial Estate, Gravesend, Kent, DA12 2PS
Tel. +44 (0)1474 363012
www.ustigate.co.uk

Nurseries
Landford Trees, Landford Lodge, Landford, Salisbury,
Wiltshire, SP5 2EH.
Tel. +44 (0)1794 390808
E-mail: trees@landfordtrees.co.uk
www.landfordtrees.co.uk

Chew Valley Trees, Winford Road, Chew Magna,
Bristol, BS40 8HJ.
Tel. +44 (0)1275 333752
Fax. +44 (0)1275 333746
E-mail: info@chewvalleytrees.co.uk

Thornhayes Nursery, St. Andrews Wood,
Dulford, Cullompton, Devon EX15 2DF.
Tel. +44 (0)1884 266746
E-mail: trees@thornhayes.demon.co.uk
www.thornhayes-nursery.co.uk

Architectural Plants, Cooks Farm, Nuthurst, Horsham,
West Sussex, RH13 6LH
Tel. +44 (0)1403 891772.
Fax. +44 (0)1403 891056
E-mail: enquires@architecturalplants.com
www.architecturalplants.com

Langley Boxwood Nursery, Rake, Nr. Liss,
Hampshire, GU33 7JL.
Tel. +44 (0)1730 894467.
Fax. +44 (0)1730 894703
E-mail: langbox@msn.com
www.boxwood.co.uk

Chris Pattison, Brookend, Pendock, Glos., GL19 3PL.
Tel./Fax. +44 (0)1531 650480
www.chrispattison.fsnet.co.uk

Sarah Raven's Cutting Garden
Perch Hill Farm, Willingford Lane, Nr. Brightling,
Robertsbridge, East Sussex TN32 5HP
Tel. +44 (0)845 050 4848
www.thecuttinggarden.com

The Romantic Garden Nursery, Swannington, Norwich,
Norfolk, NR9 5NW.
Tel. +44 (0)1603 261488
Fax. +44 (0)1603 864231
E-mail: enquiries@romantic-garden-nursery.co.uk
www.romantic-garden-nursery.co.uk

Robert Mattock Roses, The Rose Nurseries,
Lodge Hill, Abingdon, Oxon, OX14 2JD
Tel. +44 (0)1865 735382
www.robertmattockroses.com

David Austen Roses Ltd., Bowling Green Lane, Albrighton,
Wolverhampton, WV7 3HB
Tel. +44 (0)1902 376300
E-mail: retail@davidaustenroses.com
www.davidaustenroses.com

Blackmore and Langdon Ltd., Pensford,
Bristol, BS39 4JL.
Tel. +44 (0) 1275 332300
www.blackmore-langdon.com

Jekka's Herb Garden, Rose Cottage, Shellards Lane,
Alveston, Bristol, BS35 3SY.
Tel. +44 (0)1454 418878
E-mail: farm@jekkasherbfarm.com
www.jekkasherbfarm.com

Jacques Amand & Living Colour, Long Rock,
Penzance, Cornwall, TR93 0WG
Tel. +44 (0) 1736 333333
Fax. +44 (0) 1736 364636

Lighting (see p.84)
Lighting Design International, Zero Ellaline Road,
Hammersmith, London W6 9NZ
Tel. +44 (0) 7381 8999
www.lightingdesigninternational.com

John Cullen Lighting, 585, King's Road,
London SW6 2EH.
Tel. +44 (0) 7371 5400
www.johncullenlighting.co.uk

Tents (see p.81)
The Raj Tent Club, 14, St. Alban's Grove,
London W8 5BP
Tel. +44 (0)207 376 9066
E-mail: www.rajtentclub.com

Index